# Dubious Pundits

## POLITICS AND COMEDY: CRITICAL ENCOUNTERS

Series Editor: Julie A. Webber, Illinois State University

This series brings scholars of political comedy together in order to examine the effect of humor and comedy in a political way. The series has three main components. Political Comedy Encounters Neoliberalism aims to look at how comedy disrupts or reinforces dominant ideologies under neoliberalism, including but not limited to: forms of authority, epistemological certainties bred by market centrality, prospects for democratic thought and action, and the implications for civic participation. Political Comedy as Cultural Text examines the relationship between the more bizarre elements of contemporary politics and comedy, including but not limited to countersubversive narratives that challenge or reinforce anti-democratic political authority and market thought, radical social movements that seek to undermine it, and political comedy's relationship to the cultural unconscious. Lastly, the series welcomes proposals for scholarship that tracks the context in which comedy and politics interact. Political Comedy in Context follows the intersection of politics and comedy in viral, mediated, and affective environments.

### Titles Published

*Political Satire, Postmodern Reality, and the Trump Presidency: Who Are We Laughing at?* by Mehnaaz Momen

*The Joke Is on Us: Political Comedy in (Late) Neoliberal Times* by Julie A. Webber

*Taking Comedy Seriously: Stand-Up's Dissident Potential in Mass Culture* by Jennalee Donian

*Dubious Pundits: Presidential Politics, Late-Night Comedy, and the Public Sphere* by Nickie Michaud Wild

# Dubious Pundits

## Presidential Politics, Late-Night Comedy, and the Public Sphere

Nickie Michaud Wild

LEXINGTON BOOKS
*Lanham • Boulder • New York • London*

Published by Lexington Books
An imprint of The Rowman & Littlefield Publishing Group, Inc.
4501 Forbes Boulevard, Suite 200, Lanham, Maryland 20706
www.rowman.com

6 Tinworth Street, London SE11 5AL, United Kingdom

British Library Cataloguing in Publication Information Available

**Library of Congress Cataloging-in-Publication Data**

Names: Wild, Nicole Michaud, author.
Title: Dubious pundits : presidential politics, late-night comedy, and the public sphere / Nicole Michaud Wild.
Description: Lanham, Maryland : Lexington Books, 2019. | Series: Politics and comedy : critical encounters | Includes bibliographical references and index.
Identifiers: LCCN 2019012156 | ISBN 9781498567367 (cloth : alk. paper) | ISBN 9781498567381 (pbk. : alk. paper) | ISBN 9781498567374 (electronic)
Subjects: LCSH: Television and politics—United States. | Television broadcasting of news—United States. | United States—Politics and government—1981–1989—Humor. | United States—Politics and government—1989—Humor. | Presidents—United States—Election—Humor. | Political satire, American—History and criticism. | Saturday night live (Television program) | Daily show (Television program) | Colbert report (Television program)
Classification: LCC PN1992.6 .W437 2019 | DDC 791.43/6581—dc23
LC record available at https://lccn.loc.gov/2019012156

# Contents

Introduction: The Political Comedy Public Sphere     1

1   Political Comedy in the Reagan/Bush Era: Unkind and
Not So Gentle     15

2   The Clinton Era: Humor Below the Belt     33

3   *Bush v. Gore* and the Comedy of Chaos     55

4   The 9/11 Era: "Now They Are Pundits"     83

5   The 2008 Election: Authenticity (Or Lack Thereof)     105

Conclusion: The Structural Transformation of Political Humor     141

Methods     159

Bibliography     161

Index     165

About the Author     173

# Introduction

## The Political Comedy Public Sphere

A defining moment of the 2008 election was Tina Fey's portrayal of Sarah Palin on *Saturday Night Live*. *SNL* has been a mainstay of political humor about presidential candidates for decades; caricatures of political figures have ranged from the pitch-perfect parody of George H. W. Bush by Dana Carvey, to Chevy Chase's simple physically comedic falling down, meant to convey Gerald Ford. But Fey's satire was different. It was so adept that once it aired, practically no serious news coverage about Palin was complete without some reference to it. The most famous line from the parody, "I can see Russia from my house!" was never actually uttered by the real vice presidential candidate, but if you asked most people who vividly remember the 2008 campaign, it's likely that they would not believe this was the case.

Fey's caricature is a perfect representation of how political comedy on late-night TV transformed from the culturally relevant to the politically indispensable. During the 2000s, after 9/11 and the ill-conceived Iraq War, substantive political humor was elevated to a more serious status. It has always functioned as a social/cultural bonding mechanism, where we could discuss Johnny Carson's latest barbs, or Darrell Hammond's skewering of Bill Clinton with each other over the water cooler on Monday morning. What changed was political humor's function. During the run-up to the war, and thereafter, there was a strong sense in the United States that our news media had failed us, and that Jon Stewart of the *Daily Show* was doing a better job questioning what was going on than serious journalism. This was especially true for younger, left-leaning audiences who felt left out of the mainstream news discourse at a time when it was considered unpatriotic to question the president, and even mild criticism would get you boycotted (as the Dixie Chicks could attest to). Once it had become clear that what the

Bush Administration had said about how quick, easy, and profitable the war would be was not true, Stewart was hailed as a pundit and ultimately on the right side of history. When the 2008 election came around, the more superficial parodies of presidential candidates on *SNL* that had entertained us in the past no longer sufficed. The *Daily Show* had upped the ante.

In many ways the *Daily Show* benefited from changes in the structure of television. As the number of channels increased from just three networks to a multitude of choices on cable and satellite, political humor on television in the United States became more critical of politicians and their policies. Earlier examples of political comedy focused primarily on political or personal scandals (like President Clinton's affair with his intern, Monica Lewinsky), or personal characteristics (such as George W. Bush's malapropisms), rather than policies or substantive issues (Moy, Xenos, and Hess 2006; Peterson 2008). This kind of humor about politics was tried and true, and always had been the driving force. It served to humanize politicians, and when well executed, left a lasting impression on public consciousness. In other arenas of television and the public sphere in general, there was serious criticism of scandals, but not as much in political comedy. Shows that attempted to criticize politicians or serious public issues using satire, irony, or invective were routinely censored by network executives, such as the *Smothers Brothers Comedy Hour* (Bianculli 2009). In short, political criticism on television comedy shows had to be innocuous or extremely subtle to go out for broadcast.

However, with the expansion of cable, and the entrance of the *Daily Show* with Jon Stewart, the show quickly adopted a critical stance on the Bush administration that was widely discussed in serious outlets such as the *New York Times* and the *Washington Post*. One of the things that was so different and effective about the *Daily Show* from other political humor on TV was that it provided context about the issues it was satirizing; viewers could approach the program without prior knowledge of important, newsworthy incidents. Later, a spin-off show, the *Colbert Report*, produced a character that was not only critical within the confines of the show, but also carried out a legendary satirical tirade against the Bush administration right in front of them at the White House Correspondent's Dinner in 2007. This form of "critical comedy" has proved popular; examples from more recent elections include Tina Fey's notable *SNL* mocking of the perceived incompetence of vice presidential candidate Sarah Palin; Alec Baldwin's portrayal of Donald Trump; and Jimmy Kimmel's insertion into the healthcare debate.

Entertainment media is of specific importance due to the number of people that consume it. While critics of politicians and policies have been able to voice their opinions in the public sphere all along (mostly in newspapers), and serious political talk shows have presented all sides, the public does not consume these outlets as widely as popular entertainment programs. A 2007 Pew Research study confirmed that people who watched television shows that dealt with political topics were more informed about politics in general; this included not only serious shows like PBS's *NewsHour with Jim Lehrer*, but *also* found that the same held true for regular viewers of the *Daily Show* and the *Colbert Report*, even if they did not also watch other news. They concluded that the use of footage and its focus on very specific political news stories was a new kind of narrative that was "close to journalistic in nature— getting people to think critically about the public square"[1] despite Stewart himself denying that his show actually *was* journalism.

The role of media in civil society, specifically the role of television, has been a subject of intense debate for academic scholars. A space for intellectual, rational debate may not be best exemplified in the one-way communication style that is television. But entertainment media galvanize individuals in civil society to converse about "matters of common concern" (Jacobs 2012). Like all forms of entertainment that the culture industries produce, such as novels, music, and movies, television supplies common narratives that are publicly accessible to everyone due to its large rate of consumption, perhaps more so than any other form. Parodic and satirical ways of looking at the news, through entertainment media such as the late-night comedy shows *SNL* and the *Daily Show*, contribute to a critical stance on authority.

Also, it was a matter of timing. Cable news ratings had been steadily increasing over that of network news over the previous three decades.[2] Clearly, according to the Pew study cited above, people were getting news and information from the *Daily Show* and the *Colbert Report*. The overall failure of traditional journalism to fully inform the public and present alternate viewpoints after September 11, 2001, led to a hole in the fabric of adequate news coverage that was filled by political comedy (McClennen 2012). However, not all theorists have had a high opinion of political comedy's potential. It can give an opportunity to some speakers to use comedy to marginalize minority groups, and may be misconstrued, as in the case of some conservatives taking Colbert's rhetoric at face value (LaMarre, Landreville, and Beam 2009).

## LATE-NIGHT COMEDY'S TRANSFORMATIVITY

Although the use of satire certainly has a long history in television, and those who made political satire in the past had good ratings and/or positive critical acceptance (and in this sense, the *Daily Show* and the *Colbert Report* were picking up where the Smothers Brothers left off), never before was it allowed such license. There are a couple of important structural reasons for this. One is the anatomy of cable itself—language, violence, and sexual scenes are permitted here that would never be permitted on broadcast television due to its control by the FCC. Long-time late-night comedy show host, Conan O'Brien, put it this way:

> The censorship *The Smothers Brothers* were up against in the late sixties is almost inconceivable today. There are, like, 900,000 shows on TV now . . . If you have a funny and interesting idea, yeah, you may get some letters, but there's so much to choose from, people will just watch something else. (Provenza and Dion 2010, 54)

A second and historically contingent reason that the shows became more politically critical is the well-documented lack of critique of the policies of the Bush administration from the mainstream media in the wake of 9/11 and the run up to, and beginning of, the wars in Iraq and Afghanistan. Although programs like *The Simpsons* and *South Park* have parodied political figures, as does *SNL*, entertainment programs that made strong statements against contemporary political administrations tended to vanish from the airwaves. But the programs on Comedy Central not only did not get the ax, but also thrived and received prestigious journalism awards, like the Peabody. In the book *Colbert's America*, Sophia A. McClennen sums up the part humor played: "post–9/11 satire appeared in a complex moment for both the media and the state of the nation. A consequence of this was that satire became one of the few ways that the public could experience dissent" (2012, 65–66). Many writers in the mainstream press, including *New York Times* columnist Frank Rich, as well as writers in academia (Peterson 2008), attributed the shows' success to strongly critical standpoints when much of the press was not as critical of Bush 43. They filled in for the journalists who should have been more critical, especially before the Iraq War in 2002–2003: "Jon Stewart and company at least refused to join the Patriot Parade in which their competitors—in both the mainstream comedy and 'real' news realms—seemed to be marching" (Peterson 2008, 203). Political comedian Lewis Black explains it this way: "Once the *New York Times* apologized for not giving us information on Iraq—for not *doing their job*—because of *The Daily Show*, Colbert, and others, all of a sudden comedy in essence became a place where information actually became disseminated at least as well, if not better" (Provenza and Dion 2010, 16). Cable allowed different ideas to be marketed to niche audiences, which might start off small, and potentially grow larger, in ways that the networks, which must appeal to the broadest base possible from the start, could not. Indeed, even now, the *Tonight Show* (now handed off to Jimmy Fallon) had been largely number one in the ratings for the twenty-two years it had been on before Leno left. Conversely, David Letterman became much more political over the years (highlighted by the incident when John McCain failed to appear after the 2008 financial crisis), but trailed in the ratings. Yet more recently, after Stephen Colbert took over from Letterman, the show was not as successful when it was less political in its early months, and surpassed Fallon when it became so. Following suit, *Jimmy Kimmel Live!* increased in ratings after the host entered the health care debate.[3] In a more partisan political climate, viewers want their comedy to take a strong stance.

Another notable development in the history of satire on television is that it made character-flaw based political humor appear insufficient to meet the needs of the more critical media consumer. This process was evident in Tina Fey's impression of vice presidential candidate Sarah Palin during the 2008 election, for which she won the Kennedy Center's Mark Twain Prize for American Humor in 2010. Although Jon Stewart rarely enacted such deadpan satirical style himself, the show's parodies of the structure of the media itself—the correspondents' "interviews" with people with strange ideas who do not seem to know they are being mocked, the use of the same graphics as CNN, amplified only slightly to reveal their absurdity, etc.—fit well with the way in which audiences were used to getting their news. The *Daily Show*, the *Colbert Report*, and Fey's performances were successful in part because the much of the public's perception of the news media, especially in regard to their coverage of politics and elections, has increasingly included an awareness of its frequent inadequacy. Audiences wanted something more meaty than personal scandals in their humor.

One other notable development over the years is the need, whether real or perceived, for politicians to appear on the comedy programs in order to be politically successful. When John Anderson appeared on *SNL* in 1980, the first presidential candidate to do so, commentators lamented this as a blow to the seriousness of the political process. Over time, many other candidates began to appear on the show, mainly to seem like they could poke fun at themselves, and not be so distant to those they wanted to vote for them; in other words, to seem like a "regular guy." There was historical precedent for this: Richard Nixon's September 16, 1968, appearance on *Laugh-In* on CBS, done entirely to seem less stiff than in his losing 1960 televised debate.[4] Famously, in June of 1992, Bill Clinton appeared on the *Arsenio Hall Show* to play the saxophone. Although some questioned whether this appearance aligned with the expected dignity of someone running for president, it arguably helped him win over younger voters. Part of the "successful political performance" was to go on *SNL*, late-night talk shows, or the *Daily Show*, and, if not actually manage to be funny, be able to at least be in on the joke. Though it is beyond the timeframe of this book, it is worth noting that Mitt Romney did not appear on *SNL*, the *Daily Show*, or the *Colbert Report*, despite invitations to do so in

2012. Candidates who do not have a televisually appealing personality have always tended to do worse (famously going back to the first televised debate between Kennedy and Nixon in 1960), and what it means to *be* televisually appealing has changed to include going on comedy programs.

The phenomenon of having to prove one's self in this manner reflects a change in the public sphere that some theorists have regarded as having a negative effect on democracy itself: not only are politicians debasing themselves, but they are cheapening the very democratic process. This is the perspective of critiques such as Postman's (1985) and Putnam's (2001). Conversely, one could see the changes taking place not as just news being polluted by entertainment, but see the transforming media environment as evidence that politics is moving into entertainment (Delli Carpini and Williams 2001; Jenkins 2008; Schudson 1998; B. A. Williams and Delli Carpini 2011), and that all members of society are getting greater exposure to it, and have a greater interest in it. It's arguable that had these transformations not already been occurring before September 11, 2001, that the public would have had far less access to alternative critical discourses (McClennen 2012). Thus, journalists' acceptance and use of satirical narratives to reflect and bolster their own critical discourses would not have been possible otherwise. Although historical factors and changes in the media industry allowed for these types of shows to proliferate and become important to the way citizens and opinion leaders, like journalists, talk about politics in the early twenty-first century, contemporary satire on television has a long line of precedents that were less successful in directing narratives outside of them. However, there were specific predecessors and influences on them.

## POLITICAL COMEDY ON TELEVISION:
## A HISTORICAL BACKGROUND

Like many cultural institutions, comedy began to become more politically and socially aware in the 1960s. Many credit the comedy of Lenny Bruce, and subsequent legal battles over the content of that comedy, who pushed the envelope and paved the way for future politically controversial comedians (Zoglin 2008). Others who followed him that had a reputation for similar social commentary, like George Carlin and Richard Pryor, started off on Ed Sullivan as television friendly stand-ups, but later changed their acts as their personal politics evolved and became more radical. Like Bruce, they became the most daring truth-tellers of their time. These mid-twentieth-century comics met opposition, and often faced other demons; alcohol and drug addiction, poor personal relationships, and violence. Making inroads to television, especially before cable, proved most difficult. Even Carlin's groundbreaking 1983 HBO special faced concern, due to the performance of his infamous "Seven Words You Can Never Say on Television" routine, despite the fact that it was on pay cable.

Television in the United States has always had a complicated relationship with political satire. On one hand, comedians and social commentators have often attempted to use satire to make intelligent points about the news, politics, and the medium of television itself. Early examples include *That Was the Week That Was* (NBC, 1964–1964), *Rowan and Martin's Laugh-In* (NBC, 1968–1973) and performers like Ernie Kovacs, Sid Caesar, Victor Borge, and Jack Paar. Later, in 1977, Richard Pryor had a variety show, which of course had controversial content. In a move that nearly guaranteed its failure, possibly on purpose from network executives balking after giving Pryor a contract, it was put on at 8 p.m. Eastern against popular shows *Laverne and Shirley* and *Happy Days*, though it had initially been given the time slot of 9 p.m. (Silverman 2007). Not only did it not do well in the ratings, but also many viewers complained about it. On the other hand, there are notorious examples of television executives censoring satirical content, even when it is popular with viewers. This second instance seems to directly contradict the purpose of network, profit-motivated television in the United States—if people are watching, the company is making money. However, pressure from sponsors and politicians have often served as catalysts for the altering of program content and the outright cancellation of successful programs if their creators, writers, and performers pushed the envelope too far, too fast. Additionally, similar to some people not recognizing that they even were the target of satire as has happened with the *Colbert Report* (LaMarre et al. 2009), the 1970s program, *All in the Family*, did not always make its ironic stance obvious. The character Archie Bunker spouted the most racist, sexist things, typical of white men of his generation and class, but was meant to make these things appear sad and banal. However, liberals watching the program understood that, while conservatives watching it came away with the impression that he was championing their views (Ozersky 2003, 69).

Prior to the emergence of cable, there was a tendency among television executives to pre-censor program content that might be objectionable to those in political power. Interestingly, this was not always done to appease politicians, but sometimes was aimed at appeasing program sponsors who were presumed to not want to be associated with political criticism. There are two cases that illustrate both reasons for censorship. The first took place in the case of the *Smothers Brothers Comedy Hour* which aired on CBS from 1967 to 1969. The show often aimed criticism at those in power, and politics and politicians generally. Ultimately, the show was canceled not because it offended viewers and suffered in the ratings—in fact, "rather than offending a majority of viewers, the program spoke to it—particularly to those Americans who felt disenfranchised by an establishment that still supported the Vietnam War" (Silverman 2007, 61). Tom and Dick Smothers objected to having to submit a preview of the show to the network censors ten days before it was to air, and despite the show having been renewed for a third season, it was canceled due to their ultimate failure to do this on time. Most intriguingly, there is some vague and circumstantial evidence that they show may have been targeted by the Nixon administration. Notorious for going after people who mocked him or with whom he disagreed, could the Smothers Brothers and their show have been a target? Bianculli (2009) writes that "Nixon covered his tracks well" but that the show's stars and producers had always believed the president had something to do with it (324). However, in wake of their show's cancellation, the Smothers Brothers read an excerpt on the air from a letter they received from President Lyndon Johnson, whose policies had also been a target of theirs, in support of what they did. It read, "It is part of the price of leadership of this great and free nation to be the target of clever satirists." It seems as if JBJ was aware of the type of abuse of power that could take place, and wished to distance himself from it, while Nixon covertly embraced it.

The second case, that of network censorship due to fear of offending sponsors, is illustrated by the pre-censorship of *Monty Python's Flying Circus* by the television network ABC. Although the British show was aired in its entirety on PBS in the United States later on, there was a little-known foray into network showings. In 1975, ABC re-packaged and edited together episodes from the fourth season of the program. It was an unmitigated disaster. The programs were heavily censored by the network. One of the things that was removed was in an episode called "Mr. Neutron" (MacNaughton 1974). The title character, an alien superhero, is called "the most dangerous and terrifying man in the world!" for reasons that are never quite explained. Nevertheless, the American government becomes extremely concerned when they lose track of his whereabouts. A military commander is sitting at a desk directing the search by phone. He is alone in a room issuing orders ("I want a full-scale Red Alert throughout the world! Surround everyone with everything we've got! Mobilize every fighting unit and every weapon we can lay our hands on! I want three full-scale global nuclear alerts with every Army, Navy and Air Force unit on eternal standby!"). As he grows increasingly paranoid throughout the episode, he is shown removing parts of his clothing and checking himself for body odors.

These scenes were deleted with the suspicion that they might be offensive to American sensibilities: "Whether out of sensitiveness to the American supreme command, whose troops had been finally bundled out of Vietnam that April, or to the cosmetic companies whose deodorant ads filled in for the missing bits of *Monty Python*, the joke almost completely disappeared" (Hewison 1981, 44). This and other cuts resulted in an unintelligible mish-mash of several of the episodes, with punchlines missing, and sequences presented out of order which made audiences unable to follow the plot. The members of Monty Python sued the network and got a settlement which pro-hibited the airing of the edited version ever again. Although this was a land-mark legal case which ensured many future artists creative control over their work, the importance for this project lies in the fact that on PBS, the shows were not edited, while on commercial television, censorship was inevitable.

Although the *Monty Python* incident occurred in the 1970s, very little changed regarding politically sensitive satire on broadcast television into the twenty-first century. Due to the controversial comments Bill Maher made on his ABC show, *Politically Incorrect with Bill Maher*, about 9/11, his show was taken off the air. In a nutshell, Maher agreed with his guest, former Reagan aide Dinesh D'Souza, that the men who crashed the planes that day were not cow-ards. These remarks were taken out of context by right-wing talk radio com-mentators. Eventually several local ABC affiliates across the country refused to air the show under local pressure, and the network followed their lead, not renewing Maher's contract. The show was canceled due to controversial com-ments he made, but these were not of a parodic or satirical nature. However, it is likely that the network was looking for an excuse to pull the show due to a pattern of controversy that it generated over its run on the network beginning in 1997, which did center on Maher's political humor (Silverman 2007). The show began on cable on Comedy Central, and ended up back on cable in the form of *Real Time with Bill Maher* on HBO, where it is still produced, despite more recent controversies surrounding his use of racist language.

Some writers contend that *SNL* became more and more conservative in its parodies of politicians and lost its bite after its initial seasons (Gray, Jones, and Thompson 2009; Peterson 2008). Late-night talk shows, such as those hosted by Johnny Carson, David Letterman, Jay Leno, and Conan O'Brien, over the years on network television have always provided an ample sup-ply of humor about politics and politicians, but these have most often taken the form of jokes about their personal foibles or imitations. Paul Krassner, counter-culture icon and co-founder of the alternative "YIPPIES" party in the 1970s, says of them that they "joined in on all the demonizing of Saddam Hussein in the run-up to the war, and only when public opinions shifted did they start to really go after Bush. They *follow* opinion; they don't really care to *lead* it" (Provenza and Dion 2010, 23–24).

Late-night talk shows have been notorious for avoiding meaningful top-ics. When comedians who appeared on the shows made comments about

abortion, gun control, etc., the set might be censored. One infamous incident, involving the only time a comedian's set was cut entirely from a show,
involved the late comedian Bill Hicks. Hicks, who died in 1994, was well-
known in the U.K. where his powerful, biting jokes about the Gulf War,
right-wing radio talk show rhetoric, and racial strife in the United States
made him quite popular, but he did not go over as well domestically. On
October 1, 1993, Hicks' entire performance was cut by Letterman and his
producers (True 2002). Five months later, Hicks died of pancreatic cancer.
The editing was mainly due to a joke about the hypocrisy of pro-lifers,
and the fact that (in Hicks' opinion) a pro-life group was running an ad on
the program at the time. Although at first blaming CBS's standards and
practices department, Letterman took responsibility for the incident years
later, when he showed the performance in its entirety close to the fifteenth
anniversary of the comedian's death (where Hicks' mother was present to
receive an apology in person). The incident highlights the concern of producers of network television, not of government-mandated restrictions, but
of losing commercial sponsorship money.

Instead of addressing topics that are politically controversial, talk shows
often engage in "mimicking the external characteristics of politicians, but
only rarely thrust a critical knife into their inner fraudulences, [a practice
which] lost its force when it was realized that at least some politicians of the
television age felt flattered by parodies that reinforced their own brand images" (Hewison 1981, 8). We can see this at work when Dana Carvey of *SNL*
was invited to the White House by the very man he was parodying, President
George H. W. Bush, who approved of the performance; politicians can use
late-night comedy shows to enhance their images (Zoglin 2008).

Another network program that engages with politics on a humorous level is
the long-running Fox show, *The Simpsons*; however, it does not engage in the
sort of invective that got Bill Maher in trouble with network affiliates (Gray
et al. 2009). Additionally, stand-up comics whose acts are or were almost
entirely comprised of strong political or social commentary (as in the case of
Patton Oswalt, David Cross, Eddie Murphy, or Redd Fox) compartmentalize
this to their live performances or albums, and steer clear of controversy in
their mainstream work, as in the case of Cross and Oswalt doing voice-overs
for cartoons and sitcoms.

## INTO THE TWENTY-FIRST CENTURY

It is accurate to state that political comedy in the twenty-first century follows
a direct line from at least the mid-twentieth century. When *SNL* satirized

Sarah Palin for being fake, inauthentic, and only pretending to be knowledgeable about domestic and global affairs, this way of portraying her resonated with the already existing narrative and discursive structures that have been in place for nearly half a century on television. Those mocking her are familiar with *Monty Python*'s way of doing this, and so is much of the audience. But political comedy on television has also evolved. Not only is there the changing media environment to consider, but also politicians' interactions with the media and concepts like "spin" have come to be satirized. There is a growing cynicism in comedy, perhaps because people are more aware of what happens behind the scenes. Social media and scandals have revealed how the sausage is made. Shows like *The Thick of It* (2005–2012) in the United Kingdom on the BBC, and *Veep* in the U.S. on HBO (2012– ), depict the behind-the-scenes machinations in an ironic, if not at all understated, manner. *The Thick of It* can draw a direct line of heritage from the much more staid and dignified *Yes, Minister* on the U.K. in the 1980s. Although in both shows, the parties that are in charge are never specifically mentioned, it is all too obvious who they are from the descriptions of their policy positions; the point, however, is that it doesn't matter who is in charge, the plotting and skullduggery remain the same. Image is of prime concern over substance.

Although in the latter part of the twentieth century, journalists often wrote about how the news was becoming more like entertainment, essentially agreeing with the critical media theorists, in the twenty-first century, they are more likely to use the narratives on the late-night comedy programs when they want to make critical points about politicians. Once these narratives have disseminated throughout the public sphere, it would be naïve of them *not* to use them. Evening news broadcasts, Sunday morning news programs like *Meet the Press*, and cable news used commentaries and clips from the *Daily Show* and the *Colbert Report*; skits and parodies of political candidates from *SNL* appear frequently as well, especially in the Trump era. These new ways of combining news and entertainment challenges the assumptions that news is simply becoming more like entertainment, because the news narratives are utilizing the comedic narratives as a resource that the audiences not only understand, but also further serves to make them more acceptable as a serious form of editorial information (Jacobs and Michaud Wild 2013).

In an interview in Provenza and Dion's book, *Satiristas* (2010) Roseanne Barr stated, "I always say if Johnny Carson was still on the air, we never would've gone to Iraq. He was the conscience of the whole TV community" (74). Even though no late-night comedy host of the chat-show format ever rose to such prominence again,[5] other formats became just as potent. Writers in the newspapers begin to emphasize the shows' commentaries as being influential on public opinion and dialogue. There is an increase in writers' usage of commentary from the shows to "stand in" for and give additional credence to their own viewpoints, especially when their opinions are controversial or critical of other segments of the media (such as TV news, which the programs often satirize), demonstrating a greater reliance upon and importance of political humor in the contemporary public sphere. The phenomenon of candidates appearing on the programs grew over time, and went from being taken as a shallow attempt at seeming like the everyman, to something candidates are expected to do in order (ironically) to be taken seriously. John Anderson (who ran as an independent candidate in the 1980 election, after failing to win the Republican Primary) appeared on *SNL* on January 26 that year, with a cameo appearance in a sketch, and a few commentators speculated that this might help his campaign. Compare this to the several times candidates made such appearances on *SNL* in the 2008 campaign, including Obama, John McCain, Sarah Palin, and Hillary Clinton (during the primary) as well as Clinton and Obama appearing on the *Colbert Report* and Obama, Clinton, and McCain appearing on the *Daily Show*. Candidates needed to appear on the programs, and writers discussing these appearances demonstrated the continued increase in the shows' importance in the political landscape. Additionally, failure to do well under a sometimes performatively challenging environment had a negative effect on the campaign.

Comedy on *SNL* has progressed, either gradually or abruptly, from the non-substantive, personality-characteristic focused forms of the past (Gerald Ford tripping, Bob Dole's advanced age) to the *politically* meaningful critical parody of Sarah Palin by Tina Fey during 2008. It is difficult to make the argument that showing a president as physically inept impugned his ability to govern; however, Fey's parody of Palin focused on her inability to construct cogent arguments and her lack of political knowledge which, if one buys the basis for the parody, would either reinforce one's rational belief that she could not govern, or could convince someone who was on the fence about it. This is not at all to say that the jokes about age, clumsiness, personal relationships, etc., aren't funny or necessary—they simply don't do the narrative heavy lifting that the more substantive humor does. The *Daily Show* was taking something of a risk with format. Shows that had tried it in the past paid the price and were censored, and there was no guarantee that audiences would even care for it. But when the types of jokes changed, the commentary in newspapers (in this study, the *Post* and the *Times*) adjusted accordingly, paying more attention to the substantive issues about the candidates that the shows satirized. The crux of the argument about the transformation of late-night comedy is this: that as the television shows increasingly offered serious criticisms, presented in a humorous, and thus accessible way, other parts of the public sphere began to discuss their criticisms as well. Therein lies their agenda-setting effects.

## STRUCTURE OF THE BOOK

Aside from the introductory section, the main body of the project consists of six chapters. Due to the lack of data to perform a content analysis prior to the beginning of Jon Stewart's version of the *Daily Show*, the small amount of analyzable content that does exist with *SNL*, and the probable corresponding small sample size of journalistic commentary about such programs in this period, the analysis of the first three election cycles in chapter two—1980, 1984, and 1988—are collapsed into one chapter. The second chapter documents a crucial time for the media in the United States—the Clinton era. This chapter covers the 1992 and 1996 elections. Williams and Delli Carpini (2000) wrote that this period marked a turning point for journalism, when the rise of "multiple news outlets (cable news/talk shows, radio call-in shows, conservative publications like *American Spectator*), semi-news outlets (*Hard Copy, A Current Affair*), entertainment media (*The Tonight Show, Late Night with David Letterman*), and the internet (most notably, the *Drudge Report*)" began to erode the traditional distinctions between news media and entertainment media, a trend which assuredly has only continued to increase in the first decade of the twenty-first century (78). The third chapter covers the 2000 election, the first for which there is *Daily Show* content. The fourth chapter covers the 2004 election, during which the *Daily Show* had by now become an important source for public discussion about political events (Jacobs and Michaud Wild 2013). The fifth chapter, which covers the 2008 election, includes not only *SNL* and *Daily Show* content, and the mainstream press coverage about them, but also is the first election cycle that the *Colbert Report* was being broadcast. The final chapter discusses the findings and provides an overall picture of their significance for further research. Due to the popularity of cable, its successful market-based experiments in substantive satire, the dissemination of clips of those shows on the internet and in other areas of the public sphere, and the extensive commentary that serious journalists have made about it, late-night comedy has transformed from an amusing distraction to a meaningful force in twenty-first-century political commentary.

## NOTES

1. http://pewresearch.org/pubs/829/the-daily-show-journalism-satire-or-just-laughs.
2. *The State of the News Media*: "Evening News Viewership Over Time" http://www.stateofthemedia.org/2009/.
3. O'Connell M. (2017) "Kimmel Shakes Up Late Night Ratings Race as Fallon Sinks." *The Hollywood Reporter*. Available from: https://www.hollywoodreporter

.com/live-feed/kimmel-shakes-up-late-night-ratings-race-as-fallon-sinks-1047419 (accessed January 16, 2018).

4. Murray, Noel (2012). "Nixon Gets Socked in Laugh-In's Most Famous, and Influential, Five Seconds." *A.V. Club*, September 13. Accessed March 12, 2014. http://www.avclub.com/article/nixon-gets-socked-in-ilaugh-inis-most-famous-and-i-84881.

5. After he took over for Carson, Jay Leno remained first in the ratings the entire time he was on the air; however, many comedians do not respect him for "dumbing down" his act, or "selling out" for doing many commercial endorsements, and certainly never held him in as high regard as his predecessor.

## Chapter One

# Political Comedy in the Reagan/Bush Era

## *Unkind and Not So Gentle*

Generally, there was not a lot of substantive political humor on *SNL* in the 1980s. When the show did get into political matters, the personal crept in anyway, and it was not pretty. A prime example of a sketch where there was a little substantive criticism on *SNL* was from February 16, 1980, titled "Debate Substitute," in which President Carter's Press Secretary, Powell, was fielding questions instead of the president at a debate with Ted Kennedy. This sketch mocked Carter's tendency to retreat to the confines of the White House when the going got tough. A character named Burton, a townsperson at the New Hampshire debate, asks a question about what Carter might be doing about important matters of the day, like "inflation and the energy crisis and Iran." Powell answers in a way that encapsulated citizens' unhappiness with Carter:

> Well, I can assure you the president is working very hard at this moment. In fact, here's a picture of the President working very hard [holds up picture of Carter rolling up sleeves]. See, he's rolling up his sleeve there. I don't know if you can see, but his brow is knit. I wish that I could give you more details but unfortunately that would into the area of the President's performance in office during the last four years, and this is a subject I'm not at liberty to discuss.

They satirized Carter's poor communication style—he would not even represent himself and sent his Press Secretary instead. He gave the impression of "working hard" for the country, but it was all appearance and no substance. Although this is a good example of substantive humor on *SNL*, the sketch devolved into personal attacks against Ted Kennedy's marital and personal problems. After being stonewalled by Powell, the characters in the sketch then asked what they could discuss. Powell, the Press Secretary, said, "I'm

15

prepared to discuss the crisis of spirit in this country. I'm willing to talk about government as good as its people, [Kennedy's] wife, and Chappaquiddick."

A sketch called "Presidential Hopefuls Do Household Chores" from January 26, 1980, brought up the drowning incident as well. All of the candidates from both parties were mocked as groveling and desperate enough to do household tasks for an Iowa voter before the primaries, featured Ted Kennedy being portrayed as "accident prone." The Iowa voter, Mrs. Voekler, is handing out chores at her home:

> **Mrs. Voekler**: Well, my daughter Ellen should be finished with band practice soon, you could take the car and pick her up.
>
> **Kennedy**: I would be glad to pick her up.
>
> **Mrs. Voekler**: Senator Kennedy, I think it would be better if Rosalynn [Carter] took the car. [Big laughs from audience, realizing they were talking about Chappaquiddick] You just rest your back, relax here for a while.

Although the show made jokes about all the other candidates—Carter sends his wife instead of coming himself, Reagan is too old and needs his rest—the focus on the personal life of Ted Kennedy is especially notable. The 1980 season contained less of the elements of true satire, and was comprised of shallow parody and "cheap shots."

During the election cycles of 1980, 1984, and 1988, political humor on late night TV mostly consisted of Johnny Carson, *Saturday Night Live* (*SNL*), and later, David Letterman. Commentary about these programs in the *New York Times* (*NYT*) and the *Washington Post* (*WP*) often compared and contrasted these shows and commentators. When writing about late night television comedy in these election cycles, journalists made distinct statements about why they did not like it, and what, in their opinion, it should be saying instead, as if they were qualified to do so (a bit of a stretch, even by todays' standards). In general, writers for these papers found Carson's humor to be more astute and more reflective of public attitudes toward politics. However, they often dismissed *SNL*'s humor as juvenile and indicative of a turn toward a crass, less insightful public discourse that focused too much on trivial personal characteristics; this type of humor could be directed at any well-known person or public figure and did not differentiate itself as particularly "political" humor. One could make the argument that Carson better reflected the type of person the writers were themselves—largely older, white men. It is no surprise then that many of the laments from academia about the conflation of entertainment and news arose at this time, also from this same demographic (Postman 1985). *SNL* represented younger, generally more racially and gender diverse voices.

In an era when political comedy was not particularly substantive or critical, critics saw it as a distraction from real issues and information; if we are too

busy laughing at Reagan's bouts of forgetfulness or Ted Kennedy's checkered past, we may pay less attention to policy issues (which, after all, are not
by definition particularly entertaining). This complaint would be dismantled
after the rise of the *Daily Show* and the *Colbert Report* in the next century
as the critical comedy they deployed became part of the language of how the
journalists discussed elections, politicians, policy, etc. But for this era, from
the perspective of the journalists of the time, it was a valid criticism, as this
chapter will show. They valued substantive, critical humor in this medium
and disparaged the personal. They understood its influence as a sort of "piling on" and making politicians a laughingstock in a way that they could not
recover from, but that was the extent of its power in their observations.

Yet contrary to the feelings of the majority of *NYT* and *WP* journalists,
beginning in 1988, *SNL*'s humor began to exhibit signs that it was becoming
a more politically directed program. A Republican had been in the White
House for eight years, with the real possibility that another Republican—
George H. W. Bush—would be there for a further eight. The show became
more overtly left-leaning *and* substantively critical at this juncture. Were the
writers of *SNL* attempting to use their public forum to influence citizens'
political opinions? It is difficult to say with a significant degree of certainty
in 1988, but this would not be the case twenty years later. This change
foreshadowed the show's rise to a more central focus in American political
discourse, the pinnacle of which would be the 2008 election cycle. But in the
1980s, it would be hard to say that it was even the same show that it would
later become. Consequently, journalists that talked about *SNL*—when they
talked about it at all—characterized it as largely unimportant, despite the fact
that even then, it was shaping the popular imagination about any given politicians' character. Their disconnect from younger discourses shows. Answers
to the two central research questions of this study overall—one, what kinds
of satire did the shows mobilize to make claims about candidates and/or policies, and two, how this satire did or did not become part of public debate—began to form in these twentieth-century election cycles. This chapter examines
these three elections of the "Reagan-Bush" era, looking at all political humor
on *SNL*, mentions of late-night humor in the *NYT* and *WP*, and covers the
dates January 5, 1980, to November 4, 1980, February 23, 1984, to November
6, 1984, and July 1, 1987 to November 8, 1988.

## *SNL* IN THE 1980S

In 1980, 1984, and 1988, the content of *SNL* was balanced in its lack of substance, mostly having no political slant at all with a slight Democratic slant
in each year. This slant shows in an analysis of the narratives. There were a

couple of examples of a "Progressive Slant," that mocked both parties for not being sensitive enough to the needs of minorities, for example.

> Vernon Jordan, Head of the Urban League, denounced both the Republican and Democratic Presidential candidates, for turning the other cheek to problems of America's minorities. Jordan complained that candidate failed to respond to the needs of urban blacks and virtually ignore minority organizations. None of the candidates had any comment and claimed to never have heard of Jordan or of the blacks. (*SNL* "Weekend Update," January 26, 1980)

There were some sketches and jokes in 1980 that slanted strongly toward the Republicans, in that they targeted Jimmy Carter as being out of touch with the country's problems, and actively hiding from them, such as a sketch from April 5, 1980, called "ABC News: Frank Reynolds Reports on President Carter as White House Hostage." However, with most sketches having no slant (Table 1.1), the show made almost no attempt to sway audiences politically.

A recurring theme that was a source for commentary by the comedy shows as well as the newspapers throughout the 1980s was Ronald Reagan's advanced age. The question is, was this the subject of substantive or personal humor (Table 1.2)? There were plenty of opportunities here for substantive criticism of Regan on the basis of his age. Was he capable of making difficult decisions involving tense relations between the Soviet Union and the United States? During a time of recession, could he comprehend the complicated economic policies that his advisors were surely discussing with him? However, these early *SNL* episodes did not take advantage of such possibilities, usually mocking him for having almost a cartoon version of "senility." Two typical examples from the "Weekend Update" segment: "Reagan went on to reiterate his belief that he is not getting too old or senile to run for the Presidency. He then abruptly ended the press conference, put a bowl of rice pudding on his head, and took three umbrella steps out of the room" ("Weekend Update," February 16, 1980); and another that claimed, "Scientists now say they are convinced that increased sunspot activity in recent weeks is the cause

**Table 1.1.   Slant Toward?**

|                                    | None    | Democrats | Republicans | Progressive |
|------------------------------------|---------|-----------|-------------|-------------|
| 1980, Whole Election Cycle (26)    | 13      | 8         | 2           | 3           |
|                                    | (50%)   | (30.77%)  | (7.7%)      | (11.53%)    |
| 1984, Whole Election Cycle (18)    | 9       | 7         | 2           | 0           |
|                                    | (50%)   | (38.89%)  | (11.11%)    | (0%)        |
| 1988, Whole Election Cycle (78)    | 50      | 18        | 10          | 0           |
|                                    | (64.1%) | (23.1%)   | (12.8%)     | (0%)        |

**Table 1.2.   Personal or Substantive?**

|                                      | Both       | Personal    | Substantive |
|--------------------------------------|------------|-------------|-------------|
| 1980, Whole Election Cycle (26)      | 1          | 22          | 3           |
|                                      | (3.85%)    | (84.61%)    | (11.54%)    |
| 1984, Whole Election Cycle (18)      | 0          | 10          | 8           |
|                                      | (0%)       | (55.56%)    | (44.44%)    |
| 1988, Whole Election Cycle (78)      | 12         | 45          | 22          |
|                                      | (15.39%)   | (57.7%)     | (28.21%)    |

of erratic radio transmissions, inconsistent weather reports, and occasional lucid statements by Ronald Reagan" ("Weekend Update," April 12, 1980).

Even when there was quite a good opening to joke about Reagan's lack of understanding about the issues, potentially due to him being out of touch or even mentally compromised, *SNL* merely went after him for stumbling on his words. Former presidential candidate and Civil Rights leader Jesse Jackson hosted *SNL* on October 20, 1984, and even his commentary was no exception to this superficial trend. One sketch, called "Saturday Night News with Jesse Jackson," involved him analyzing answers that Reagan gave during a debate in the '84 election cycle, when Reagan mentioned that some money in the defense budget went to pay for the military's "wardrobe," and Jackson quipped that "Wardrobe is for a war movie. Uniforms are for a war." This was also a subtle dig at Reagan's past profession as an actor, yet another near-meaningless personal characteristic. Jackson goes on to say, "And I'm glad only a small portion of the defense budget goes to weapons." Although one might interpret this as a structural comment about how the budget was allocated, Jackson did not offer any thoughts as to whether or not Reagan was being entirely truthful or had a good understanding of the issue. However, in his monologue, Jackson made a few comments about the structure of the media's coverage of the campaign, and how it was more critical of him, in his view, than any of the other candidates. He joked that if he walked on water, the next day's newspaper headline would be, "Jesse can't swim."

The theme of media coverage, or lack thereof, was also evident in John Anderson's run during the 1980 election cycle, who was described, in a "Weekend Update" joke, as having had "yet another newspaper article written about him describing his inability to get any press coverage. This brings the total number of news articles about John Anderson up to 7 million, ten times the number that have been written about all the other candidates put together" ("Weekend Update," February 23, 1980). During these early years of the show, *SNL* did a few jokes and sketches that satirized media coverage of presidential elections, but it was not particularly critical of the structure of media. Rather, it focused on the concept that news media would do anything for ratings, and would squeeze the campaign for its last drop of material that audiences would conceivably watch (a prescient complaint, to be sure). *SNL* did several sketches in the 1988 election cycle with Al Franken going out with a satellite dish on his head trying to cover the election from the campaign trail, and breaking up while trying to transmit, in a satire of campaign-coverage gimmicks. The show also characterized television election coverage as generally dull:

> People who listened to the legendary Kennedy/Nixon debate . . . felt that Nixon had won, while those who watched it on TV felt that Kennedy won. People who listened to the Bush/Dukakis debate on radio called it a draw, and those who watched it on TV felt they had listened to it on the radio. ("Weekend Update," October 15, 1988)

*SNL* parodied specific political talk show hosts and veteran newsmen as well. In an attempt to get ratings for a flagging program, a sketch depicted talk show host Tom Snyder interviewing the brothers of presidential candidates to see if they are as embarrassing as Billy Carter ("Prime Time Saturday," February 23, 1980). An appearance by veteran NBC newsman Edwin Newman, who hosted the "Weekend Update" segment on November 3, 1984 (then called "Saturday Night News with Edwin Newman"), made fun of the Fairness Doctrine: "if I tell a joke about Mr. Reagan and a joke about Mondale, and only one of those jokes gets a laugh, it might affect the outcome of the election and determine the make-up of the Supreme Court for years to come, and frankly for one joke, I don't want that responsibility."

## POLICY CRITIQUE OR PERSONAL HUMOR?

When did *SNL* satirize actual policies of political parties? There were few sketches or "Weekend Update" jokes in the early years of 1980 and 1984 that were deeply critical of particular Republicans or their policies. Rather, there was a general sense that the Republicans were out of touch with the people and were more inclined to support the interests of the richest Americans. Occasionally, there was an offhand joke here and there that portrayed them as slightly evil, as in this joke from "Weekend Update," February 23, 1980: "Imagine that some Republicans were holding a cockfight. The moderate Republican is the one that brings the duck. The conservative Republican is the one that bet on the duck. And the senile reactionary Republican is the one that tells the story about the cockfight." This comment was in reference to a joke that Reagan told while on the campaign trail in February 1980, during the Primary, that some construed as an ethnic joke against the Polish and the Italians, for which he was asked to apologize ("Nation: Duck!" *Time*, March 3, 1980).

Later on, however, after eight years of the Republican Party being in charge of the White House, the gloves began to come off. During the 1988 election cycle, there were many more jokes and sketches that were critical of Republicans in a substantive way, and revealed a general sense that all of the Republican candidates that voters had to choose from during the primary were bad choices for the voters: "a new third place finisher, Drew McLemore . . . classifies himself as an anti-ruralist, and has promised, if elected, to destroy Iowa with a thermonuclear device. McLemore edged Bush by a scant eighty votes" ("Weekend Update," February 13, 1988). "Weekend Update" jokes were more likely to go after Republicans in this way, while sketches were more likely to go after specific Republicans; however, in the sketches, the jokes were much more frequently directed at personal characteristics, rather than substantive policy issues. There were some exceptions, such as this sketch from April 14, 1984, called "Very, Very Hungry Man Dinners":

**Mother**: Dinner! Everybody hungry?

**Father**: You bet! After a day of hopeless job-hunting, I could eat a bear! Oh, not surplus cheese-loaf again! This is the eighteenth day in a row!

**Mother**: But how can I plan an interesting menu on $11 a week? What's a welfare mother to do?

**President Ronald Reagan**: Sound familiar? Well, we here at White House Foods don't believe that poverty-line cuisine has to be boring. That's why we've collected starvation-level cooking from around the Third-World for our Very Hungry, Hungry Man Dinners.

. . .

**President Ronald Reagan**: And now, try Very, Very Hungry Man Dinners for the Elderly! Featuring low-sodium Cat Food! And Very Hungry Kid's School Lunches, complete with two vegetables—ketchup and salt! Enough to meet 100% of my federal nutrition standards!

Mostly, however, *SNL* made fun of specific candidates and their personality characteristics during this time period once again. In particular, Dan Quayle stood out as a specific target. He provided ample fodder for all political commentators, humorous or otherwise, during the years he was in office or running for office, with his many gaffes. Jokes were aimed at his or his wife's haircuts ("Weekend Update," October 8, 1988, October 22, 1988), or his likely surprise and shock would George H. W. Bush die, and if he would wake up to find himself president ("Dan Quayle: President," October 22,

1988). But although his age and inexperience were mentioned briefly, they were never satirized as serious issues.

*SNL* stayed away from critically mocking either Mondale or Ferraro during the 1984 election cycle. There was one sketch, called "TVs' Foul-Ups, Bleeps, Blunders, Bloopers, Practical Jokes, and Political Debates" where for some reason, Mondale cannot stop accidentally swearing during a Democratic debate (April 7, 1984), and another bit in which Rich Hall actually followed the real Mondale around to fundraising dinners and gently mocked him for doing so many ("Rich Hall's Election Report," October 6, 1984). Perhaps because she was the first major-party female vice presidential candidate or perhaps because of *SNL*'s general slight Democratic-positive slant, the show did not mock Ferraro at all. However, they also did not discuss any of her policy positions. The show only focused on the fact that she was female, and did not treat her candidacy seriously. In what most people might now regard as a sexist piece of commentary, Billy Crystal, in his monologue as host of the show in October 6, 1984, said, of Ferraro's hypothetical "old boyfriends"—"They feel a little jealous. And when guys feel left out, they make up stuff about women. These guys in Brooklyn, watching her up on a bar TV screen, 'It's Jerry. I slept with her.'"—and then he makes a so-so motion with hands. Ferarro herself appeared on the show during "Weekend Update" (then called "Saturday Night News") on October 13, 1984. She was there to respond to a comment Barbara Bush had made about her, calling Ferarro "a $4 million word that rhymes with rich but I can't say it." Jokingly, Ferarro interpreted this as Barbara Bush calling her a "snitch," which she humorously disputed. Again, this reinforces an anti-feminist dialogue, which advances the idea that women in politics will always resort to name calling and "cat fights" that have nothing to do with policy.

Another prime target during these years was Gary Hart. Two main aspects of Hart's candidacy were satirized the most on *SNL*—his sex scandal with model Donna Rice, and his dropping out, getting back into, and second drop-out of the presidential race. Both "Weekend Update" jokes and sketches focused on these two aspects. A typical comment from Dennis Miller: "So, Gary Hart wants back in the race . . . This guy sleeps with every dame on the planet, I'm supposed to forgive and forget . . . I just don't know how stable this Hart cat is. I'd hate to think we got into World War III because this guy saw a cute chick in the Kremlin" ("Weekend Update," December 18, 1987). Miller frequently targeted the indecisiveness of Hart's campaign with quick one-liners starting with the phrase "This just in," making it appear that one cannot keep up with all the times Hart changes his mind: "This just in: in the last 3 minutes, Gary Hart was caught in a Washington, D.C. condominium with a twenty-three-year old model, and announced he is dropping out of the race again" ("Weekend Update," November 5, 1988). Hart was acting irrationally, allowing his personal desires to get in the way of running a viable campaign. Like with Dukakis, these personal aspects, and how they affected the campaign, were of primary focus, and no substantive comments were ever made about either of their policies. Once the comedians could heap derision upon a candidate for a personal characteristic, there was little room to go after them for substantive policy issues or ability to govern. This process actually *prevented* the potential for critical comedy to emerge, and was interpreted by the newspaper writers as cynicism. This type of humor is akin to Bakhtin's (1968) conception of a type of false satire that is only capable of negating and invalidating the politician's place in the Democratic process, without going deeply into the issues or questions of competence.

One of the most ironic statements on *SNL* appeared on the "Weekend Update" segment on November 21, 1987. Regarding Gorbachev coming to the U.S. to speak to Congress, which Republican leaders opposed, Dennis Miller said, "Now if the Fox network still had the late show on, we could make him host that for a night. Really put the screws to him. But it's off the air now, and I hear they're going to do a late-night comedy news show. Trust me, boys, that's an impossibility, it'll never fly." Of course, as we know, late-night comedy news shows became incredibly popular after the beginning of the twenty-first century with the advent of the *Daily Show* and the *Colbert Report*. Miller here was possibly joking about *SNL*'s low ratings, or the feeling that such a show could not make it in the ratings more than one night a week, and that only in a very small segment, such as "Weekend Update." But the main difference is that this type of show has been and is extremely successful, but only after the shift toward a much more critical form of comedy that aims its satire at substantive issues more than personal ones. *SNL*'s formula had become tiresome, not political comedy itself. The show at this point in time characterized Republicans as "bad"—out of touch with people's real-world economic concerns, more likely to represent the interests of the rich, etc. However, specific Democrats, like Ted Kennedy, Carter, Hart, Biden, Dukakis, Mondale, and others, were parodied for being liars, cheaters, indecisive, greedy, and ineffective as leaders. But the criticism was only a cartoon version of who the people were or what they did. The show exaggerated one or two incidents to represent the whole of their political life.

## HUMOR COMMENTARY IN THE *WASHINGTON POST* AND THE *NEW YORK TIMES*

If *SNL*, Carson, Letterman, or other comedians were making fun of general impressions about the candidates, Democratic or Republican, or staying within the realm of superficial personality characteristics, it would not fit into the narrative structure of true critical satire. To achieve this, the comedy would need more specificity; a satire of not just the characters, but what they were doing, and of their policies. The "plot" of what the candidates have done, or what their policies indicate they *will do*, was rarely even brought up. Besides a few brief mentions of Republican policies that negatively affect the poor or minorities, *SNL* and other late night comedians stuck to non-substantive criticism in the 1980s. While this was a perfectly adequate form of comedy in and of itself, it was unlikely to motivate voters to think about the issues. The commentary in the "official" public sphere, represented here by the *NYT* and the *WP*, showed a disdain for these programs that reflected the traditional binary between "news" as good and "entertainment" as bad. In their opinion, the shows had the opportunity to say something important, since they were so widely watched, but they fell short. Other than early 1980s respect for Johnny Carson's place as a satirical pundit, who was recognized as setting the tone for the campaign, the journalists largely expressed the view that political comedy on television, and *SNL* in particular, detracted from the Democratic deliberative process and rational debate. Since only John Anderson appeared on *SNL*, there was not much discussion about candidates appearing on the shows. The negative feelings toward *SNL* meant that journalists in this era did not often use television political humor narratives to express their own opinions, as they would in later years.

In 1980, neither the *WP* nor the *NYT* had much to say at all on the topic of political comedy on television during the election cycle. There were only eight mentions in the *NYT* and thirteen in the *WP* at all. When they did talk about it, the focus was mainly on Johnny Carson. They described him as "perhaps the nation's most prominent political commentator" and said his monologue was a "bellwether" for the nation's overall political climate at this time. From the coverage in these papers, it would seem like Reagan's landslide victory was not a predictable outcome: "[Carson] asked his studio audience if it thought [third party candidate] Mr. Anderson should withdraw. A sizable number applauded. Then Mr. Carson asked, 'How many think Carter and Reagan should withdraw?' Almost everyone clapped" (Adam Clymer, "News Analysis; Stakes Turn National," *New York Times*, October 20, 1980). Perhaps the papers gave Carson more credit than they should have. For the most part, the papers agreed with what Carson was saying about the elections and the politicians in it, that they were not terribly impressive. There was an incident involving a League of Women Voter's debate that was to take place in September 1980, in which Carter said he would not attend if Anderson was invited, wanting instead to debate Reagan alone. The group at first stated that they would place an empty chair on the stage to symbolize his absence.

The papers credited a joke of Carson's—"Suppose the chair wins?"—with the League changing their mind about doing this. It was too close to the truth and might bias the election. Writers for the papers were themselves biased *toward Carson*, perhaps because of his long-standing position as a respected voice in televised political comedy. They were using his jokes to back up their own viewpoint, despite the fact that they turned out to be factually incorrect, in that Reagan ended up being far more popular than either the newspaper writers or Carson gave him credit for being. One exception to the writers agreeing with Carson was a *WP* writer defending Reagan against the barbs of Carson: "contrary to the needles of Johnny Carson, it is not Jerry Brown who is the prototypical laid-back, unflappable and mellow California. Brown is quite driven and uptight, like Jimmy Carter. Reagan is the true Californian" (Mark Shields, "The Real Californian," *Washington Post*, July 20, 1980). But this type of comment was not common, with the writers in general holding Carson's satirical political commentary in high regard.

If the papers typically agreed with Carson, and valued his opinions, the opposite was true for their evaluation of *SNL*. There was a general agreement that *SNL* had the ability to accurately point out that the candidates were self-parodying at times: "The charm of Campaign '80 (I guess) is that everything it touches it turns into parody. This is true even of deadly issues of war and peace, which by the time the candidates get through with them, seem to be coming to us direct from 'Saturday Night Live'" (Meg Greenfield, "The Real Military Issue," *Washington Post*, October 1, 1980). In general, though, they did not write about *SNL* in a positive light. One *WP* writer felt that the show had a negative effect on other reporters:

> In some ways, today's younger reporters who cover [Ted] Kennedy reflect the feeling that for most Americans "there are no heroes today" as George Gallup Jr. states. They are nurtured on "Saturday Night Live" where taste has never been a criterion for humor. Kennedy and Chappaquiddick are spoofed unmercifully; a Bill Murray imitation of Kennedy with seaweed dripping from him, mumbling incoherent and unintelligible sentences. (Myra MacPherson, "Teddy the Underdog Flies into the Maine Event," *Washington Post*, February 10, 1980)

Of course, this criticism was aimed these other "younger reporters" and not the writer of the article, who was presumably exempt from *SNL*'s effects. This was a trend that would continue in the 2000s after the establishment of the *Daily Show* and the *Colbert Report* as a resource for establishment newspaper journalists to distinguish themselves from television news (Jacobs and Michaud Wild 2013).

There were, in fact, several rather brutal jokes on *SNL* during this period that made fun of the incident where Ted Kennedy's actions caused the death of the young woman, Mary Jo Kopechne, described above. They might seem shocking in a more politically correct era, though it is possible to credit this incident to Kennedy's inability to win the Democratic nomination—an over-arching piling on of abuse on the loser. If Carson was the presumed cultural indicator of where the election will go, *SNL* was the weathervane for the decline in the tone of public discourse, according to the writers in the *WP* and *NYT*. The papers could not see through the surface-level parody and did not see any substance beneath it.

In the *WP*'s and the *NYT*'s coverage of political comedy on television, there was a slight shift that began to take place between 1980 and 1984. There was an increasing relevance of political candidates appearing on *SNL*, and an agreement that candidates who went on the show and did well got a general career boost, but there was a decreasing relevance of its political satire in general; although they paid much attention to Jesse Jackson's appearance on the show, the writers all basically agreed that *SNL* was not funny in those days. Despite the fact that there were many actors and actresses that went on to later success, such as Julia Louis-Dreyfus and Eddie Murphy, the loss of the old "classic" cast members and change in producers sent the show adrift.[1] Ratings were bad, and it seemed the show would not come back on more than one occasion. In 1984, *SNL* Producer Dick Ebersol was quoted in the *NYT* as saying that half the writers would leave, and that the election provided an opportunity to revive a truer form of political satire. Peter W. Kaplan commented that, "If that happens it may be the first time in a long time that satire becomes what *opens* on 'Saturday Night'" (Peter W. Kaplan, "TV Notes; Role of Networks in Election Results," *New York Times*, June 9, 1984). Harsh criticism indeed. Tom Shales states that the 1984 season's *SNL* was one "for young Republicans." Yet journalists hailed Jesse Jackson's appearance as an important one and mentioned it in four articles. In the *WP*, Shales wrote that Jackson could count as a substitute for a black cast member, which the show lacked at the time, and that he "revitalized and energized 'Saturday Night Live' with a performance that was sure, funny and accomplished . . . ratings indicate the former Democratic presidential contender attracted larger audiences than are usual for the program in its post-hip era" (Tom Shales, "And Now, Here's Jesse! Jackson Scores a Hit On 'Saturday Night Live,'" *Washington Post*, October 22, 1984).

Another interesting departure from the previous election cycle was some criticism of Carson's stance on Reagan. In 1980, the papers agreed with the talk show host's stance that all the candidates were pretty uninspiring, and they turned out to be wrong when Reagan won in a landslide that year. Then, in 1984, when Carson mocked Reagan, even when it was deserved (such as when Reagan does poorly in a debate) it did not go over well with his audience:

When Johnny Carson makes fun of a public figure, it is generally safe to assume that the person has become fair game. The theory is that when Carson is ready to kid, Middle America is ready, too. But several nights after the Mondale-Reagan debate, Carson attempted a few pleasantries about President Reagan's undisputed flop in Louisville. He noted that when the next debate takes place, Reagan "will be two weeks older." Instead of the cascade of laughter that he usually gets from his doting audience, Carson was met with heavy silence . . . If the "Tonight" audience is the electorate writ small, American voters are terribly sensitive about Reagan on the ropes. They were embarrassed and disturbed by seeing 100 unedited minutes of the man they intend to reelect. (Mary McGrory, "No Laughing Matter," *Washington Post*, October 18, 1984)

Reagan was possibly showing early signs of dementia during this debate, and the public and the audience, though perhaps not consciously aware of this potential problem, may not have thought it funny to make fun of an elderly man showing signs of confusion. However, the papers still portrayed Carson as an uncanny predictor of the political climate. When Gary Hart won the New Hampshire primary on February 28, 1984, defeating Mondale, Carson made a joke about it *before* the results were even in. The *WP* called him a "prescient" commentator when he said, at midnight on "The Tonight Show," "Well, Mondale kind of had a Hart attack tonight in New Hampshire," even though the show was taped six hours earlier in Los Angeles (Tom Shales, "TV's New Tune: Play It by Hart," *Washington Post*, February 29, 1984).

The 1988 presidential campaign participants provided fertile ground for jokes on late-night comedy programs and commentary about them in the mainstream press. This was true for both parties. On one hand there were many more gaffes by Vice President Dan Quayle ("The Holocaust was an obscene period in our nation's history. No, not our nation's, but in World War II. I mean, we all lived in this century. I didn't live in this century, but in this century's history."—Press conference, September 15, 1988). There were many comments by Carson and Jay Leno (while filling in for Carson) about Quayle joining the Indiana National Guard to avoid going to Vietnam. There was the general fear about putting someone like Quayle second in line for the presidency (a theme that would be repeated in the 2008 campaign regarding Sarah Palin): "Johnny Carson jokes that a kid 'scared the hell out of me' on Halloween when he came to his door dressed as 'President Quayle'" (Juan Williams, "Why America Doesn't Vote," *Washington Post*, November 6, 1988). There was George H. W. Bush's "wimp factor" to be mocked: "The press writes about it, pollsters ask voters about it (51 percent agree that the 'wimp' image will be a serious problem, Newsweek reports in self-fulfilling prophecy), Doonesbury, Carson and Letterman have their fun with it" (Paul Taylor, "Election '88: Sullen Voters and the Cult of Personality," *Washington*

*Post*, October 18, 1987). In fact, there were two mentions, one in both papers, of quantitative measures of jokes on late-night comedy, and they both found that comedians mocked Republicans more often than Democratic candidates: "U.S. News & World Report found that television comedians told twice as many jokes about Republican candidates as they did about Democratic candidates in February, with Mr. Bush the prime target" (AP, "Politicians are Fair Game," *New York Times*, March 7, 1988). Additionally, "The Center [for Media and Public Affairs] found that in Carson monologues from January 1 through June 7, Republicans were the targets of seventy-three jokes, compared with forty-one about Democrats" (John Carmody, "Make-Believe Companions," *Washington Post*, July 19, 1988). On the other side, earlier in the primaries, Joe Biden was a frequent target. Eventually, Biden dropped out of the race due to accusations of plagiarism (Biden had lifted, more or less unacknowledged, a few lines from a speech from a British Labor party leader, when Biden gave a speech at the Iowa State Fair in August of 1987). This, combined with revelations that Biden had stretched the truth a bit about his college accomplishments, resulted in an avalanche of media criticism, including by late-night comedians: "Once he becomes the butt of a hundred jokes heard in a million bedrooms—Senator Biden tried to cheer up his staff, said Mr. Carson; he told them they had nothing to fear but fear itself—it is hard for any mere politician to survive" (R. W. Apple Jr., "Candidates' Transgressions Loom Large on Home Screen," *New York Times*, September 27, 1987). It is worth noting at this point that the writer in this *Times* article *did* attribute a causal force of the satire to the "decline" of the politician. However, it was merely an *additional* force to influences that already existed; it was not perceived as the instigating factor.

More important than the plagiarism accusations leveled against Joe Biden, and certainly falling into the category of scenting blood about a candidate's falling place in the minds of the public, was the alleged affair that Gary Hart had with twenty-nine-year-old model Donna Rice, on his yacht aptly named "Monkey Business." This caused Hart to drop out of the race on May 8, 1987, only to re-enter it briefly from December to March, when he dropped out for a second time. Writers mentioned his character, and its relevance to the campaign, as an overly obvious choice of target: "These have to be the cruelest days, because they are the dismissive days. Gary Hart, national joke. Just say those two words in certain quarters: Gary Hart. Ha. Ha. Please, please, stop it, you're killing me" (Paul Hendrickson, "Gary Hart & the Journey to the Trail's End," *Washington Post*, February 8, 1988). Nevertheless, other writers characterized it as clearly fair game for late-night television comedy, because of the importance of a candidate appearing as if they were an easy target who could not be taken seriously: "Many feel, as Johnny Carson said, that Mr. Hart's trying to ignore his past reputation is akin to Carmen Miranda's asking people not to notice that she is dancing with a bowl of fruit on her head" (Maureen Dowd, "Hart's Campaign Igniting Emotions," *New York Times*, January 13, 1988). Again, the way that writers in the paper treated the commentary by comedians shows that once you have made yourself into a laughingstock, the campaign is effectively over. "Mr. Orren [of Harvard's Center on Press, Politics and Public Policy] said the troubles of . . . Democratic candidates had made the party a target for the nation's most devastating political critics: television comedians. 'It's the Johnny Carson jokes that may hurt most . . . You go from ridicule to derision'" (E. J. Dionne Jr., "Some Perceiving Self-Destruction for Democrats," *New York Times*, October 2, 1987). The main difference between jabs at Quayle's competence and Hart's infidelities was that Quayle was not running for president himself.

The other Democratic candidate besides Hart who was mocked the most out of all three of these years was Michael Dukakis, and the papers took notice of this as well. *SNL* portrayed Dukakis as an extraterrestrial due to his lack of emotionality and dullness ("Alien Dukakis," October 22, 1988) and, as the nominee, the show cast him as someone who could not win: "Out in Euclid, Ohio this week, following the debate, and the latest poll results, Michael Dukakis picked up his trumpet and played his newly-adopted official campaign song. Let's hear a little of it [plays 'Taps']" ("Weekend Update," October 22, 1988). Once it became clear the Dukakis would be the Democratic nominee, according to the *WP* and the *NYT*, the coverage of the campaign tilted toward mocking Dukakis most frequently, despite the earlier empirical evidence that Republicans were targets of jokes more often: "In the early months of the campaign, Mr. Carson's jokes were full of references to Mr. Bush as a wimp. Now they are full of jabs at Mr. Dukakis as boring" (Michael Oreskes, "TV's Voter Influence Extends Beyond Ads," *New York Times*, November 7, 1988). The writers largely attributed this shift to Dukakis' infamous tank ride. In September of 1988, he was photographed riding in an M-1 Abrams tank, smiling and waving. This goofy image, with the candidate wearing a too-big helmet and giving the thumbs-up, was used by the Bush campaign in an attack ad, claiming that Dukakis was soft on defense due to his voting record, and, like the tank ride, was all appearance, and no substance. However, it is arguable that Carson's jokes about it may have had a devastating impact on his candidacy as the Bush anti-Dukakis ad did: "'Obviously everyone knew it was a mistake, except the Dukakis campaign,' said KRC pollster Gerry Chervinsky . . . 'Even Johnny Carson made jokes about the ride'" (Maralee Schwartz, "An Image-Making Flop," *Washington Post*, September 21, 1988). Although it was likely that at least some of those who said they were less likely to vote for Dukakis "based on what they had seen or heard about the tank ride" got Carson's perspective as the most influential thing they heard about the entire incident, it was also possible that Carson was just going along with the prevailing winds of opinion. Thus Carson's (and the other comedians') shift from concentrating on the Republican candidates to subsequently focusing on Dukakis, made them opinion followers and *not* opinion leaders.

## CONCLUSION

The idea that television comedians were following prevailing sentiment was the opinion of legendary comedian Mort Sahl, known to be a strong critic of conventional and conservative politics. Speaking about Carson and those comedians who appeared on his show, Sahl said:

> In the phrase of Graham Greene, the comedian is a dangerous man. Well, they're not dangerous men. What they're trying to do is sell-in; they're not trying to overthrow . . . They want to be part of that commercial success, they want to join it. The Carson show is a ticket to join it. The healthy attitude for them would be to be skeptical of that, as a protector of the status quo, which he is. (Peter J. Boyer, "Hold the Borscht, Here Comes Mort Sahl," *New York Times*, October 4, 1987)

Did *SNL* fall into this category as well? The lack of real substantive humor about the elections, the parties, the candidates, or their policies put *SNL* on equal footing with Sahl's opinions about Carson in these years. They could impact the way people thought of the candidates, but the humor was drifting along the same course of public opinion anyway, taking advantage of it and not setting the agenda in a critical way. Perhaps the humor was the final nail in the campaigns' respective coffins, but it was not distinct in the way that it spoke about any substantive issue. This would change in the future, but for now, the humor was mired in the mundane. Journalists and other commentators, like Sahl, criticized the lack of substance as having missed an opportunity; that is, when humor about politicians is on the same level as humor about any other public figure or celebrity, it does not reach its potential. It makes no difference if a politician speaks oddly or looks strange, but they *can* influence citizens' lives in a unique way. Thus the stakes are higher for political humor than any other type.

Given the lack of critical humor on *SNL*, especially in the early 1980s presidential election cycles, it is difficult to understand how they became such an important cultural force in politics in the late 2000s. The writers in the *Post* and the *Times* did not see much of a future for *SNL* in this period. Here we see what Moy et al. (2006), Niven et al. (2003), and Peterson (2008) wrote about: a lack of substantive criticism that presumably functions as "mass distraction." But the show plodded on through the Reagan-Bush era and became slightly more critical of conservative policies. But when the pendulum swung back, and the Clinton era began, the primary target would inevitably become liberals and Democrats (as Tom Shales caustically alluded to above). The deep divisions in the United States after September 11, 2001, and the emerging "War on Terror" would cause the pendulum to swing back yet again. Only this time, the influence of the critically acclaimed *Daily Show* would set the stage for a much more substantively satirical *Saturday Night Live*. Jokes about a political candidate's personal life or mere malapropisms can become tiresome and make the viewer more sympathetic to them in the end. In the years that this chapter examines, we can clearly see this effect in the writers' attitudes towards *SNL* in regards to Gary Hart and Dan Quayle. In future election cycles, Bill Clinton and George W. Bush filled these roles. Jokes about Ronald Reagan's age fell flat; Bob Dole would suffer the same jokes. If the *Daily Show* or the *Colbert Report* had adhered to this formula, they would never have lasted, let alone won Peabody Awards.

## NOTE

1. Original Producer Lorne Michaels was replaced by Jean Doumanian in 1980, who was in turn replaced by Dick Ebersol. Ebersol was replaced when original Producer Michaels came back.

## Chapter Two

# The Clinton Era

## Humor Below the Belt

Part of the reason why personal humor was so much at the forefront in the 1990s was because of the odd personality of the third-party candidate, Ross Perot, in the 1992 election. This set the tone for political humor in the decade. Not much was known about Perot's policy positions, because he had such a hard time explaining them to the public. First, there was his heavy Southern accent and propensity to talk fast, coupled with the many numbers he would spout, and rapid-fire changing of topics he engaged in, which made his real ideas hard to pin down. Second, he had the stigma of buying his way into the election, as no one without political experience would have made it to a national election and gotten their name on the ballot in all fifty states without an enormous personal bankroll: "Ross Perot filed a financial disclosure statement on Friday, putting his personal fortune at 3.3 billion, or 800 million more than previously estimated. As a result, yesterday Perot was awarded an honorary Dr. of Money degree at Oklahoma State University" ("Weekend Update," May 16, 1992). Third, he was of short stature, which *SNL* mentioned a few times as a reason not to take him seriously, however wrongly: "While campaigning this week, Ross Perot was startled when he was continuously picked up and kissed by babies" ("Weekend Update," October 31, 1992), and his supposed resemblance to chicken-selling businessman Frank Perdue ("Weekend Update," May 16, 1992). Finally, there was a great deal of contention among his campaign staff and indecision on Perot's part on whether he would run or not. In July of 1992, after his campaign manager resigned amid "emptiness and chaos" (Anthony Lewis, "Abroad at Home; Why Perot?" *New York Times*, October 2, 1992). Perot claimed on the CBS newsmagazine program *60 Minutes* that his family was the target of a George H. W. Bush-directed CIA plot to disrupt his daughter's wedding, and that he

33

needed to drop out of the campaign to spare her embarrassment (Richard L. Berke, "The 1992 Campaign: The Overview; Perot Says He Quit in July to Thwart G.O.P. 'Dirty Tricks,'" *New York Times*, October 26, 1992). These factors made him more susceptible to jokes about his personality, appearance, and wealth, which is exactly what *SNL* engaged in the most in 1992; the show highlighted his propensity for bizarre accusations and the public perception of them: "Alright, this . . . astrologer to the stars had a premonition. She told me that the Republican Party was planning to drug me and my family, yank all our dental work, and replace them with transmitters inside our fillings" ("Ross Perot Press Conference," October 31, 1992).

Perhaps most memorably, *SNL* mocked Perot's selection of an unusual running mate, the sixty-nine-year-old Admiral James Stockdale. During an October debate appearance alongside Quayle and Gore, Stockdale seemed unprepared to discuss policy, and had difficulty hearing the questions. His opening statement began with the lines, "Who am I? Why am I here?" While meant to be a rhetorical introduction, it was clearly open to misinterpretation. This debate performance resulted in arguably the most memorable campaign sketch of the 1992 election cycle. In a devastating portrayal of the admiral, *SNL* performer Phil Hartman played him as a confused, senile old man who Dana Carvey's Perot desperately wanted to get rid of by dropping him off in the middle of nowhere. The phrase "gridlock," used by Stockdale to indicate that government was unable to operate efficiently, was also satirized.

> **Perot**: You wanna hear some music? You'd like that, wouldn't you? . . . Aw, I don't believe it! You see? Is that how the game is played, Admiral? They can't put a transmitter out here so good, honest, decent American people can hear some nice country music. And I just think that's sad!
>
> **Stockdale**: GOVERNMENT'S IN . . . ! IN GRIDLOCK!
>
> **Perot**: Well, there you go! Now, that was vintage! That was one of the finest moments in any debate I've ever seen. . . .
>
> **Stockdale**: WHO AM I?! WHY AM I HERE?!
>
> **Perot**: Well, you're the Admiral! You're taking a joyride! Oh, I get it! You're quoting yourself, right? "Who am I?" Now, that line there, that was precious! And you know, Admiral, when you were wandering around there—remember that? When it looked like you were gonna go over to Gore's podium? . . . And the part where you were stopping and stuttering—grand slam, I'll tell you! Shows you weren't rehearsed. . . . And the way your mind drifted—showed you're open to new ideas. And, Admiral . . . when you forgot your hearing aid was off, like you didn't know where you were—well, that was just stunning! ("Perot-Stockdale," October 24, 1992)

Although it is easy to claim that *SNL* was just being incredibly unflattering in their portrayal of Stockdale, the show was following its standard practice of highlighting personal characteristics in this election, and his debate performance was simply too easy of a target to pass up.

There was some extremely brief substantive humor about Perot—one "Weekend Update" joke about the fact that he had to pay his campaign "volunteers" (October 3, 1992); and one sketch where he outlined his policy to improve unemployment that showed he did not understand the economy and often tried to sound smarter than he really was. A somewhat racist May 9, 1992, sketch showed how he might deal with the Los Angeles; riots: "Now, here's what I'm gonna do—I'm gonna rebuild every building, state-of-the-art technology, put computers in every one of them, train the Crips, train the Bloods to operate the computers, put them to work competing against the Japanese." Dana Carvey's Perot character then went on to spout many confusing and unsupported claims about business statistics (parodied in an *SNL* sketch on October 3, 1992, where he talked about how much money the country would save if everyone wore the same style shoe).

If the 1980s was typified by jokes about Ronald Reagan's age, that theme was repeated and greatly amplified in the 1990s by jokes about Bob Dole's age. The tawdriness of jokes about Bill Clinton's presumed sexual improprieties crept in as well (and this was before the Monica Lewinsky scandal). Newspaper commentary in the *NYT* and the *WP* often focused on the trend toward the vicious personal humor on the shows. This era included *SNL*, David Letterman, newcomer Conan O'Brien, the departure of Johnny Carson, and the rise of Jay Leno. But at the same time, journalists also began to take note of the public's increasing attention to these shows as a source of news. However, the journalists who wrote about it were unable or unwilling to understand why this change was beginning to occur, a trend that would only increase. The writers in the papers saw the comedy as boring, formulaic, and safe, which was not an unfair assessment. In 1992, jokes about Dan Quayle's intelligence would be seen as hurting the Bush campaign (a foreshadowing of what happened with Sarah Palin in 2008). In 1996, journalists saw the constant harping on Bob Dole's age as hurting his campaign. Once his poll numbers began to slip, the jokes about him intensified. The jokes about Clinton's moral character, however, were seen as something he could more easily brush off, especially in the 1996 election cycle, since the economy was doing well.

Substantive humor, to the extent that it happened at all, was directed at George H. W. Bush, and more secondary candidates like Pat Buchanan. Much of the humor on *SNL* in particular was directed at Perot, a strong third-party candidate, thus taking away from other chances to mock the main party candidates. There were opportunities for substantive humor in the 1990s—incidents like the Congressional "Government Shutdown," the L.A. riots, and the U.S. involvement in the Bosnian conflict were missed chances for truly critical comedy. It seemed like substantive humor was beginning to form in the 1980s election cycles, especially on *SNL*, but the process got derailed during the Clinton era. This was largely due to the personalities that hosted *SNL*'s "Weekend Update" segment—Kevin Nealon in 1992, who was bland and conventional in his humor, and Norm MacDonald, who was savage in his personal critiques. Nealon's and Mac-Donald's humor were opposites in comedic demeanor, though neither of them were substantively critical. The show's overall tone of personality-based humor in the 1990s was driven by these personalities to the detriment of substantive humor (Day 2012). This would change after more substantively critical comedians like Tina Fey emerged in the 2000s, but for now, *SNL* remained weak in its satire. This chapter examines the 1990s election cycles of the "Clinton" era, looking at all political humor on *SNL*, and mentions of the late-night talk show hosts and *SNL*, and includes the dates from February 29, 1992, to November 3, 1992, and October 11, 1995, to November 6, 1996.

## THE DOMINANCE OF PERSONALITY-BASED HUMOR IN 1992 AND 1996 ON *SNL*

Humor in the 1992 and 1996 election cycles was mostly about personality; when the show brought up substantive issues at all, they were usually combined with personality-based humor. This weakened the satire. There were far more "Weekend Update" segment jokes than sketches, and, as mentioned above, these jokes were largely driven by the type of humor that the comedians who delivered them employed.

Even when substantive jokes stood alone, they were not effectively critical, as in this sketch about Clinton's economic policy, where they portrayed

**Table 2.1.  Slant Toward?** *SNL*

|  | *None* | *Democrats* | *Republicans* |
|---|---|---|---|
| 1992, Whole Election Cycle (62) | 27 | 20 | 15 |
|  | (43.5%) | (32.3%) | (24.3%) |
| 1996, Whole Election Cycle (61) | 11 | 37 | 13 |
|  | (18%) | (60.7%) | (21.3%) |

Table 2.2. **Personal or Substantive?** *SNL*

|  | Both | Personal | Substantive |
|---|---|---|---|
| 1992, Whole Election Cycle (62) | 3 | 47 | 12 |
|  | (4.8%) | (75.8%) | (19.4%) |
| 1996, Whole Election Cycle (61) | 7 | 51 | 3 |
|  | (11.5%) | (83.6%) | (4.9%) |

him in a debate exchanging questions and answers with Ted Koppel and a perplexed voter:

> **Leon Norwood [a voter]**: Hello, Governor. My name is Leon Norwood. I heard you say in a speech you were gonna cut middle-class taxes to increase consumer spending . . . isn't that the same old tax-and-spend we *always* hear?

> **Clinton**: Well, Leon, I meant we would cut *your* taxes, so *you* would have more to spend.

> **Leon Norwood**: There it is! "Tax" and "Spend."

> **Ted Koppel**: Excuse me, Governor, if I may, Sir. Just because the words "tax" and "spend" appear in the same sentence, it doesn't make it a bad thing. There are *other* words in there—verbs and modifiers that *change* the meaning. ("Nightline," October 26, 1992)

This exchange highlighted the confusion of the average voter about (somewhat) complex economic policy. But it was not particularly a substantive joke about Clinton's policy propositions, other than that they might be difficult to understand; but this could just as easily have been the case because voters were willfully ignorant and not paying close enough attention to matters that could impact their financial lives.

Republican candidate George H. W. Bush had the most substantive satirical jokes directed at him in the 1992 election cycle, with a total of eight. These were all "Weekend Update" segment jokes, so none were extensive or went into great detail. They covered four main topics. One was the L.A. riots (which was just represented by Adam Sandler's character Operaman singing about Bush falling asleep during the L.A. riots because he was old, from a segment on "Weekend Update," May 16, 1992). The second was about Bush being dishonest about his poll numbers: "And President Bush today attacked journalists for their left wing bias against him. When asked for examples, Bush cited all the polls that showed him trailing Gov. Clinton" ("Weekend Update, October 24, 1992). The third topic was the Iran-Contra scandal, and about Bush's dishonesty about it: "Today the President admitted he lied, but added, 'That's only 6 times I've lied. Clinton has lied 11 times, so I'm 5 points ahead of him'" ("Weekend Update," October 31, 1992). The fourth topic, and the most joked about in the substantive category, was the poor state of the economy after the Reagan-Bush years: "President Bush took to the rails last week, campaigning . . . by train so he could take his message directly to those Americans most affected by his presidency . . . the hobos riding in the freight car" ("Weekend Update," October 3, 1992). Additionally, a simple misstatement became a chance to criticize economic policy, albeit weakly:

On Thursday, President Bush greeted a crowd in NJ with this Freudian slip:

Bush: And so today, I don't want to run the risk of ruining what is a lovely recession, a lovely reception by . . .
   He also complimented them on their delightful deficit, and promised never to give up his fight against jobs. ("Weekend Update," October 24, 1992)

However, there were not many substantive jokes overall, despite the possible choices that could have been made after twelve years of Reagan-Bush economics.

*SNL* made one substantive joke about Gingrich: "Asked why so few Republicans were involved in Rubbergate, House minority whip Newt Gingrich explained, that's what S&Ls are for" ("Weekend Update," March 21, 1992). The House Banking scandal of 1992 (in which House members overdrew their accounts) was likened to the Savings and Loan Scandal of previous years. This joke was similar to the allusion to the Iran-Contra controversy referenced above. The point was that Republicans could not be trusted to be honest about a range of topics due to their history of lying about involvements in important institutional issues. But old scandals were not as relevant as fresh ones, and some viewers may not have even remembered the details of these clearly. Why didn't *SNL* take advantage of current problems as satirical fodder during this election cycle? In later years, *SNL* put much more effort into pulling specific current events and parodies of what the candidates were saying and doing in the week that the show would air. But in these years, the show relied much more on easier targets of personality-based jokes and references to things that happened in the past that viewers would potentially be more familiar with.

The personal humor mainly targeted Perot and Clinton, with some targeted at Jerry Brown and Paul Tsongas, and also at Bush and Quayle. The Clinton humor focused on his claim that he "didn't inhale" when he tried marijuana in college ("Weekend Update," April 18, 1992), his alleged "draft dodging" during the Vietnam war, and his perceived propensity to pursue women other than his wife (March 21, 1992, and April 11, 1992), which would of course become a major subject of mockery in subsequent years. *SNL* parodied Clinton and Brown discussing the way the culture perceived them:

> **Clinton**: I just want you to know that I think you got a raw deal with that marijuana party thing in California, and I'm not going to bring it up . . . I mean, I don't think either of us is being served by drug stories at this point in the race, I mean it hurts the process, and it hurts the party.
>
> **Brown**: I agree, Bill, and it would be like bringing up old nicknames that really weren't fair. And I know that you're not interested in referring to me as Governor Moonbeam, or Spaceman Jerry, or Governor Spaceman, or Captain Weirdo.
>
> **Clinton**: Well, exactly. The last thing America wants to dwell on is something that happened years ago. Like who registered for what draft, and how they got out of it. ("Clinton-Brown Debate," April 18, 1992)

Tsongas (the only candidate to appear on the show this election cycle, on April 18, 1992, but only to deliver the "Live from New York, it's Saturday Night!" opening line) was mocked for having a "nerdy" voice and was portrayed as having a certain kinship with *Star Trek* fans ("Star Trek Democrats," March 14, 1992). Personality-based humor about George H. W. Bush was also about his wealth that made him out of touch with the voters: "the candidates have finally agreed on the debates, over Clinton's objections that the dates conflicted with World Series play offs . . . Bush agreed, providing the dates don't conflict with the New England Horseshoe Pitching Finals in Kennebunkport" ("Weekend Update," October 3, 1992). Humor also dealt with his "uncoolness": "President Bush Thursday unveiled the Bush League, his new line of sportswear for dorky white guys" ("Weekend Update," May 16, 1992) and that he gave people "the creeps" ("Weekend Update," October 24, 1992). Also in the "uncool" category were both Quayle and Gore: "Vice President Dan Quayle and Senator Gore agreed the Madonna book was offensive, but couldn't agree which page was most offensive" ("Weekend Update," October 24, 1992).

Nothing was more stiff and backward-looking in this election cycle than Quayle's commentary on the fictional television character Murphy Brown. When the character decided to bear a child alone, after the father decided not to be in its life, Quayle commented (in a speech to the Commonwealth Club in May 1992) that it was indicative of the increasing propensity of American culture toward "ignoring the importance of fathers." It seemed silly to criticize the lifestyle choice of a fictional person, and made Quayle sound critical of single mothers, who often had little choice in the matter. However, *SNL* only mentioned it briefly, and mocked the media for continuing to bring it up in the six months between the comment and the election: Adam Sandler's "Operaman" character sang: "Enuffo! Enuffo! / Topico over exposo!" ("Weekend Update," September 26, 1992).

One sketch, a parody of a debate between Bush and Clinton, provided a good example of the dichotomy between personal and substantive humor. A debate moderator questioned Bush about how he would bring down the deficit, and brought up his failed promise to not raise taxes which he famously broke in his first term ("Debate '92: The Challenge to Avoid Saying Something Stupid," October 10, 1992). But in regard to Clinton, in the same sketch, another moderator merely brought up Clinton's anti-war past and echoed the "I didn't inhale" line for which he was so frequently mocked: "I tried to burn an American flag *once*. I didn't like it. It gave off toxic fumes, so I didn't inhale." Although some have argued that *SNL*'s satire had become more conservative by this time period (Gray, Jones, and Thompson 2009; Peterson 2008), this election was characterized as a bad choice between almost equally bad candidates (a sentiment the show strongly echoed in 2000), giving Clinton a slight edge because he was the least objectionable in comparison. Kevin Nealon, who anchored the "Weekend Update" segment in this year, summarized the problems with the candidates in his "Subliminal Editorial" bits, where he says one thing in a normal voice, then says what he really thinks in a softer one:

> Some think that Bush has reached an all-time low in his campaign. As a mature adult, I've actually never seen grown men so childishly attack on another (*Three Stooges*). The mud-slinging doesn't really benefit anyone (*Clinton*). Why don't they just you know deal with the real issues effecting America (*Madonna*)? I mean Clinton's been working with a lot of good people (*KGB*) and I think he's got some really good ideas (*wife swapping*). But on the other hand, Bush has his priorities too (*fishing*) and of course he has had a lot of experience (*hookers*). And of course there's Perot (*elephant ears*) I'm sure he has a good wavering (*Alzheimer's*), he's back in the running. (*SNL*, "Weekend Update," October 10, 1992)

It's hard to imagine that this bland shooting-fish-in-a-barrel style comedy could have had much impact on viewer's opinions. But *SNL* did not take much of a side this election. The candidates were either "weird" like Perot, "uncool" like Bush, Quayle, and Gore, or had a morally questionable past, like Clinton and Brown.

In the 1996 election cycle, substantive jokes were almost nonexistent. As indicated in table 2.2, there were only three purely substantive jokes; two were about Pat Buchanan, and one was about Dole not wanting minority voters to come to the polls. There was a brief sketch in the last episode before the election that was a parody of a political ad "Paid for by Dole/Kemp," where a black man, a gay man, and a woman told the viewer, "Your vote doesn't make a difference. Don't vote if you are a woman, black, or a gay man" ("Dole/Kemp '96," November 2, 1996). Regarding Buchanan, there were two jokes on "Weekend Update" that suggested he was a Nazi and a racist:

> Meanwhile Pat Buchanan warns that if frontrunner Bob Dole chooses General Colin Powell as a running mate, his followers will march out of the Republican convention. Later Buchanan admitted that actually his followers march everywhere they go. (*SNL*, "Weekend Update," March 16, 1996)

> In Colorado this week Bob Dole warned that if Pat Buchanan is the Republican nominee the party might lose both the presidency and control of congress. In response Buchanan warned that if anyone other than himself becomes president, blacks will retain the right to vote. ("Weekend Update," February 24, 1996)

Arguably, joking about a candidate's attitude toward minorities was a joke about personal characteristics, but compared to the dull jokes that *SNL* normally made then, jokes about a candidate having strong negative attitudes about minorities rose to the level of a substantive criticism.

There were *no* purely substantive jokes about President Clinton in this election cycle. Some substantive areas were mentioned, but they were always tempered with a joke about his personal characteristics. The prime example of this is a sketch where Clinton was sitting in the White House kitchen late at night calling people randomly on the phone trying to get reassurance about his policies:

> Hello? You don't know me, I just dialed your number at random. . . . Look, I don't know what your politics are. I don't know if you're a Democrat or a Republican. But if you'll just tell me what to do, I swear to God I'll do it! I'm not kidding! If you want Welfare eliminated I'll do it. If you want it expanded I'll do that too, I don't care, it's your call. I just want one person to tell me that I'm doing a great job. ("White House Kitchen," November 11, 1995)

*SNL* characterized Clinton here as indecisive and worried about the fact that he had betrayed his base. But even though these are clearly substantive issues, they portrayed Clinton ordering pizza and eating everything in sight. Although in the present day, Bill Clinton appears to be at a very healthy weight after undergoing quadruple bypass surgery in 2004, jokes about his love of fast food were prevalent in popular culture when he was president. Additionally, the U.S. and NATO intervention in Bosnia was occurring during this time, and could have been a target for substantive criticism on *SNL*, if it were in fact a politically progressive show. However, the jokes were barely substantive and the punchlines were about personal issues. In the 1996 election cycle, there were fifty-one personal jokes, three substantive, and seven that were both personal and substantive. This joke was an example of one that brought up a substantive issue, but the punch line was related to drug use, a personal issue: "Should the situation [in Bosnia] deteriorate, he'll have all 20,000 troops airlifted to England and smoking pot within twenty-four hours" ("Weekend Update," December 9, 1995). This weakened the joke and undercut it ability to be truly critical of a real, serious issue. Another "Weekend Update" joke that mentioned Bosnia was not even directed at Clinton at all:

> Republican hopeful Phil Gramm says that Bob Dole should not get the nomination because he backed President Clinton's plan to send troops to Bosnia. Dole responded that Gramm should not be nominated for President, because, well, look at him. Take a gander at the fella. ("Weekend Update," February 10, 1996)

President Clinton at this time was also embroiled in the Whitewater land deal scandal and was also the subject of conspiracy theories about the death of former Deputy White House Counsel Vince Foster in 1993, who committed suicide. Both of these issues could be considered either personal or substantive issues; however, even though they rose to a level of gravity that sex scandals or jokes about personal appearance did not, they were not about policy positions, knowledge, or competence. Both issues were the target of some "cheap shots": "The president may have secretly intimated that he would pardon the whitewater swindlers, 'But only after making every effort to have them killed in Prison'" ("Weekend Update," October 5, 1996).

It is also worth noting at this point that the host of the "Weekend Update" segment during this election cycle was Norm MacDonald. His tenure at the desk was characterized by cruel jokes about public figures, most notably about Michael Jackson and O. J. Simpson. Most of the political humor at this time originated from him, either on "Weekend Update" or in the form of his Bob Dole impression (discussed below). His time at the desk was in direct contrast to the 1992 election cycle, occupied by Kevin Nealon, who, while not afraid to joke about the candidates, did not rise to the level of viciousness that MacDonald did. Many times, MacDonald's most extreme jokes were met with dead silence by the audience; however, his targets were arguably deserving of the vitriol he cast (like Simpson).

One major difference between this election cycle and the last one was the amount of jokes directed at the candidates' wives, with ten about Hillary Clinton and two about Elizabeth Dole. However, these jokes were entirely personal. The jokes about Elizabeth Dole were about her appearing unable to seem relaxed in interviews and her drive as a woman making her appear to be "a bitch on wheels" ("The Barbara Walters Special," October 26, 1996). The jokes about Hillary Clinton were primarily about Bill Clinton's presumed dislike of her, going along with the prevailing sexist sentiment that women who have their own opinions are inherently disagreeable (and certainly setting up anti-Hillary cultural narratives that would impact the future). Twice, Clinton, played by Darrell Hammond, appeared on "Weekend Update" to review movies about a fictional president whose wife was dead, including *Independence Day* ("Weekend Update," October 5, 1996) and *An American President*: "the story of a young, idealistic president, who has not only a hostile Congress and a nasty Republican contender to deal with, but also has to raise a twelve-year-old daughter on his own, because, you see, his wife is dead. I love this movie!" ("Weekend Update," December 9, 1995). Norm MacDonald's use of the O. J. Simpson murders trope came full circle when he inserted it into a "Bill hates Hillary" joke: "On Friday, the Juice officially endorsed Bill Clinton for President, adding, 'I'd like to help him any way I can.' To which the President replied, 'Well, there is one thing'," and then they cut to photo of Hillary Clinton, implying that the president would like Simpson to murder his wife as well ("Weekend Update," May 18, 1996). The Whitewater scandal, in which Hillary Clinton was also implicated, played into the theme as well: "When asked if he would pardon First Lady Hillary Clinton the President was crystal clear. 'She does the crime, she does the time'" ("Weekend Update," October 26, 1996).

There were also a few personal jokes about Steve Forbes and Pat Buchanan during the primaries. *SNL* portrayed Buchanan as mean-spirited, and Forbes as the out-of-touch wealthy man who wanted to buy his way into the election out of boredom, similar to Perot's campaign in 1992. One sketch depicted them having a physical altercation. In the sketch, Forbes and Buchanan were checking out of the hotel after the Iowa Caucuses. Buchanan made fun of him for having a gold credit card, but Forbes let him know it was actually a platinum card. Buchanan snatched it from him.

**Forbes**: Now if you will excuse me I have a plane to catch.

**Buchanan**: What, your own private jet?

**Forbes**: Well if you must know it's a one man space shuttle. But I have to get to the bank first. ("Bully Pat Buchanan," February 24, 1996)

As with many of the candidates, Forbes also had many personal characteristic-based "Weekend Update" jokes directed against him: "Finally some good news for Steve Forbes, in his sputtering campaign this week, he picked up the endorsement of *Forbes Magazine*" ("Weekend Update," February 17, 1996).

A potentially rich source of substantive humor was the government shutdown instigated by Newt Gingrich, due to what essentially amounted to interpersonal conflicts between the Speaker of the House and President Clinton. An *SNL* sketch depicted Gingrich and Dole having a childish fit over not being able to fly in the "First Class" section of Air Force One (which is of course a fictional concept). But it was only briefly mentioned in one sketch ("Flying Coach," November 18, 1995). In contrast to the 1992 election cycle, where there was either no favoring of political parties, or mostly equal mocking of both, the 1996 election cycle *SNL* political humor was mostly slanted toward the Democrats, presumably because they show at this point tended to favor the incumbent. There was no slant or equal mocking of candidates in both parties in ten jokes/sketches, thirteen that slanted toward the Republicans, and thirty-seven that slanted toward the Democrats. This was mostly because of humor directed against Bob Dole. Earlier in the election cycle, there were many jokes about Dole being mean, old, physically frail, and frightening to children. But later, as it became obvious that he was going to lose because of his poor poll numbers, the humor began to include jokes about his impending loss as well. Dole was portrayed throughout the election as unable to connect with the voters. In one sketch, he was shown practicing speeches in front of the mirror:

> **Dole**: I'm President Bob Dole, I'm President of the United States, nice to meet you, Ambassador! (laughs). This must be your lovely wife? Assistant? Sorry. Oh, your wife passed on? . . . Rest assured, you have the condolences of the President of the United States, I'm President of the United States, I'm President Bob Dole, I'm President and I live in the White House! ("The Real World," March 16, 1996)

Another sketch depicted him meeting with and talking to former President George H. W. Bush about why he was behind in the polls. One of the main real-world criticisms President Clinton's detractors was about his morals. Although Dole did not have a problem with the "character issue," he was unlikable by comparison:

> **Bush**: Your campaign, an embarrassment. Your image, scary! Spooky! Children run away!
>
> **Dole**: Why do people vote for him? Why do people like him so much?
>
> **Bush**: Well, Clinton is like a laid back uncle. The guy who will buy them beer when they're under age. Bob Dole, scary old neighbor. Guy who cuts up Nerf footballs that accidentally fall in his yard.
>
> **Dole**: But don't they know Bob Dole is the better man?

**Bush**: Tough sell, Bob. Economy is strong, you claim it should be stronger. Crime low, you claim it should be lower. Status quo good, you claim it should be gooder.

**Dole**: I can beat Mondale! ("The Fishing Dock," November 2, 1996)

This sketch also included the point that Clinton was doing a fairly good job as president, so the voters were not compelled to change direction (as they had done with Bush, who had broken his economic promises). Additionally, it carried the theme that Dole was a confused old man (with the "Mondale" line). *SNL* did an entire sketch devoted to mocking Dole for falling off a stage at a campaign rally in September 1996. The fact that Dole seemed poised to lose to Clinton, both because of the poll numbers, and his having to go up against the charismatic Clinton in debates, was the subject of many sketches—"Mr. Dole, we also appreciate you taking time out from your grueling and hopeless campaign to talk with us tonight. For a man your age that can't be very easy" ("ABC News Election Report," September 28, 1996) and numerous "Weekend Update" jokes: "according to a new CNN poll Republican candidate Bob Dole now trails President Clinton by 15 points. A Dole campaign spokesman says that despite this numbers it is possible for them to reach their ultimate goal, to lose by 7 points." ("Weekend Update," October 19, 1996). Several of the personal jokes and sketches were actually about both Dole and Clinton. They summarized the contest between the men as Dole being more morally upstanding and a war hero, but so stiff and unable to connect with the voters, that Clinton could do or say anything he wanted and still win: "Hey America, guess what? I inhaled! I inhaled, then I exhaled, then I inhaled again. In fact, I filled a scuba tank with dope smoke and swam the English Channel ("ABC News Election Report," September 28, 1996). As it turned out, *SNL* was correct in these suppositions. Although Republicans themselves, along with late-night comedians, continuously mentioned Clinton's "character issues," they were not enough to cost him either election. The need to change direction from the Reagan/Bush years in 1992, and the relatively good state of the economy in 1996, made the "character issue" less relevant, despite Republicans trying to start a "Culture War" (as Pat Buchanan essentially called for in his 1996 Republican National Convention Keynote Address). Personality-based humor was the norm on *SNL* in 1992 and 1996.

## JOURNALISM EXAMINES ROLE OF COMEDY PROGRAMS IN THE ELECTIONS

Although there was not a lot of utilization of the narratives on late-night television comedy by the journalists to stand in for their own opinions, during these election cycles, there were two more pertinent changes from the 1980s. Besides examining the very personality-based humor, they realized and discussed the effect the programs were having on public sphere conversations about the elections, questioning the more prominent role of late-night comedy on television in the democratic process, and increasingly began to reflect on politicians appearing on the programs. Was it "undignified" for the politicians to appear on them in order to gain exposure and seem more relatable? Would it somehow "cheapen" our democracy? Would celebrity status be more important than policy positions? Tom Shales of the *Post* certainly thought so in 1992:

> But surely dignity was one of the first victims of the 1992 presidential race as it was run on television, where all campaigns are now fought. The talkshowfication of America continues apace; now the political process is conquered too. Perhaps when 1996 rolls around, presidential candidates will take turns popping up . . . just to show they're regular Joes. And Janes. They can play themselves on "Saturday Night Live." . . . Four years ago, this sort of thing didn't happen. The scaling down and informalizing of everything hadn't gone quite so far. . . . It is true that John Kennedy, Richard Nixon and other political figures appeared with Jack Paar on "The Tonight Show" and on Paar's prime-time hour in the late '50s and early '60s. . . . But the Paar show wasn't the center ring for the entire political process. No other talk show was, either. (Tom Shales, "On the Tube: All Talked Out," *Washington Post*, November 2, 1992)

It is true that politicians would make an increasing amount of appearances on *SNL* and other comedy programs in later years, at least in part for the reason that Shales gave here—to make them seem like "regular people." However, Shales either changed his mind or contradicted himself, when he said four years later that, "Some people may worry that Forbes did something to damage his dignity by appearing on the show . . . dignity? The guy was part of a presidential primary! What could be less dignified than that?" (Tom Shales, "Saturday Night Comedy Wars: Roseanne Bores, Forbes Scores," *Washington Post*, April 15, 1996). It is as if it had become less of a problem, or that he simply accepted its inevitability. But by contrast, other journalists saw it as simply the way things were changing in the election in an increasingly mediated public sphere: "In 1992, such appearances are becoming so commonplace that some viewers would not be surprised to see President Bush pay a visit to Jay Leno" (Elizabeth Kolbert, "The 1992 Campaign: Media; Whistle-Stops a la 1992: Arsenio, Larry and Phil," *New York Times*, June 5, 1992). This was a prescient comment. Candidate appearances on talk shows did in fact increase after this; more on the reasons why in later chapters. Other than to seem like they were "regular Joes," which was only part of the story, *why* were politicians increasingly going on the comedy programs? This question remained unanswered by journalists in the 1990s.

Contributing to knowledge about the political process in the public sphere was also something that talk shows actually did in greater and greater amounts as time went on. But in the 1992 and 1996 election cycles, the journalists merely observed the phenomenon, and did not attempt, or were unable, to explain why it was happening. When, then, did Tom Brokaw go on the *Tonight Show* to say what he really thought about the Democratic National Convention, as was discussed in the *Times* in 1992?

> "I did an actual calculation," Mr. Brokaw quipped in a live report to Mr. Leno from Madison Square Garden early yesterday morning. "If he had spoken for another 10 minutes, his speech would have been longer than Ross Perot's Presidential campaign." Welcome to the new world of political broadcasting, where viewers may have learned as much about the Democratic convention on Music Television, Comedy Central and even The Tonight Show as from the network news programs. . . . In this year of talk-show politics, the melding of news and entertainment was probably inevitable. . . . On Comedy Central, a cable network whose "Indecision '92" offered more coverage than ABC, CBS and NBC. . . . Those who were not sated by NBC News's coverage could switch on "Late Night with David Letterman" to see Gov. Ann Richards of Texas, who presided over the event. (Richard L. Berke, "The 1992 Campaign: Convention Humor; When TV Turns Politics into a Laughing Matter," *New York Times,* July 18, 1992)

Was Ann Richards on Letterman's show just because of "the melding of news and entertainment"? Why was this phenomenon occurring? The journalists did not offer an explanation. Since these questions went unexamined, and certainly because they were part of it, the journalists failed to see what was happening; namely that it was not adequately exploring the candidates and the issues surrounding them. It has become clear that "legacy" media values access over critique, a job that was increasingly becoming the role of entertainment media. No surprise then that they began to see it through bitter eyes. Although much of the humor on *SNL* in particular was personal, and not substantive during these election cycles, the severity of the commentary and vitriol against the Republican candidates in particular may have reflected more of the national feelings toward them than the journalists dared to write about. Accordingly, often journalists did not see the comedy as either interesting or contributing to democratic process. A commentary in praise of Bill Maher's then-new ABC show, *Politically Incorrect*, included a comparison to *SNL*'s "Weekend Update" segment, which was said to have "become tame and unfunny" (Caryn James, "Critic's Notebook; Giggles Intact, Political Satire Is Back on TV," *New York Times* February 22, 1996, p. C13). This is contradictory, given that other commentators found *SNL*'s and the talk show hosts' humor to be mean.

Late-night comedy at this time was so incredibly focused on personal characteristics of the politicians, and made it seem to some journalists formulaic, repetitive, and completely unfunny: "Now all Leno wants to joke about . . . is politics . . . endless variations on gags about George Bush's failures, Dan Quayle's incompetence, Ross Perot's lack of stick-to-itivity, Teddy Kennedy's sex life" (Tom Shales, "Jay Leno Missing His Funny Bone," *Washington Post*, July 30, 1992). While this was a fair criticism, there were other factors that made journalist hate it—it was becoming a news source for younger people who did not often consume traditional news sources. The *Times* noted that, "A recent survey for the Pew Research Center for the People and the Press found that 40 percent of people under 30—and 25 percent of adults overall—say they learned something about the 1996 campaign from late-night television humor" (James Bennet, "Word for Word/Late-Night Comics; Joking About Bill, Bob and Hillary With Dave, Jay and Conan," *New York Times*, July 14, 1996). If the shows were so unfunny and predictable, why were so many people getting news about the elections from them? There was scarcely any discussion about this, which would seem like an obvious question. Journalists in these election cycles were either not yet able or were unwilling to be reflexive about the changes that were taking place in people's consumption of news, a change that would only intensify in subsequent years.

## THE PAPERS EXAMINE PERSONALITY-DRIVEN HUMOR

Ross Perot and Dan Quayle were late-night comedy's prime targets in the 1990s. Although he ran in both 1992 and 1996, Ross Perot was a much greater factor in the former of the two election cycles. His appearance, speech, and demeanor were tailor-made to be satirized on *SNL*, as the previous analysis indicates. Journalists in the *WP* and the *NYT* saw his candidacy through the lens of late-night political humor. Perot's indecisiveness about running and bizarre accusations about the Bush campaign were seen as ultimately harmful to democracy, and the jabs were well-deserved: "Letterman took note of the feckless mood in a top 10 list of voter pet peeves. "You spend a week painting 'Ross Perot for President' on your family car and he drops out. You spend a week scraping 'Ross Perot for President' off your family car and he's back in" (Maureen Dowd, "The 1992 Campaign: Political Week; When Trust Is at Issue, The Trusted Are Scarce." *New York Times*, September 29, 1992). One thing that only increased over time, both on *SNL* and the newspapers' commentary about it and other late-night political comedy, were jokes about the intelligence of Vice President Dan Quayle. In the 1988 election cycle, he had only begun to commit gaffes and say strange things. But the "potatoe" incident, and his criticism of the fictional television character Murphy Brown's life choices, increased mentions of him dramatically: "David Letterman immediately booked William Figeroa, the 12-year-old who had spelled the word correctly" (Howard Kurtz, "Why Quayle's 'Potatoe' Gaffe Won't Fade; For the Media, Simple Misstep Can Be Metaphor for a Larger Flaw," *Washington Post*, June 21, 1992). In fact, comedy about Quayle in the 1992 election cycle was so prevalent, there was practically none about Bush by comparison. Often, the journalists used quotes from late-night comedians to reinforce and editorialize about Quayle without directly having to do so: "Quayle is still more than capable of pulling a stunning boner. His recent misspelling of the word 'potato' prompted Jay Leno to remark: 'Maybe the Vice President should stop watching "Murphy Brown" and start watching "Sesame Street."'" (Andrew Rosenthal, "Quayle's Moment," *New York Times*, July 5, 1992). In a close election, this type of comedy was in fact seen as a potential deciding factor. Bush could not afford even the slightest negative impact on the Republican ticket:

> S. Robert Lichter, the director of the Center for Media and Public Affairs . . . [said Quayle] . . . had been relegated to occasional use as the symbol of any stupid or childlike behavior. . . . Clearly he had worked hard to try to rehabilitate his image. But his face just went back up on the dartboard [when he was the] subject of [Letterman's] nightly top 10 list: "Dan Quayle's top 10 other complaints about TV." (Bill Carter, "CBS Is Silent, but Then There's the Next Season," *New York Times*, May 21, 1992)

The trend of the journalists using the comedy as a stand-in for their own opinions would only increase in future election cycles. Still, it is important to note that the comedy here was still almost entirely personal, and not policy-based or substantive, even if it may have had an influence on voters. As the *Times* noted:

> Millions of late-night viewers surely do not receive the most uplifting impressions of their leaders—one man known variously as Tubby and Fat Boy, who could become the first President to ride in a limousine with license plates made by the First Lady; and another so old his Social Security number is 2, and so crotchety his top priority is sitting on his porch in his bathrobe, shaking his fist at cars. (James Bennet, "Politics: The Laugh Meter; Did You Hear the One About the '96 Campaign?" *New York Times*, July 9, 1996)

Personality-based humor colored Jerry Brown's primary run, as perception of the candidates' personalities overrode attention to their actual policies. *SNL*'s portrayal of "Mr. Brown at a 'Star Trek' convention, that [seizing] upon the image [of 'Governor Moonbeam']" is mentioned in the same paragraph as voters being unable to think of him otherwise, and that 'He hasn't changed that perception' (Richard L. Berke, "Brown Renews His Battle Against the Moonbeam," *New York Times*, April 12, 1992).

Non-substantive political humor was observed by journalists in the 1996 election cycle, and they agreed that the comedy on *SNL* and the late-night talk shows had grown even *more* personal over the last four years, and was influential, but not informative to the political process: "Clinton jokes fall into two categories: 'cheatin' and eatin',' as one wit put it. Mr. Dole is . . . very, very old. . . . Many political strategists think the late-night comedians have an uncanny ability to peg which candidates' qualities and what public miscues will stick in people's minds" (James Bennet, "Word for Word/Late-Night Comics; Joking About Bill, Bob and Hillary with Dave, Jay and Conan," *New York Times*, July 14, 1996). In 1996, the Republicans took the brunt of the humor on the TV programs and the papers took note of it. Dole supposedly tried to temper his image as particularly abrasive a bit after his losses in the 1992 Primary campaign after he successfully became the nominee in 1996. But his old image lived on and was intensified in the way Norm MacDonald both parodied him and talked about him on *SNL*'s "Weekend Update" segment. First and foremost, late-night comedy programs portrayed Dole as being as old as Methuselah. This clearly was an easy, if lazy, way to characterize him and certainly had nothing to do with his policies. But even the Clinton campaign used the image, furthered by the comedy, to their advantage, which the journalists noted: "The old-guy bashing of Mr. Dole in political cartoons and late-night comedy routines has reached an intensity that makes the jokes about Ronald Reagan in the 1980s seem like gentle kidding" (Richard L. Berke, "Still Running; Is Age-Bashing Any Way to Beat Bob Dole?" *New York Times*, May 5, 1996). As a result, Elizabeth Dole went on a Public Relations campaign on Letterman and Leno to try and counteract the image of the mean, old fogy that *SNL* especially characterized her husband as being. The papers noted her going on the programs, including presenting David Letterman's "Top Ten List" in October 1996. Additionally, she appeared on Jay Leno in "jeans, a black leather jacket and boots and roared onto the Jay Leno show on the back of Mr. Leno's motorcycle. If she could convince late-night viewers that she was hip, the theory went, they might take another look at her husband" (Katharine Q. Seelye, "Politics: The Spouse; On the Trail, Dole's Wife Seeks Votes of Women," *New York Times*, October 5, 1996).

Even though he was mentioned only a handful of times, no one received as much direct vitriol as Pat Buchanan on *SNL* and the other programs. His unsuccessful primary campaigns were significant, in that they increased the focus on the "culture war" (which was the subject of his Keynote Address at the 1992 Republican National Convention[1]). Journalists in the *Times* and the *Post* used the remarks on the comedy shows as a substitute for their own opinions: "David Letterman said Buchanan is 'going to take a couple of days off after the New Hampshire primary and then invade Poland.'" Jay Leno said Buchanan's campaign was generating the most heat—"It's mostly from burning books and crosses," he said, "but it's heat" (Marc Fisher, "Buchanan's Brash Rhetoric Ruffles Convention," *Washington Post*, February 22, 1996). If the Clinton campaign was able to use television comedy to make points about Dole, then the Republicans certainly were able to do the same thing:

> Last December, Letterman cracked that if Clinton gets any higher in the polls, "he's gonna start dating again." Soon afterward, Democratic Sen. Ernest Hollings repeated the joke to the Sumter, S.C., Item, whose article was faxed to White House reporters by local Republicans . . . the line was later used by Pat Buchanan, Rep. Robert Dornan, California GOP Chairman John Herrington and Newsweek's Howard Fineman. (Howard Kurtz, "Clinton's Caricature Sketch; Political Opponents Make Their Point with Barbed Wit," *Washington Post*, June 4, 1996)

But in comparison to what was said on *SNL* and other shows about the Republicans, despite all the jokes about his sexual proclivities, weight, drug use, draft-dodging, and "hatred" of his wife, the jokes about Clinton on late night television did not cut as deeply as those directed at the Republicans: "Clinton now enjoys a 15- to 20-point lead over Dole in the national polls, despite the fact that jokes about his morals have become standard fare on late-night television" (*Washington Post*, June 16, 1996, p. X05). The *Times* noted that "the Clinton and Dole campaigns are taking the late-night jokes seriously" and that "that the jokes are increasing, and growing harsher"; further, "Political humor has long served as at least a lagging—if not a leading—indicator of public attitudes" (Kevin Phillips, "Prelude to a Presidency," *New York Times*, July 9, 1996). But even though there was a lot of silly personal humor about him, Clinton laughed it off in both election cycles: "He laughed especially hard at [an SNL] sequence that portrayed him as a bead-wearing hippy defending himself against accusations that he evaded the draft" (Gwen Ifill, "Leading in the Homestretch, Clinton's Campaign Grows More Confident," *New York Times*, October 18, 1992).

## CONCLUSION

Although a larger target of the humor during this era did become Democrats, and Bill Clinton in particular, as journalists predicted in the previous election cycles, the humor remained personality-based, and was not particularly critical of policies, so did not do much to damage to them politically. Other than serious questions about Dan Quayle's intelligence that did not probe more deeply than his spelling abilities, these types of jokes did not appear to hurt the campaigns (according to the journalists in the *Times* and the *Post*). When an increasing amount of the politically-based humor on *SNL* came from the "Weekend Update" segments, and not the sketches, the tone of the jokes were so dependent upon the host of the segment (Day 2012). Ross Perot's insertion into the 1992 campaign was a significant reason why *SNL* was so distracted with personality-based humor in the 1992 election cycle, and Norm MacDonald's constant emphasis on Bob Dole's age and "crankiness" was the reason in 1996. This led to missed opportunities to make substantive jokes about real issues and politicians' responses to them that were going on in the country during these years.

In the 1992 and 1996 election cycles, we have begun to see the groundwork laid for what would come in 2000, 2004, and 2008: the mainstream media, the "serious" journalistic sphere, was beginning to erode as a primary source of news, and legacy media was not happy about it. After September 11, 2001, when the "news" did little to question what George W. Bush's administration was doing in response to the war, and late-night comedy in the form of the *Daily Show* began to increasingly fill a critical gap in questioning the official discourse, it is reasonable to see why. But as noted in this chapter, the process had already begun, even before the *Daily Show* or the War on Terror. The journalists had begun to see the comedy as much more influential on voters' attitudes, for better or worse, rather than just a reflection of them in contrast to the 1980s. The *Times* noted that "political analysts often seem to view the comics as rollicking successors to the late Walter Lippman" (James Bennet, "Did You Hear the One About the '96 Campaign?," *New York Times*, July 9, 1996). But this was really the only attempt to contextualize what was beginning to happen with humor, but as for the "political analysts" that are mentioned, they go unnamed and their ideas go unspecified. In future election cycles, after the *Daily Show* and the *Colbert Report* begin to challenge the quality of news journalism, both on television and in print, journalists in these papers accept and are reflexive about the criticisms about TV, but not about their own failings and shortcomings (Jacobs and Michaud Wild 2013). This tendency has its roots in their general confusion about why democratically involved citizens were beginning to turn to satire as a source of news.

Increasingly in the 1992 and 1996 election cycles, journalists began to question the role of late-night comedy on television in the democratic process, and their appearances on them (as Tom Shales did, above). These attitudes reflected the "news is becoming more like entertainment" lament of Postman (1985) and others; but this perspective soon becomes an oversimplified view of things. In the 2000 election cycle, there would be a shift toward entertainment becoming more like news because of two primary reasons. One, because of some structural changes in the landscape of such "entertainment media," namely *SNL*'s "Weekend Update" segment going to a two-"anchor" format, as it had not been since its inception, and the premiere of the *Daily Show* (which just as often came to be critical of the media's coverage of politicians as well as their policies). And two, because of historical events, including the contested 2000 election and, later, traditional news journalism's failures after September 11. As it has become clear after the 2016 election as well, legacy media would rather continue to rebuff critics rather than face its own weaknesses, but this tendency has been long in its development.

## NOTE

1. http://buchanan.org/blog/1992-republican-national-convention-speech-148.

## Chapter Three

# *Bush v. Gore* and
# the Comedy of Chaos

Humor on *SNL* in the 2000 election cycle was most memorable for the impression of George W. Bush by Will Ferrell. Bush often used malapropisms like "misunderestimate" and "subliminable," and mixed up phrases ("Families is where our nation finds hope, where wings take dream"—October 18, 2000) while speaking in public, and Ferrell capitalized on these as a cornerstone of his impression. A vacant stare and an overly self-assured demeanor despite appearing to know very little were the physical characteristics of Ferrell's parody. There were two main personal stereotypes of Bush that comprised the majority of the content of sketches Ferrell was in as Bush: his reputation as a former "partier" and drug user, and his seeming like "the dumb guy" (Marshall Sella, "The Stiff Guy vs. the Dumb Guy," *New York Times*, September 24, 2000). These types of jokes were prevalent in sketches and "Weekend Update" jokes, both during Colin Quinn's "Weekend Update" era and Tina Fey and Jimmy Fallon's time at the desk. A typical joke about Bush's drug use by Quinn:

> George W. Bush vowed to stick to his $483 tax cut by insisting on quote, "Tax cuts, so help me God." Some pundits felt this was a hollow claim, however, believing Bush probably used up all his favors from God in the 1970s when he was lying on bathroom floors with his heart racing. ("Weekend Update," January 8, 2000)

Although "Weekend Update" during the Fey/Fallon time referenced his policy positions on capital punishment, it mostly kept to jokes about Bush's past. This one, about revelations that both Bush and Cheney had past drunken driving arrests, is still mainly personal:

> Bush says he kept the story of his arrest secret because he felt it did not set a good example for his daughters, preferring instead that they see him as a

failed businessman who executes people. . . . "That was a turning point in my life," said Bush. "I went home, took a long, hard look at myself in the mirror and decided then and there to quit drinking in 10 years." . . . Bush did question who was behind breaking the story just days before the election, saying, "I bet it was one of those creeps I used to do coke with." ("Weekend Update," November 4, 2000)

The 2000 election was unlike previous election cycles in many other keys ways; of course, the most important difference was the contestation of the Florida voting results from the Gore campaign, which led to the landmark *Bush v. Gore* Supreme Court decision; the fact that the popular vote went to Gore, and the Electoral College went to Bush; and the resultant entrenchment of the political divisions in the United States that continues (and has intensified) to this day.

Television comedy about the election of 2000 started off like many of the previous years; on *Saturday Night Live*, there was a single male comedian at the "Weekend Update" desk, who drove most of the comedy with his own characteristic tone; the jokes on all the late-night shows were very personality-driven; the programs tended to favor the Democratic candidate, although not by much. However, it was also a transitional election cycle for late-night comedy as well. The year 2000 was the first election cycle that the *Daily Show* with Jon Stewart at the desk covered. Journalists in the *Washington Post* and the *New York Times* noticed the uniqueness of the type of contribution that the *Daily Show* was making to political discourse during this election, but only on a very superficial level. Although some commentators remarked that studies showed more of the younger viewers were likely to get political knowledge from "entertainment" programs, most of the commentary that was made on the newspapers during this time were negative comments about the saturation point of news becoming more like entertainment.

This year marked the transformation of the "old" *SNL* to the "new" *SNL*. In the first half of the election, the "Weekend Update" desk was anchored by Colin Quinn. But the second half of the 2000 election cycle, beginning with the fall season, saw a major departure; the desk was anchored by Jimmy Fallon, who was relatively young, and Tina Fey, the first woman to appear in the primary role (albeit as co-anchor). Journalists did not take note of this development at all, which would prove incredibly significant to political discourse in later years. Instead, they primarily focused on the perception that the candidates were becoming increasingly required to appear on late-night comedy, including *SNL*, the *Tonight Show*, and *Late Night*, in order to seem more authentic. *SNL*'s "Weekend Update" segment also transitioned to a more substantive straight-news parody, most especially after Election Day had passed and the country still did not have a president-elect. The effect that this disputed election would have on late-night comedy would only be surpassed in later years by the effects of the terrorist attacks on September 11, 2001; but the dispute served as a catalyst for structural changes in late-night television comedy that still exist. Two factors, the historically contingent events of this election (and later 9/11), and the structural changes in the industry came together to produce this transformation. In the 1990s, cable news had permitted greater enclaves of news and information ideological polarization to emerge, and the *Daily Show*'s change to a more substantive-based kind of satire program was a direct reaction to it (and later, the *Colbert Report* would make this even more obvious). Even though the program's effects would not be obvious until the next two elections, the irregularities of 2000 would provide an opening for it to become more influential in the future.

## LATE NIGHT COMEDY IN THE 2000
## ELECTION: THE TRANSITION

Over the entire election cycle on *SNL*, 31 percent of Weekend Update Jokes and sketches were directed at both or neither of the parties; 54.6 percent favored Democrats; and 14.4 percent favored Republicans. Unexpectedly, there were many more jokes that favored Democrats during Colin Quinn's time on "Weekend Update" than in the Fey/Fallon weeks. Of these jokes on this segment during Quinn's time, 8.7 percent were directed at both or neither of the parties; 19.6 percent favored Republicans; and 71.7 percent favored Democrats (Table 3.1). During the Fey/Fallon episodes, 45.5 percent were directed at both or neither of the parties; 45.5 percent favored Democrats; and 9 percent favored Republicans. Although the general trend was to favor Democrats, the Fey/Fallon weeks were clearly more balanced in their satire. Of all sketches and jokes before the election was held, 57.8 percent were directed at both or neither of the parties; 28.2 percent favored Democrats; and 14 percent favored Republicans. However, of all sketches and jokes after the election was held, during the *Bush v. Gore* debacle and just leading up to it, a slight shift toward favoring Democrats occurred: 38.5 percent of jokes and sketches were directed at both or neither of the parties; 46.1 percent favored Democrats; and 15.4 percent favored Republicans. It should be noted that this set of jokes and sketches were entirely during the Fey/Fallon weeks, and as most of the information being analyzed were jokes on "Weekend Update," there could be an effect due to this change.

**Table 3.1.  Slant Toward?** *SNL*

|  | None | Democrats | Republicans |
|---|---|---|---|
| 2000, Whole Election Cycle (97) | 30 | 53 | 14 |
|  | (31%) | (54.6%) | (14.4%) |
| Colin Quinn at Weekend Update | 4 | 33 | 9 |
| Desk (46) | (8.7%) | (71.7%) | (19.6%) |
| Tina Fey and Jimmy Fallon at | 15 | 15 | 3 |
| Weekend Update Desk (33) | (45.5%) | (45.5%) | (9%) |
| 2000, Before Election Disputed (71) | 41 | 20 | 10 |
|  | (57.8%) | (28.2%) | (14%) |
| 2000, After Election Disputed (26) | 10 | 12 | 4 |
|  | (38.5%) | (46.1%) | (15.4%) |

But even though there was a stronger favoring of Democrats in the Quinn weeks, it is also important to note that there was a large increase in substantive jokes after Fey/Fallon took over, and also after the election was disputed. So, even though Quinn appeared to favor the Democrats more, in general, he (and the accompanying sketches during his time period) relied upon the older formula of going after the personal characteristics of those running, rather than their competence or policy positions. Over the whole cycle, there were practically no substantive jokes that favored Republicans and were aimed at Democrats, but the reverse was true when looking at substantive jokes favoring Democrats and against Republicans (7.2 percent versus 35.8 percent)

**Table 3.2.  Personal or Substantive?** *SNL*

|  | Both | Personal | Substantive |
|---|---|---|---|
| 2000, Whole Election Cycle (97) | 12 | 45 | 26 |
|  | (16.5%) | (56.7%) | (26.8%) |
| 2000, Whole Election Cycle, | 3 | 10 | 1 |
| Republicans (14) | (21.4%) | (71.4%) | (7.2%) |
| 2000, Whole Election Cycle, | 7 | 27 | 19 |
| Democrats (53) | (13.2%) | (51%) | (35.8%) |
| 2000, Whole Election Cycle, | 6 | 18 | 6 |
| No Slant (30) | (20%) | (60%) | (20%) |
| Colin Quinn at Weekend Update | 5 | 30 | 11 |
| Desk (46) | (10.9%) | (65.2%) | (23.9%) |
| Tina Fey and Jimmy Fallon at | 4 | 18 | 11 |
| Weekend Update Desk (33) | (12.1%) | (54.6%) | (33.3%) |
| 2000, Before Election Disputed (71) | 12 | 45 | 14 |
|  | (16.9%) | (63.4%) | (19.7%) |
| 2000, After Election Disputed (26) | 4 | 10 | 12 |
|  | (15.4%) | (38.5%) | (46.1%) |

**Table 3.3.   Slant Toward?** *Daily Show*

|  | None | Democrats | Republicans |
|---|---|---|---|
| 2000, Whole Election Cycle (47) | 14 | 23 | 10 |
|  | (29.8%) | (48.9%) | (21.3%) |
| 2000, Before Election Disputed (41) | 12 | 21 | 8 |
|  | (29.3%) | (51.2%) | (19.5%) |
| 2000, After Election Disputed (6) | 2 | 2 | 2 |
|  | (33.3%) | (33.3%) | (33.3%) |

Similar to *SNL*, on the *Daily Show*, the jokes were mostly slanted toward the Democrats and aimed at Republicans (48.9 percent). Only 21.3 percent of jokes were aimed at Democrats, with 29.8 percent favoring neither party and aimed at candidates and policies from both of them (Table 3.3). This was more so the case before the election dispute—after the Election Day fiasco (which did not contain as many shows to sample from), jokes targets were evenly distributed among both candidates and parties.

The distribution of personal versus substantive jokes in the 2000 election cycle was similar between the shows as well, with 29.8 percent being substantive, 53.3 percent being personal, and 14.9 percent including elements of both (Table 3.4). Of these, there were 70 percent of personal jokes that favored Republicans, and 20 percent substantive jokes that favored them, while there were only 47.8 percent of these that favored Democrats and 34.8 percent substantive jokes that favored them. Here we can see that more substantive jokes were aimed at Republicans, again similar what was happening on *SNL*. Bush was primarily mocked for his presumed past drug and alcohol

**Table 3.4.   Personal or Substantive?** *Daily Show*

|  | Both | Personal | Substantive |
|---|---|---|---|
| 2000, Whole Election Cycle (47) | 7 | 26 | 14 |
|  | (14.9%) | (55.3%) | (29.8%) |
| 2000, Whole Election Cycle, Republicans (10) | 1 | 7 | 2 |
|  | (10%) | (70%) | (20%) |
| 2000, Whole Election Cycle, Democrats (23) | 4 | 11 | 8 |
|  | (17.4%) | (47.8%) | (34.8%) |
| 2000, Whole Election Cycle, No Slant (14) | 2 | 8 | 4 |
|  | (14.3%) | (57.1%) | (28.6%) |
| 2000, Before Election Disputed (41) | 7 | 24 | 10 |
|  | (17.1%) | (58.5%) | (24.4%) |
| 2000, After Election Disputed (7) | 0 | 3 | 4 |
|  | (0%) | (42.9%) | (57.1%) |

use and his poor usage of English, but Gore was presented as stiff, boring, and uninspiring. After the election was disputed, the percentage of substantive jokes went up (24.4 percent substantive before, and 57.1 percent substantive afterward), again similar to the pattern on *SNL*. The stakes had gotten higher due to the fact that there was a major threat to democracy because of the potential for corruption in the state of Florida.

George W. Bush as unintelligent was also a significant part of Ferrell's impression of him and the subject of numerous "Weekend Update" segment jokes. However, they were almost entirely superficial, and did not address his competence as a politician or policymaker. One sketch portrayed Dana Carvey reprising his role as George H. W. Bush, trying to help his son seem less incompetent and more like him, but realizing that it might be a fruitless endeavor: "I know you're not quite right in the head, son. Maybe it's this dyslexia they keep talking about. Back when you were born, Babs and I called it 'retardation.' I guess no one says that anymore" ("Father and Son Go Hunting," October 21, 2000). In another sketch, Bush's father was portrayed as helping the son with his "own" opinions, which should always be vague; this was a little bit substantive, in that it did mention policy, but it was not about the substance of the policy, thus making it more personality-based:

**Son**: What about Social Security?

**Father**: Should be very social . . . and very secure . . . Slip-sliding, that's what I'm doing.

**Son**: Dad, you are awesome!

**Father**: That's right. Now, you try . . . Should we send the Gonzalez boy back to Cuba?

**Son**: I don't give a rat's ass!

**Father**: No! No, no, no! You can't say that! You should have said, "The little brown one—should he go or stay? Don't know. Can't say. Wouldn't be prudent! ("Father and Son Bush," April 8, 2000)

All of these characterizations made Bush seem flaky, but did not specifically address his capabilities as a political actor. The one substantive area that candidate Bush was mocked for was the State of Texas' propensity to execute many people while he was governor:

An entire school showed up at a George W. Bush rally in Dearborn, Michigan this week to complain to the governor that their building is unsafe and they lack books and teachers. A sympathetic Bush promised that if elected, he'll take care of the students the best way he knows how, by executing them. ("Weekend Update," October 14, 2000)

But these were mere exaggerations for comedic effect and did not get at the potential policy implications should he become president.

While *SNL* mainly focused on Bush's personal characteristic of seeming like "the dumb guy," and making fun of his rumored college-age drug use, the *Daily Show* was more likely to focus on Bush appearing mean or unsympathetic. While this was also not a substantive issue, it demonstrates that the *Daily Show* was more interested in issues about his character that *were* relevant, timely, and empirically demonstrable. Arguably the most memorable example of Bush's unpleasant demeanor which the *Daily Show* commented on that was actually pertinent came when Bush appeared on *Late Night* and had an extremely awkward interview via satellite with Letterman. In January 2000, David Letterman famously underwent emergency heart surgery, and had a quadruple bypass; he returned a few weeks later. In March, during an interview with the candidate, Bush made an incredibly tasteless joke referencing Letterman's near-death health scare, which was met with boos from the audience. The *Daily Show* highlighted this:

> Bush's Letterman appearance was quickly hailed as "A train wreck the likes of which America hasn't seen since The Fugitive, and showed the Texan brandishing his very own form of compassionate conservatism:
>
> **Bush**: It's about time you had the heart to invite me. (audience boos)
>
> **Letterman**: You keep saying you're a uniter, not a divider . . .
>
> **Bush**: That's true.
>
> **Letterman**: What exactly does that mean?
>
> **Bush**: It means that when it comes time to sew up your chest cavity we use stitches as opposed to opening it up . . .
>
> **Stewart**: Bush's aides reassured the governor that he killed, and when the audience groans, it's a sign you're really getting through to them. (March 2, 2000)

Later, the *Daily Show* also showed how Bush's character was demonstrated when he was overheard talking to running mate Dick Cheney at a campaign stop about a *New York Times* reporter who was in the audience:

> This weekend, George W. Bush gave us a glimpse of how wars might start if he was president, when a microphone picked up this comment he made to running mate Dick Cheney about a New York Times reporter:
> "There's Adam Clymer, Major League asshole from the New York Times."
> Now, we can't be 100% sure what that bleeped word was, but the NY Daily News reported that Bush called the reporter a quote: "@$#&*!" We here at the Daily Show think that may be just a dreadful misspelling of "asshole." We're not sure. (September 5, 2000)

Here, Jon Stewart was focused on linking Bush's character issues to his competency to be president, and not just about scoring points about his past or intelligence.

Bush as the "rich guy" who was more easily able to overcome his past alcoholism because he most likely had access to adequate treatment and counseling was highlighted when he appeared on the *Oprah Winfrey Show* in an interview satirized by Jon Stewart on September 20, 2000, where Oprah asked him softball questions (as one would expect), and Bush tried to appear more genuine by bringing up his struggles:

**Bush**: Alcohol was beginning to compete for my affections . . . for my wife and my family . . .

**Stewart**: But Oprah didn't pull any punches with the candidate, as she throttled the Texas Governor with questions like, "What was the best gift you've ever given?"

Bush responded that he gave his wife Laura the Promenade to the SMU library (to be named after her), thus totally negating his effort to seem normal. In contrast, the portrayal of Bush as the "dumb guy" on *SNL* made him more relatable to the general public.

Will Farrell's parody of Bush in the 2000 election cycle was best represented by a sketch on October 7, 2000, in which Bush and Gore were having their first debate. It included Bush being questioned by the moderator about political crises in Eastern Europe and Slobodan Milosevic's policies, but Bush would not answer. Instead he said, "I'm not going to pronounce any of their names tonight, because I don't believe that's in our national interest." Bush as "dumb guy" was cemented when Chris Parnell, playing debate moderator Jim Lehrer, asked the candidates "to sum up, in a single word, the best argument for his candidacy" at the end of the sketch. Bush/Ferrell simply replies "strategery." Although this was not a malapropism Bush himself actually used, it came to represent all of his vocabulary mistakes. But even though being unintelligent and mixing up words is not a positive trait for a presidential candidate, it was balanced by Darrell Hammond's portrayal of Al Gore, depicted as wooden and uncharismatic. Was *SNL* trying to convince the audience that neither candidate was a good choice? Both of the parodies were mainly about personal characteristics. The *New York Times* described the race, and the parodies of the candidates, as "The Stiff Guy vs. the Dumb Guy" (September 24, 2000). The portrayal of Gore as being boring, impersonal, and using jargon was also evident in the "First Presidential Debate" sketch, when, asked by Parnell/Lehrer to sum up *his* campaign, simply replied "lockbox," referring to Gore's plan to only allow Medicare payroll taxes to strengthen Medicare, and not be used for Congress members' "pork barrel" projects. Darrell Hammond would also appear on "Weekend Update" playing soon-to-be-former President Clinton, and commenting on the race, and the poor choices that the voters had between Bush and Gore: "Look, I love this guy. You know that, but come on. English is Al Gore's second language. His native tongue is binary code" ("Weekend Update," February 5, 2000). They portrayed Gore as emotionless, but little was said about his policies: "During an interview this week on '60 Minutes', Al Gore denied that he was angry about the election, saying, 'Anger? What would be the point of feeling that way? . . . Seriously. Tell me. I am fascinated by your human emotions'" ("Weekend Update," December 9, 2000). Similar to *SNL*, the *Daily Show* mocked Gore for being boring and difficult to listen to for a sustained period of time: "Al Gore's speech was described as 'electrifying,' in as much as it made listeners want to climb into a bathtub with a space heater" (May 31, 2000). Gore's association with Bill Clinton, who was ending his second term in scandal and impeachment hearings, was portrayed as a deficit to his public image: "With his crucial victory in the New Hampshire primary, insiders feel Vice President Al Gore might be getting a tad bit overconfident. Earlier today he actually allowed his photograph to be taken with this man (showing a picture of Clinton)" ("Weekend Update," February 5, 2000).

Ultimately, though, the thread that ran through most of *SNL*'s parodies of both Bush and Gore (before the election dispute took place) were that they were very similar in their personal backgrounds, and that it did not matter much who the voters chose, because both would be the wrong choice. Several sketches characterized them as basically the same; two combined satire of substantive issues, but the rest were personal. In the sketch that parodied the third presidential debate, a person in the audience questions Bush as to how his policies on abortion, climate change, and other issues differed from Gore's, but he could not articulate an answer, either because he was not good at discussing his own policies, or, more likely, he was perceived as not being very different from Gore in the first place: "Bush: . . . that's a very good question . . . and uh . . . there are differences between the Vice-President and myself on those issues" ("Third Presidential Debate," October 21, 2000). This sketch was both a parody of Gore's difficulties in articulating his differences from Bush, as well as mocking voters who were not paying close enough attention to something very important. On "Weekend Update," their "political correspondent," Kevin Brennan, discussed the personal characteristics of Bush and Gore's similar backgrounds:

> So, it looks like we're down to two candidates—Republican George W. Bush, and Democrat Al Gore. Let's look at how they're different: Gore went to Harvard, whereas Bush went to Yale. Bush's father used to be President, but Gore's father used to be a Senator. They both served in the military during Vietnam.

Gore was a roving reporter who never roved near enemy lines, and Bush served in the Texas National Guard where he did an excellent job keeping the Viet Cong out of Dallas. (March 11, 2000)

One major difference was that the *Daily Show* did *not* emphasize the sameness of the party nominees' policy positions as much as *SNL* did. One sketch portrayed both Gore and primary challenger Bill Bradley as puppets:

**Stewart**: The State of New Hampshire turned into a political Thunder Dome last night, one that two men entered, and 500 desperately wanted to leave. Vice President Al Gore and Presidential hopeful Bill Bradley sparred in the first Democratic Town hall of the 2000 campaign. Since CNN was kind enough to impose a media blackout on the event, the Daily Show's in-house political puppeteer was asked to capture the essence of the debate.

**Puppet 1**: Me too!

**Puppet 2**: Me too!

**Puppet 1**: And me too! (October 28, 1999)

But the *Daily Show* did not make the choice between Gore and Bush later on as more or less the same, as did *SNL*.

An important substantive area that the *Daily Show* pointed out was Bush's campaign tactic of emphasizing that he would be very different from Clinton. However, Clinton's policies led to economic growth that was well above average. It was strange that Bush would try to use this to his advantage. At the Iowa caucuses after his victory, Bush remarked: "And tonight also marks the beginning of the end of the Clinton era." Stewart responded to this by stating, "Yeah, he added, an era when Iowa's unemployment level fell to below 2%, and y'all made more money than ever imaginable. Enough is enough!" (*Daily Show*, January 25, 2000). Stewart joked about Bush's allegiance to special interest groups like the National Rifle Association, a substantive issue that was not brought up by *SNL*:

The George W. Bush campaign is scrambling to defend itself against a new advertisement released by a pro-gun control lobby group. The ad shows behind the scenes footage of an NRA meeting, where officials boast of the influence that they'll have should Bush be elected . . . (they talk of having "unbelievably friendly relations) . . . how friendly you ask? Let's just say by Bush's inauguration, history books will be saying JFK slipped in the shower. (May 8, 2000)

The *Daily Show* also pointed out times when Bush was being hypocritical about substantive policy issues. Bush accused Gore of being insincere because of his changing stances on campaign finance, Medicare, and tobacco; however, Bush pandered to the Log Cabin Republicans, a cynical and duplicitous move if one took into account his policy positions on issues like same-sex marriage and gays serving in the military: "Bush claims it's all part of an effort to reach out to non-traditional Republican voters. You know, without actually touching them" (April 13, 2000). Perhaps presaging the problems that would emerge in the Florida election results, the *Daily Show* also discussed Bush's problems with African Americans. His appearance at an NAACP event was described as having "provided him with a refreshing chill on a hot July evening," and trying to link the modern GOP with past Republicans like Abraham Lincoln, pandering hypocritically once again (July 13, 2000).

A main reason the *Daily Show* distinguished itself from *SNL* was its satirical engagement with the actual candidates. During the Primary, Correspondent Steve Carell tried to go on McCain's campaign bus, but was disappointed to find that he had to go on the "overflow" bus instead—not for major journalists. However, by the end of the sketch, he convinced McCain's wife Cindy to let him on the real bus. He then interviews McCain, feigning seriousness about economic policy after several softball questions:

**Carell**: Let's do a lightning round. Your favorite book?

**McCain**: For Whom the Bell Tolls.

**Carell**: Favorite movie?

**McCain**: Viva Zapata.

**Carell**: Charlton Heston?

**McCain**: Marlon Brando.

**Carell**: Close enough. If I were a tree, I would be a . . . ?

**McCain**: If I were a tree I'd be a root. What does that mean?

**Carell**: Senator, how do you reconcile the fact that you were one of the most vocal critics of Pork Barrel Politics, and yet, while you were chairman of the Commerce Committee, it set a record for unauthorized appropriation? (McCain looks uneasy.) I'm just kidding! I don't even know what that means! (December 16, 1999)

Even though Carell backed off at the end, the exchange showed that the *Daily Show* was not afraid to take risks. This exchange would be noticed by journalists in the mainstream press, which I discuss below, though they fail to understand its full significance. Additionally, it showed that McCain could be taken off guard and made to look less confident than he would like. This would become a major weapon in the show's narrative arsenal in later years.

A handful of *SNL* jokes and sketches were devoted to particular concerns should George W. Bush become president; fears that, in retrospect, turned out to be quite prophetic. One joke on "Weekend Update" seemed to predict the election controversies and point out the connections in the Bush family that could give him undue advantage (albeit in California, and not in Florida, and focusing on his father, and not his brother, as it turned out: "Despite trailing Al Gore in polls in California, Governor Bush says that he does not plan to let the Vice President win that liberal state in November. When asked how he plans on doing that, Bush replied, 'My father ran the CIA. We'll think of something'" ("Weekend Update", April 15, 2000). Another hinted at the economic disasters that would befall the U.S. later on in his administration ("Weekend Update," May 20, 2000). Finally, there were two instances, one "Weekend Update" joke, and one sketch, that hinted at unease and worry about what another Bush in the White House might do in terms of going to war over oil, a perception that was held by some in regard to President George H. W. Bush's Gulf War in the early 1990s: "Bush this week blamed President Clinton for the recent increase in gas prices and said if he were president, he'd abolish the gas tax, and if necessary, go to war with Alaska and steal their oil" ("Weekend Update," March 18, 2000). In the episode right before the election was held, *SNL* showed three sketches spoofing what each of the three major candidates' presidencies might look like (Bush, Gore, and Nader). The sketch about Bush's presidency was uncanny. Will Ferrell's Bush was being made to give a press conference by an advisor about the problems that he had caused in his first two weeks in the Oval Office:

> **Bush**: Hey, America! So, how we all doing out there, huh? Yeah, not so good. I broke the Hoover Dam . . . we had that war thing happen. But I mean, who ever heard of a Civil War, anyway? What is that? (he grabs a pair of fake binoculars, unscrews the lens, then pours alcohol from it into his mouth) I have missed you, ol' buddy! . . . Whoo! I think we can agree, Americans, that these have been a difficult first two years of my presidency.

> **Advisor**: You've been President for two weeks! ("A Glimpse of Our Possible Future Part I," November 4, 2000)

Although Bush did not cause an actual Civil War, the war against Iraq that he and his administration started divided Americans and erased the feeling of unity many felt after the attacks of September 11, 2001.

## SATIRE ON *SNL* AND THE *DAILY SHOW* FOLLOWING ELECTION DISPUTE

Although *SNL* portrayed Bush and Gore as similar to each other before the election took place, and there was a great focus on their personal characteristics, after the election did not produce a clear result, *SNL* made more substantively focused jokes than before. These dealt with the possible effects that conservative policies would have on society, and also with the perceived corruption of the Florida election decisions. After the election, there was a period of time that lasted several weeks before the election was finally decided. In this period on *SNL*, there were eleven substantive jokes and sketches, nine personal ones, and four that were both substantive and personal. Right after Election Day, *SNL* starts off as more lighthearted with their humor, exemplified by a sketch from November 11, 2000, called "The Presidential Couple," in a parody of the television sitcom *The Odd Couple*, where Bush and Gore both take up residence in the White House as co-presidents; it portrayed Gore as the man who would deal with the serious issues, while Bush would just goof off and not take anything seriously:

> **Bush**: Just think of the hilarious possibilities of having two presidents who hate each other's guts!
>
> **Gore**: For example, I might be having a crucial summit meeting to discuss foreign policy in China . . .
>
> **Bush**: And then I'll leave my laundry lying around in humorous piles!
>
> **Gore**: Now, what happens . . . what happens if we come to a complete standstill on an issue facing the nation?
>
> **Bush**: Like, what if Al wants to appoint a pro-choice justice to the Supreme Court, and I want to appoint the Texas Rangers?
>
> **Gore**: Well, don't worry, America . . . George W. came up with a fair and impartial system by which we can arbitrate any conceivable dispute.
>
> **Bush**: It's called Rock, Paper, Scissors. I learned it in college.

Another sketch featured Gore and Bush's brother, the Governor of Florida Jeb Bush, discussing George W.'s perceived lack of intelligence: "Jeb, let me ask you something. You seem to care a lot about this country. When you saw your brother actually had a chance of winning, were you ever tempted to tell everyone how he's . . . well, you know . . . 'special'?" ("Palm Beach," December 9, 2000). Additionally, there was a great deal of focus on the personal life, and personal characteristics, of Katherine Harris, the Florida Secretary of State who was responsible for throwing out a number of disputed ballots, which essentially decided the election: "Katherine Harris hasn't gotten this much attention since Spring Break '77 . . . She looks like the woman being cheated on in a Mexican soap opera. Katherine, honey, there's another setting on your make-up mirror. It's called 'daytime'" ("Weekend Update," November 18, 2000). Jokes on "Weekend Update" also mocked the voters of Florida for their inability to understand how the ballots actually worked, mainly because of the stereotype that many elderly people live in the state: "Online advocates say that the delays and confusion over ballot counting wouldn't be a problem if people voted on the internet . . . Sure, they can't candle punch cards, but old people love the internet. My grandfather's afraid of his answering machine" ("Weekend Update, January 11, 2000).

Another thing that distinguished the *Daily Show* early on in its run, which particularly emerged during this election cycle, was the propensity to gather news clips from many sources (cable news and network news) when a candidate or politician was speaking. Often, they did this over time, to show when a politician had made a statement in the present that contradicted what they said in the past. During the presidential campaign, however, it became increasingly clear, when the *Daily Show* employed this technique, it was done to make obvious the "talking points" that the candidates used. The show assembled clips of the candidates saying the same thing over and over again. After Election Day had passed, Gore went on several TV shows and used the same strange analogy about the inaccurately scanned votes. To paraphrase, he said, repeatedly, that supermarket checkout lines were not going to not let you buy something if it did not scan properly. Although he was certainly correct about this, this technique of showing the repetition employed by the *Daily Show* made Gore seem both dull and desperate (November 30, 2000). After the election dispute, Jon Stewart continued to frequently discuss the various aspects of the situation. The show emphasized the complexity of the issue, and expressed fears that it would be long, drawn out, and harmful to the Democratic process (which all turned out to be true). They showed a clip of Gore's campaign manager talking about the beginning of the dispute:

> **William Daley**: We're in the process of speaking with lawyers, secretary Christopher is one of the top lawyers in America. We have lawyers that have gone to Florida, and they're lawyers in Florida who are experts in elections laws . . .
>
> He continued . . . and by the way, don't think because I just used the word "lawyer" four times in fifteen seconds that this is gonna be a long process. (November 9, 2000)

As it became increasingly clear that the election would not be decided quickly, that it would come down to decisions made by the Florida Supreme Court and the Supreme Court of the United States, and that there were actually serious problems with the ballots and the way they were being counted (or not counted), *SNL* and the *Daily Show* became much more substantive in its jokes about the election dispute. Jokes about Katherine Harris also focused on her connections to the Bush family and her rumored ulterior motives for favoring Bush over Gore. In a sketch parodying Chris Matthews' show *Hardball*, Matthews questioned Harris about whether or not she felt the Florida Supreme Court will decide in Bush's favor. She said, "The Florida Supreme Court can chomp on it, I'm gettin' out of this backwater state. All I have to do now is practice smiling for my ambassador job" ("Hardball," November 18, 2000).

Similarly, at the end of the conflict, the *Daily Show* addressed the issue that there might have been "conflicts of interest" in how the election dispute was being handled in Florida, and they laid out these conflicts in more detail than *SNL* (and arguably better than most traditional news sources):

> Justice Scalia's son is a partner is the same law firm as Bush's chief lawyer, Bush's brother is Florida's Governor, the head of Bush's Florida campaign happens to be Secretary of State in that area, and Bush's cousin was the first network news official to prematurely call the election for Bush . . . in a related story, Al Gore's daughter works for Futurama, so . . . gonna have to keep an eye on that powder keg. (December 12, 2000)

This particularly substantive criticism essentially stated that Gore did not have a real chance of getting a fair outcome. Even so, the *Daily Show* also mocked how the Gore campaign dealt with the situation. After the Florida Supreme Court and the U.S. Supreme Court handed down rulings that were not good for Gore's challenge, the Gore campaign said some strange things:

> Yesterday also saw the US Supreme Court, seen her in its natural setting, put aside a ruling by the Florida Supreme Court that had allowed for manual recounts . . . Gore's lawyer, David Boies, had some strong words about the ruling:
>
> **Boies**: The United States Supreme Court has no authority at all.
>
> **Stewart [appearing confused]**: Oh that's right, he's gone batshit insane. (December 5, 2000)

Democracy itself was on the line, the elderly were effectively being disenfranchised by the confusing ballots, and African Americans directly disenfranchised, having been mistakenly purged from the rolls as felons:[1] "Jeb Bush, the Governor of Florida and Brother of George W. Bush took himself out of the Florida Recount Process, noting, look, I already threw out 19,000 ballots, hassled black voters, and confused the old Jews, my work here is done" ("Weekend Update," November 11, 2000). In the final analysis, *SNL* portrayed the controversy over the election as a terrible circumstance for Democracy, riddled with the potential of corruption, due to the close ties of the

people who had the ability to make the decisions about it to George W. Bush.
It was an embarrassing circus:

> **Tina Fey**: At eight o'clock this morning, the hand recounts start up again, then
> the Circuit Court rejects Bush's appeal, the Prime Minister of Israel resigns,
> no one notices, then this afternoon the U.S. Supreme Court got all up in it and
> stopped the recount. In light of these events, America is cancelled. Citizens are
> asked to choose between Canada and Mexico by 4 p.m. tomorrow. ("Weekend
> Update," December 9, 2000)

> **Jimmy Fallon**: The tension, the excitement, the emotions, people—it kicks
> ass! Disenfranchised voters! Oh, yeah, I said it! And I know what it means, too!
> Yeah, I'm watching CNN now, because I want to! . . . Decision 2000, that's
> what they call it. Not "The Election." You know why? Because it's a TV show.
> It's "Survivor." It's "Millionaire." It's "The Real World"—the Boston one. You
> hear that, America? For the first time ever, politics are exciting! ("Weekend
> Update," December 9, 2000)

It is clear that this incident represented a turning point for political humor. In the years to come, the disputed win of the Bush campaign would
be a source which comedy could draw upon. If Bush was an illegitimate
president, they would have greater license to be more critical of him than
any other. This, along with the later events of September 11, 2001, would
elevate the place of political humor as an alternate resource of public
discourse. Later, a *Daily Show* executive would be quoted as saying that
their "currency is one of insanity" (Jim Rutenberg, "TV Notes; News is
the Comedy," *New York Times*, November 22, 2000), meaning that politics
had become so absurd, only satire could adequately contextualize it. As
discussed below, the journalists in the *Times* and the *Post* had only a limited
understanding of this phenomenon.

## JOURNALISTS DEBATE INFLUENCE

The trend for journalists in the *New York Times* and the *Washington Post* to
place greater importance upon late-night comedy's influence on the narrative
construction of the elections continued its growth in the 2000 election cycle.
However, they debated exactly how much influence it was having, and in
what areas of the public's perception. They focused on comedy hosts like
Leno and Letterman, and the power of *SNL* to set the tone. They mentioned
the *Daily Show*, but failed to see how much of a key part of the construction
it might become, instead often either directly bemoaning the conflation of en-

tertainment and news, or quoting those who did. Although the representations of the candidates on the late-night comedy programs were humorous and exaggerated, "the [campaign] advisers say . . . the monologues are playing a crucial, if flawed, role in shaping voters' perception of candidates . . . The power of the late-night television hosts to define a candidate's political weaknesses and quirks often terrifies candidates" (Bernard Weinraub, "Election's Barometer: Barbs of Late-Night TV," *New York Times*, January 19, 2000). A case in point about Al Gore was described in the *Times*: "Mr. Clinton called . . . Gore's top strategist, a couple of weeks ago to tell him he ought to make the vice president watch a skit about the first debate on . . . 'Saturday Night Live,' in which Mr. Gore was depicted as overbearing and orange" (Melinda Henneberger and Don Van Natta Jr., "Once Close to Clinton, Gore Keeps a Distance," *New York Times*, October 20, 2000). Although Gore may or may not have possessed these qualities, they simultaneously informed the public's perception of him, and were informed by the perception that already existed.

> "It's the Jay Leno test," said David Axelrod, a Democratic strategist in Chicago. "If a salient quality of yours begins to become a frequent repeat joke in Jay Leno's monologue, then you've reached such a level of attention and penetration that that quality will begin to define you. These things are almost always unfair. People are more complex than one quality. Bush may not be a genius, but he's not a moron either—or he wouldn't be where he is." (Richard L. Berke, "The Nation: Negative Spin; Their Biggest Campaign May Be Against Type-Casting," *New York Times*, November 28, 1999)

It appeared that the shows, the journalists, and the campaign advisers were focusing on representations of these non-substantive superficial traits. However, in time it became apparent during this election cycle that the *Daily Show* was pulling away from this type of characterization and including more substantive issues; but it took the journalists some time to notice what was happening and begin to reflect on it.

Instead of meaning, journalists focused on appearances made by the candidates, and the parodies of them, on *SNL*. They noted that *SNL* had become "Hot enough that for last night's election coverage, Will Ferrell and Darrell Hammond . . . were invited to join Tom Brokaw and the NBC News team" (Bill Carter, "TV Notes; The People's Choice," *New York Times*, November 8, 2000). But even the influence of these satires was met with some skepticism:

> The late-night show's latest political sketches [with Hammond and Ferrell] have been called the most important political writing of this election year by MSNBC senior political analyst Lawrence O'Donnell. But since he works for NBC—in

addition to his gig on network co-owned MSNBC, he's a writer-producer on NBC's hit drama "The West Wing"—you might want to ratchet that hyperbole down a notch or two. (Lisa de Moraes, "Taped from New York, It's the Candidates on 'Saturday Night,'" *Washington Post*, November 3, 2000)

Even as the journalists discussed the influence of Leno, Letterman, and *SNL*, a few recognized the growing influence of the *Daily Show*, saying it was "Once an obscure cable program with a cult following," and had become "an almost legitimate though farcical news outlet for young people" (Jim Rutenberg, "TV Notes; News Is the Comedy," *New York Times*, November 22, 2000). The fact that they had to use qualifiers like "almost" and "though farcical" shows that their recognition of its influence is seen through the filter of polluting the program and Jon Stewart as "merely" entertainment (Back et al. 2012). *Daily Show* Executive Producer Madeleine Smithberg was quoted as saying, "The 'Today' show has clips of us almost every day." Why was this happening? They said that they thought it was because they were "freer than real television journalists are to point out how bizarre the situation is" . . . and that comedians were the "'only ones who can make sense of it; because our currency is one of insanity,' Ms. Smithberg said." (Jim Rutenberg, "TV Notes; News Is the Comedy," *New York Times*, November 22, 2000). After 9/11, this idea turns out to be even more relevant.

The discussion about the "freeness" of the fake show to be more truthful about the situation was truly prescient, and would exponentially increase after 9/11. But the stage was set, and viewers and creators of the *Daily Show* (if not totally the journalists writing about it) had insight as to what was beginning to happen in regard to it. The idea that people were really getting news from the *Daily Show* was one that Jon Stewart dismissed:

"What news are they getting? We're not breaking any news," Stewart says. "We're a very reactive business." The comedians don't drive the national discourse—unless, perhaps, you think all the late-night jokes on the Lewinsky scandal turned the attention of Dan Rather, Tom Brokaw and Peter Jennings to an issue, he says, that "otherwise would've been ignored." (Dana Milbank, "Tracking Laughs Is No Joke in Election Year," *Washington Post*, October 19, 2000)

But the journalists were still writing superficially about the importance of the *Daily Show* as well, noting that, "As if the line between news and entertainment on television were not already blurry enough . . . yesterday, the word on the logo for NBC's election coverage—which had been 'Decision 2000'—changed to 'Indecision 2000' . . . Was it a deliberate echo of Jon Stewart . . . ?" (James Barron, "Public Lives," *New York Times*, November 9, 2000).

## CANDIDATES ON THE SHOWS SEEN
## IN THE LIGHT OF PERSONAL HUMOR

Journalists in this election cycle gave more attention and importance to the candidates appearing on late-night comedy programs than in the past, and were distracted by it. Writers saw the appearances under the umbrella of two epiphenomena; first, their perception that news and entertainment were merging, and thus candidates had to go on them to get their message out, and second that they needed to counter the personal attacks being made against them, clear the air, and get on to more substantive matters. But there was more going on than just candidates going on the shows to burst the caricatures being made of them; the shows themselves, led by the *Daily Show*, were becoming more substantive in their satire, which the writers did not yet recognize. In this same vein, the shows had not yet shed the polluted entertainment side of the public sphere binary as they would later on, when it would diminish or become irrelevant. Journalists saw the appearances as an essential feature of the campaign, which was accurate; candidates had to appear on the shows to seem relatable and perform their competency as candidates in order to succeed. Both Bush and Gore, for the most part, were successful in their attempts in doing this. One notable exception, as the *Daily Show* noted (above) was when George W. Bush appeared via satellite on Letterman's show. His performative failure did not escape the notice of the journalists:

> "I could barely watch it," Vance DeGeneres, a veteran comedy writer and performer on Comedy Central's "Daily Show," said of the incident on "Late Show with David Letterman." . . . After weeks of goading by Mr. Letterman, Gov. George W. Bush of Texas agreed to appear by satellite on his show, an encounter that was, by most assessments, a disaster for the Republican presidential candidate. Mr. Bush, hampered by the split-second time delay and projecting an air of being led on a forced march, offered one lame quip after another, including a pun about Mr. Letterman's recent heart operation so strained that it left the host staring, mortified, into the camera. (Peter Marks, "Television/Radio; Fear and Joking on the Late-Night Campaign Trail," *New York Times*, May 7, 2000)

If Bush had many appearances like this, it would have been disastrous for him; however, this was an exception. He learned from this failure, because he did not repeat it. In fact, this was exactly how his performance was narrated in the papers; Bush managed to recover from the bad Letterman appearance by going on Leno's show and appearing confident and more authentic, "unlike an earlier appearance in the campaign on CBS's 'Late Show,' when . . . he bombed trying to match David Letterman joke for joke, Mr. Bush made no effort to go head to head with Mr. Leno. Instead, Mr. Bush gave relaxed, straightforward answers about . . . the campaign" (Todd S. Purdum and Alison Mitchell, "McCain Renews Attack on Ads as Bush Talks of Race Tolerance," *New York Times*, March 7, 2000). Thus, Bush turned the failure around to his advantage and made himself look authentic once again.

The journalists especially took note of both Bush and Gore's appearance on an *SNL* special which aired in primetime, noting that, "Bush and Gore reinforce their own stereotypes as, respectively, a habitual word mangler and a pedantic glory hog," but commenting that the remarkable thing about the candidates' bits on a show airing just two days before the election is how unremarkable it all seems" (Paul Farhi, "Al and Dubya's 'Saturday Night' Date; Candidates Follow Laugh Track to Voters," *Washington Post*, November 4, 2000). Why did they have to do this if it would perhaps make them look foolish? It went beyond simply having to seem "normal" or able to take a joke; they were "self-deprecating" on the shows but there was greater peril in *not* doing it—"In attempting to co-opt the joke, Bush and Gore may recognize some political danger in leaving parody unanswered." But although this new way of performing authenticity as a presidential candidate might have been advantageous for the candidates, it was *not* good for the narrative integrity of contemporary satire:

> Does good-naturedness by the spoofees perhaps indicate that "SNL's" satire is toothless—perhaps too good-natured itself? Maybe . . . the victims feel it behooves them to accept the joking graciously and even participate in it. As all the world knows, thanks to recent news reports, after this year's first debate Gore and Bush aides watched the "SNL" version as one way of determining where their candidates went wrong. (Tom Shales, "'Presidential Bash': Hands-Down Winner," *Washington Post*, November 4, 2000)

The general consensus in the papers was that appearing on the shows was not especially helpful to the candidates, but *not* appearing on them would be harmful, that "a candidate is serious about running but not so serious about themselves" (Peter Marks, "Fear and Joking on the Late-Night Campaign Trail," *New York Times*, May 7, 2000). Journalists wrote about quantitative measures that researchers were collecting about the number of jokes, trying to see whether there was a correlation between how well they did when appearing on the late-night programs and how many jokes were directed against them in comedians' monologues:

> In August, when Bush was still riding high, Curry counted 78 jokes about Gore and 43 about Bush. In September, when Gore was strong, the count reversed: 94 about Bush and only 34 about Gore. Now that Gore is skidding, the October count so far has the two much closer: 78 for Bush, 67 for Gore.

(Dana Milbank, "Tracking Laughs Is No Joke in Election Year," *Washington Post*, October 19, 2000)

Other than the superficial "news-is-becoming-more-like-entertainment" lament, there was almost no reflection in the papers during this election cycle about what it *actually meant* in terms of the transformation of the public sphere itself. The above-mentioned data collection only showed the slightest of engagement with the reality of the situation—a reality that the journalists did not really want to acknowledge, which was that they were being circumvented. The segment from the *Daily Show* where Steve Carell got onto the "secondary bus" for John McCain's campaign and harassed McCain's wife until he got access to the Republican Primary Candidate (described above), received a mention in the *Times*, but they missed most of the point about its true relevance: "The segment followed Mr. Carell's exploits as he tried vainly to get a seat on Mr. McCain's bus, a conceit that was inherently funny: Mr. McCain had become instantly legendary for the generous access he provided to the press" (Peter Marks, "Fear and Joking on the Late-Night Campaign Trail," *New York Times*, May 7, 2000). Carell masterfully makes fun of the news media itself, by starting to ask vacuous "fluff" personality questions of McCain, then hit him with a serious question, which confused the candidate, making him look like a deer in the headlights; but then Carrel let him off the hook, *just exactly as the journalists would do*, because they would not want to lose their access.

Several comments were made in the papers about the perception that news and entertainment were becoming more alike. Why the candidates' appearances on the show are important was seen under this light. Some writers expressed the idea that it was a normatively bad thing, and observed that the process had been going on for some time, saying it was "a boundary that has been fading since the psychedelic days of 'Rowan and Martin's Laugh-In,'" (Peter Marks, "Fear and Joking on the Late-Night Campaign Trail," *New York Times*, May 7, 2000).

> One is liable to say almost anything after too much coffee, too little sleep and too many campaign stops . . . there is the increased number of media chatterers all too willing to amplify the simple slip into epic proportions. The confluence of the entertainment and political worlds also has helped magnify these mistakes. The Leno and Letterman shows feed off them; as a result, gaffes take on a late-night life of their own, reaching young voters largely unexposed to television news broadcasts or newspapers. (Andrew Kohut, "The Vox Pop on Malaprops," *Washington Post*, September 24, 2000)

Being able to go on the programs and perform successfully under difficult conditions had become a rite of passage. The candidates must appear on the

shows; if they did not, they risked being seen as unlikeable: "America is seeing the ultimate in the fusion of not just entertainment and news, but entertainment, news and politics. And truth be told, the candidates have no choice.
They have to play. The public demands it" (Joyce Purnick, "First Lady on
Late Show: TV Rules," *New York Times*, January 13, 2000). The number of
jokes had been steadily increasing in this arena of the public sphere, a trend
which worried "Bob Lichter, who runs [a] research group. 'It's one small blip
in the gradual decline of Western civilization . . . There's no distinction anymore between news and popular culture'" (Dana Milbank, "Tracking Laughs
Is No Joke in Election Year," *Washington Post*, October 19, 2000). However,
no one tried to explain *why* the confluence of entertainment and politics was
bad; it was unquestioningly assumed to be.

Even so, some journalists still maintained that there *was* a distinction, and
that the comedy shows were throwing light on just exactly what that distinction was and why the jokes had begun to increase so much: "Because 'The
Daily Show' is far more enjoyable when compared with the traditional news-
casts, it could actually encourage young people to watch the nightly news—if
only to make fun of it" (Julie Salamon, "In the News Today: Wry Observations and Snide Remarks," *New York Times*, August 1, 2000). Thus, there was
the possibility for normatively good outcomes—such as getting "young people" (whatever that meant) to know more about the news, but the writers were
still very ambivalent about the changing situation: "Who knows, maybe the
'SNL' business even helps engage and inspire an apathetic electorate; one has
to be au courant in order to get the jokes told about the candidates on 'Saturday Night Live'" (Tom Shales, "'Presidential Bash': Hands-Down Winner,"
*Washington Post*, November 4, 2000). Others blamed the lack of engagement
on the qualities of the candidates themselves: "Perhaps watching a candidate
on the 'Late Show with David Letterman' has somehow become a substitute
for voting" (Richard L. Berke, "The Nation: Voter Tune Out; Focusing on
the Few, Blind to the Many," *New York Times*, October 22, 2000). A prime
opportunity for real analysis of how political commentary was transforming
was missed when George W. Bush, on the *Tonight Show*, jokingly discussed
the idea that "his 'little brother recognizes that Thanksgiving might be a little
chilly' if he does not deliver Florida. He repeated that line tonight in Tampa"
(Alison Mitchell, "Focus Is on Crucial States in Campaign's Final Hours,"
*New York Times*, November 6, 2000). Of course, Bush was talking about his
brother Jeb, Governor of Florida, who, historically, of course did just that; but
they took the candidates' appearances on show like Leno's so lightly that this
comment did not seem highly undemocratic, even to joke about.

While journalists acknowledged shows like "Leno and Letterman, quite
literally, have become the town squares of the campaign," because the

candidates keep appearing on them, to reach the largest number of people (Katharine Q. Seelye, "Gore Offers and Seeks Assurance in Pennsylvania," *New York Times*, October 28, 2000), they were hesitant to make a causal link between the amount of sketches and voting patterns:

> While Johnny Carson did some political humor and "Saturday Night Live" has done skits for years, the real watershed year for TV political humor was 1988, when Dan Quayle became the perpetual butt of late-night jokes . . . Since that year, he said, the number of jokes on TV about the candidates has soared. (Paul Farhi, "Al and Dubya's 'Saturday Night' Date; Candidates Follow Laugh Track to Voters," *Washington Post*, November 4, 2000)

> . . . there's no evidence that [the amount of jokes about candidates] actually has any impact on the way people vote. For its years of studying and counting late-night political jokes, the Center for Media and Public Affairs hasn't found any links between the jokes about a candidate and the candidate's electoral success. (Dana Milbank, "Tracking Laughs Is No Joke in Election Year," *Washington Post*, October 19, 2000)

But it was likely that the amount was not really what was important here; comedians could make numerous offhanded remarks about the candidates' personal characteristics, and audiences would likely experience these as more-or-less the same block of jokes; more jokes did not mean more influence, and would have the effect of diminishing returns. It was the *meaning* of the jokes that had impact; the *Times* noted the Pew study that "roughly one in ten Americans said they routinely gleaned information about the presidential race from late-night talk shows"—information did not consist of "Bush mispronounces words" or "Gore looks orange"; people already knew this. New information was what mattered for elections, especially going forward from this election cycle. The *Times* rightly pointed out that "considering that the 1996 presidential election was decided by a mere eight percentage points, what each and every consumer of comedy on television takes away from the experience can be highly significant" (Peter Marks, "Television/Radio; Fear and Joking on the Late-Night Campaign Trail." *New York Times*, May 7, 2000). But still, they did not speculate on what that would be. Perhaps the reliance upon personality-driven humor overshadowed any insight the journalists might have had.

Other than the many negative comments about the Letterman appearance, the journalists were largely dismissive about the humor on television about George W. Bush. As with Gore, most of it dwelt upon personal characteristics of his that might or might not have any bearing on his ability to be an effective president. Bush as the "dumb guy" and Bush as the former partier dominated the narrative. The former was simply regarded as the corollary to the "Gore as boring" narrative: "In the debate sketch [Will Ferrell playing George W. Bush] displays an entire range of baffled looks in response to a single question . . . Asked for a single word that sums up his candidacy he says, 'Strategery,' then gives a smug smile" (Caryn James, "Critic's Notebook; Where Politics and Comedy Intermingle, the Punch Lines Can Draw Blood," *New York Times*, November 4, 2000). The same sketch had him unsure how to pronounce the names of world leaders. This image takes over the satire about Bush, and no inroads about his political abilities or policies are made, and it was largely ineffectual: "Despite lampoons by Letterman and others, Bush as a bumbler seems ancient history in this cyclorama of a campaign" (Mike Allen, "Confident Bush Shifts Right, Goes After New Ground," *Washington Post*, October 16, 2000). The journalists specifically refuted the latter representation, that of Bush as a former drug and alcohol abuser: "There is a popular image of Mr. Bush's younger days, fueled by late-night television jokes, suggesting that he spent much of the 1970s stupefied in a drug-fueled haze . . . [but] his behavior was more callow than criminal" (Nicholas D. Kristof, "How Bush Came to Tame His Inner Scamp," *New York Times*, July 29, 2000). There was little to no impact upon the campaign.

Journalists took special note of the way that Al Gore altered his debate and media performances in reaction to how *SNL* had portrayed him. Gore had a media coach, Michael Sheehan, watch the tape of his performance and try to improve upon his "overbearing manner and jargon-laden speech" (Terry M. Neal and Ceci Connolly, "Debate Challenges Are Same as Before; Analysts: Gore Must Show an Earth-ier Side, Bush Must Display Some Intellectual Heft," *Washington Post*, October 11, 2000). Maureen Dowd described this as "a 'Clockwork Orange' moment, desperately trying to condition Mr. Gore against another such unbearable performance . . . [as] the vice president hogs the microphone for a sob story without end, delivered in punctilious tones, and wants to deliver two closing statements" ("Liberties; His Lyin', Sighin' Heart," *New York Times*, October 11, 2000). Additionally, his word choices are focused upon particularly the term "lockbox," rather than the policy positions behind them: "After 'Saturday Night Live' parodied his frequent use of that term to refer to his promise to protect Medicare and Social Security surpluses from raids by Congress, Mr. Gore avoided the metaphor today" (Kevin Sack, "The 2000 Campaign: The Vice President; Gore Again Alters Day To Meet On Middle East," *New York Times*, October 14, 2000). But again, these are not substantive issues, were not likely to sway opinions.

Certainly, one unique feature of this campaign cycle was that it lasted so long, with the extended period of time that the U.S. Supreme Court took to finally decide the disputed election. The late-night comedy programs commented upon the incident in many different ways, as outlined above; however, the journalists chose to primarily focus upon the humor about ballot problems, not the threat to democracy (largely advanced by the *Daily Show* and to a lesser extent Tina Fey and Jimmy Fallon). This was a wasted opportunity; they mainly summarized the remarks on the shows, commenting about "the matter that has caused an extended legal dispute and no end of late-night comedy on television—how to judge dimpled ballots" (Roberto Suro, Jo Becker, and Serge F. Kovaleski, "Florida Supreme Court Rebuffs Gore; Legal Moves Are Likely Past Sunday," *Washington Post*, November 24, 2000). They deplored the generalized sense of confusion and inability of the mainstream news media to sort it out: "'You sit and you watch the Lenos and Lettermans and "Saturday Night Live," and you realize that the parody captures the confusion,' said Ramon Escobar, MSNBC's executive producer" (Peter Marks, "Counting the Vote: The Media; For TV, A Story With Everything," *New York Times*, November 19, 2000). Florida as a target of humor was also discussed, but again, this was structurally insignificant: "For weeks, Floridians have seen their state ridiculed around the country, and seen it become the focus of late-night television sarcasm and comedy" (Rick Bragg, "Floridians at Last Have a Vote to Cheer," *New York Times*, December 11, 2000). Ultimately, the journalists failed to note the important points that *SNL* and the *Daily Show* in particular were making about the threats to democracy that the election dispute might have posed: "Each evening on television, scholars and pundits solemnly warn of nightmarish possibilities, only to be followed by late-night talk-show hosts who make fun of it all" (Dan Barry, "The Election: Chaos Theory; How to Stop Worrying and Love the Limbo," *New York Times*, November 12, 2000). There was so much more being discussed and satirized on *SNL* and the *Daily Show*, that to say that they were just making "fun of it all" is indicative of how little the journalists understood about the changing nature of political satire at that time.

## CONCLUSION: COMEDIC TALK AS A MEANING RESOURCE

There was a measure of progress made in this election cycle toward both substantive humor on the programs themselves, as well as recognition of this in the *Post* and the *Times*. In the election cycles in the 1980s, there was an almost total lack of substantive humor. The main criticism leveled against political comedy during this decade was that it was following the tone, rather than setting it, and thus was not truly satirical. With the structural changes in *SNL* including more gender diversity at the "Weekend Update" desk (which was always a large source of political humor on the program), an original source of the transformation is revealed. Fey's presence was not exceptionally meaningful in terms of gender dynamics in this election cycle; but if she had not been there for such a long period of time before 2008, she may well not have been such a strong satirical narrative presence when she came on *SNL* to parody Sarah Palin. Additionally, with the arrival of the *Daily Show*, and the turning point of the disputed election, the momentum begins to shift in 2000. In this year, the humor about George W. Bush's intelligence mirrored that of the humor in the 1990s about Dan Quayle. However, there were no sexual scandals as there were back then (including those of Gary Hart and Bill Clinton). This absence in 2000 made the shows have to look for other avenues of mockery, and perhaps drove them to more substantive areas to draw upon. Finally, in 2000, there were not any jokes about the candidates' wives, as there had been, especially about Hillary Clinton. As predicted by numerous commentators in the past, candidates did more regularly appear on the shows, both to reach this young, large audience of potential voters, but also to make themselves seem normal. This was especially relevant for Gore, who needed to portray a more relaxed attitude.

The journalists did not completely accept the caricatures of either Gore or Bush, specifically refuting them in some instances. And when the candidates themselves appeared on the shows, to defuse the strength of the parodies about them, appearing "in on the joke," it caused the journalist to ultimately regard the shows as "toothless," and without satirical power. But commentators about the programs missed many opportunities when the candidates really were *not* in on the joke, such as the incident described above between Steve Carrell and John McCain. These "confrontations" would only increase over the years. The *Daily Show* would eventually become the gold standard against which all other political satire would be judged because of this, among other reasons. Although it was clearly the case that news and entertainment were beginning to become more alike in the latter part of the twentieth century (Williams and Delli Carpini 2011), the journalists plainly did not recognize the fact that it was not just news becoming more like entertainment (Jacobs 2012), but entertainment becoming more like news *at the same time*. It was a blurring of the lines, not a colonization of one over the other. Politics is everywhere, as Schudson (1998) claimed. Why should it not be more of a part of entertainment, if it was becoming more incorporated into all areas of the public sphere?

Political discourse had started to change based on the historically contextualized events that brought the realm of politics into seeming more and more absurd, thus making discussion about them that was based in absurdity seem more natural. The Pew studies that showed that people were gaining more political knowledge by watching the programs (Feldman 2007; Hollander 2005; Young 2004), and other studies showed that this had a positive effect on civic engagement (Cao and Brewer 2008). But these measured effects were only part of the picture. The shows were taking a more prominent place as a source of meaning in public discourse. The *Daily Show* in particular was perfectly positioned to take on this role. Throughout the 1990s, the growing polarization of cable news made political discourse on television seem more inherently farcical. At the same time, people relied upon cable more and more to get information about political events. Combined with the contentious election dispute (and later 9/11), the *Daily Show* became both a reaction to these events, and a narrative resource for voters and journalists. In part, it came along at exactly the right time, but also carved a place for itself as an influencer unto its own.

As Jacobs and Michaud Wild (2013) argue, "If these new media formats are to have any significant influence, they need to become part of the discussions that take place within the larger public conversations organized by elite media. Without this kind of public focus and attention, it becomes extremely difficult for them to have any steering influence over civil society" (91). In the 2000 election cycle, journalists recognized the importance of the comedy programs, but it is clear from this analysis that they also made a few tentative attempts to emphasize their significance in guiding the narrative about the candidates and the election, particularly toward the end. Gore and Bush had equally failed performances in the main portion of the 2000 election cycle—there was no advantage or disadvantage to either one as the shows, especially *SNL*, portrayed them both in differently unflattering lights, but no more one than the other. Thus, there was no narrative "foothold" for elite media participants to grasp and use as a meaning structure to criticize one over the other or represent their own viewpoints. In later years, they would use *SNL* and the *Daily Show* to do these things (Jacobs and Michaud Wild 2013). Mentions of the Pew study about where people were getting their political information from were tempered by more thorough discussion of how news and entertainment becoming more alike might be a negative trend. The influence of the *Daily Show* was underexamined in this election cycle, but it was also not as strong as it would become. The program's usage of sound bite montages, and going back into the archives to show political figures contradicting themselves, had not yet begun to be seen by journalists as a new way to make rational arguments about political discourse. In subsequent years, there would be an increase in journalists, in print as well as television, using quotes and clips from the show to represent their own viewpoints.

## NOTE

1. Palast, Gregory. 2000. "Florida's flawed 'voter-cleansing' program: Secretary of State Katherine Harris hired a firm to vet the rolls for felons, but that may have wrongly kept thousands, particularly blacks, from casting ballots." *Salon.com*, December 4. http://www.salon.com/2000/12/04/voter_file/.

## Chapter Four

# The 9/11 Era

## *"Now They Are Pundits"*

September 11, 2001, cast a shadow over the 2004 election, as it was the first one since the attacks. Journalists characterized the changing face of political humor in terms of 9/11, and this was a recurring theme. The influence of the *Daily Show* in particular increased because of how political discourse changed.

> The first [campaign] since the terrorist attacks of Sept. 11 . . . has squelched much of what usually passes for political humor. The most the presidential candidates seem to be able to muster is a sardonic smile. Such is the tenor of the campaign that it has transformed Comedy Central into a serious network. Al Franken, Jon Stewart and Dennis Miller used to be comedians. Now they are pundits. (Robert Strauss, "Laugh Early and Often," *New York Times*, October 31, 2004)

In general, writers lauded the greater reliance Americans had on late-night comedy, and particularly on the *Daily Show*, because essentially, it was better than not having any guidance at all. This assistance was not being provided by the television news media as it once was, and calling the new era: "a golden age of satire. While citizens in earlier eras had Walter Cronkite . . . to help them navigate contentious and confusing matters of public import, more and more of us seem to rely on Jon Stewart and Comedy Central. Which suits me just fine" (A. O. Scott, "Moral Guidance From Class Clowns," *New York Times*, October 15, 2004). A January 2004 Pew Research Study found that "young people, by far the hardest to reach segment of the political news audience, were abandoning mainstream sources of election news and increasingly citing alternative outlets, including comedy shows such as the *Daily Show* and *Saturday Night Live*, as their source for election news."[1]

The Presidential Primaries during the 2004 election cycle were long and managed to fragment the Democratic Party. Howard Dean emerged as an early frontrunner, and made some great advances in grassroots organizing on the internet. Despite this accomplishment, some saw him as volatile and unstable, culminating in his concession speech after he lost the Iowa caucuses to John Kerry and John Edwards, in which a microphone picked him on uttering a strange "scream." John Kerry instead became the nominee; but the media and late-night television comedy programs portrayed him as not dissimilar enough from George W. Bush in terms of his educational and personal background. Both had roots in the northeast, came from wealth, and went to Yale. The primary difference in their biographies was that Kerry served in Vietnam, and Bush did not, having been in the National Guard—at the time, widely considered to be a way to get out of going overseas. Despite the highly contentious and close election, and Kerry's genuine war service, Kerry lost. Part of the reason was Kerry's inability to manage to look like a "regular guy" as well as Bush could, despite neither of them being one. Another reason was, despite the questionability of the war in Iraq, many citizens did not want to change leadership so soon after 9/11 and during a major military incursion.

Writers in the *Washington Post* and the *New York Times* began to take much greater notice of how both *Saturday Night Live*, and especially the *Daily Show*, commented on these and other issues during the campaign. A major study by the Pew Research Center for the People and the Press in January 2004, which showed a greater reliance upon such "alternative" news sources such as *SNL* and the *Daily Show*, provided a backdrop and justification for journalists who had been using the criticism provided by the comedy programs to back up their own opinions. Additionally, Jon Stewart's appearance on the CNN program *Crossfire*, which was highly critical of the way that cable news presented important political issues, where he opined that the argumentative way that the hosts narrated matters of public concern actually harmed important rational discourse itself, was something that some of the journalists had apparently been waiting for someone to come out and say for quite some time, judging by the positive reaction it received. Matters like the War on Terror, the lack of Weapons of Mass Destruction that the administration claimed they would find, and the television news media's uncritical attitude toward these issues opened up an opportunity for the *Daily Show* to begin to be taken more seriously, as they were filling this need. The fact that the newspapers themselves had been complicit in this inadequate coverage was not addressed.

In the 2004 election cycle, from May 2, 2003–November 2, 2004, there were a total of sixty-five segments of the *Daily Show* that were related to the presidential election and the Democratic Party primary. There were

**Table 4.1.  Slant Toward?** *SNL*

|  | None | Democrats | Republicans |
|---|---|---|---|
| 2004, Whole Election Cycle (58) | 17 | 28 | 13 |
|  | (29.3%) | (48.3%) | (22.4%) |

239 total shows. This analysis includes a systematic random selection of every third show date with the most relevant sketch for that day chosen, with some alterations for days that had no election covered. Earlier sketches were more likely to deal with the Democratic Primary. Despite the fact that the newspapers praised the *Daily Show* for its substantive coverage, and tended to largely ignore *Saturday Night Live* during this election cycle, a closer analysis of this program reveals that, out of fifty-eight total politically themed jokes and sketches, twenty-four were substantive, twenty-nine were personal, and five have elements of both. Jokes aimed at Bush (slant toward Democrats) were mostly substantive (out of twenty-eight, eight were personal and twenty substantive) while jokes aimed at the Democratic candidates, and eventually just at Kerry, were mostly personal (twelve were personal, one was substantive). There were seventeen jokes/ sketches aimed at all the candidates, and these were generally mixed between personal and substantive.

Although there was occasional criticism, both the *New York Times* and the *Washington Post* combined had twenty-seven articles each that spoke of comedy programs in a positive light, with nine negative articles in the *Times* and ten negative articles in the *Post*. The fact that there was such a striking similarity across the papers, and with different authors, showed the general consensus about the importance and influence of the comedy programs.

This year was a much more "normal" election year than the last one, both in terms of the actual election itself—not being contested—and also

**Table 4.2.  Personal or Substantive?** *SNL*

|  | Both | Personal | Substantive |
|---|---|---|---|
| 2004, Whole Election Cycle (58) | 5 | 29 | 24 |
|  | (8.6%) | (50%) | (41.4%) |
| 2004, Whole Election Cycle, Republicans (13) | 0 | 12 | 1 |
|  | (0%) | (92.3%) | (7.7%) |
| 2004, Whole Election Cycle, Democrats (28) | 0 | 8 | 20 |
|  | (0%) | (28.6%) | (71.4%) |
| 2004, Whole Election Cycle, No Slant (17) | 5 | 9 | 3 |
|  | (29.4%) | (53%) | (17.6%) |

**Table 4.3. Slant Toward?** *Daily Show*

|  | None | Democrats | Republicans |
|---|---|---|---|
| 2004, Whole Election Cycle (65) | 16 (24.6%) | 18 (27.7%) | 31 (47.7%) |

in terms of the television humor. Although there was a replacement at the "Weekend Update" segment, adding Amy Poehler (making it the first time there were two female comedians doing the segment), it wasn't markedly different in tone after Jimmy Fallon left. Additionally, the *Daily Show* had become more established as an alternative, satirical voice to mainstream news media after 9/11, which it had not yet done in 2000. An interesting pattern emerged in the *Daily Show* segments. Initial expectations where that most of the humor would be coded as substantive. However, there were twenty-two substantive segments, thirty-three personal-humor-focused segments, and ten that could be coded as both. Table 4.4 shows the breakdown of the humor.

The pattern that was established after the 2000 election was disputed continues in this year. As is shown, most of the personal humor was against the Democrats (coming mainly in the time dealing with the long Primary) and most of the substantive humor was based against President Bush and his Republican administration. Specifically, substantive humor about the Republicans on the *Daily Show* was mostly focused on the handling of the Iraq war, the "Swiftboat" attack ads against Kerry, and the media. Personal humor against the Democrats on the *Daily Show* was mostly focused on the interminable length of the Primary, which included the infamous "Dean Scream" incident, various jokes about the candidates having creepy facial expressions (*Daily Show*, May 5, 2003), and the generally dull nature of the numerous debates and of the many candidates.

**Table 4.4. Personal or Substantive?** *Daily Show*

|  | Both | Personal | Substantive |
|---|---|---|---|
| 2004, Whole Election Cycle (65) | 10 (15.3%) | 33 (50.8%) | 22 (33.9%) |
| 2004, Whole Election Cycle, Republicans (31) | 2 (6.5%) | 26 (83.8%) | 3 (9.7%) |
| 2004, Whole Election Cycle, Democrats (18) | 2 (11.1%) | 2 (11.1%) | 14 (77.8%) |
| 2004, Whole Election Cycle, No Slant (16) | 6 (37.6%) | 5 (31.2%) | 5 (31.2%) |

## PERSONAL HUMOR STILL INFLUENTIAL

Although the vast majority of the mentions of late-night television comedy in the *Times* and the *Post* during the 2004 election cycle consisted of writers commenting on the *Daily Show*, there were occasional mentions of other late-night comedy, such as comments about *SNL*. However, *SNL* was still in a very personality-driven humor mode in the 2004 election cycle. This type of satire could still have an influence, but it was more akin to the Gerald Ford as "klutz" humor that the show employed throughout its history, rather than the more substantive satire of the *Daily Show*. The *Post* quoted a voter who said she wished she had seen less of the Bush portrayal on *SNL*: "But she cannot help but think of the show's comedic skits when she watches Bush debate. 'It colors my feelings about the man, it does . . . And the next thing you know, you're looking at the man, and you're saying to yourself: buffoon'" (John F. Harris and Richard Morin, "Debate Helps to Sway Undecided; Third Encounter Reinforces Trends," *Washington Post*, January 22, 2004). Personality based humor on *SNL* against George W. Bush as a whole focused on the concept that he was not intelligent, but this was not necessarily about his ability to do his job. Rather, it portrayed him as merely goofy, with a checkered past. This included jokes about his admitted substance and alcohol abuse as a younger man. Most of these jokes consisted of one-liners delivered in the "Weekend Update" segment. "While speaking at a Christian Youth Center in Dallas, President Bush said that religion helped him overcome his heavy drinking and rowdiness. But it was good old-fashioned Texas willpower that got him off the cocaine" ("Weekend Update," November 1, 2003).

> First Lady Laura Bush said Tuesday that if her husband is elected to a second term, she would like to help juvenile delinquents with substance abuse problems. When asked how she would do that, Mrs. Bush replied, "Just as I always have. By marrying them and bearing their children." ("Weekend Update," October 23, 2004)

Drug humor was not limited to Bush, however: "In the 'Rock the Vote Presidential Debate' Tuesday night, Democratic presidential candidates Howard Dean, John Edwards, and John Kerry admitted that they had smoked marijuana, while Dennis Kucinich admitted that he was 'High right now'" ("Weekend Update," November 8, 2003). The "dumb frat guy" (*New York Times*, March 14, 2004, p. A22) portrayal of Bush continued to be the dominant way that *SNL* parodied the president. This was again the subject of one-liners: "In a Veteran's Day speech this Tuesday, President Bush vowed: 'We will finish the mission we have begun—period.' Afterwards, he was advised that, in the future, he doesn't have to read the punctuation marks" ("Weekend

Update," November 5, 2003). "On Monday, President Bush boarded a bus for a campaign tour across southern Michigan. The president remarked that the bus seemed a lot bigger than the one he remembered from school" ("Weekend Update," May 8, 2004).

Personal humor about Bush on the *Daily Show* aligned with *SNL*—Bush as the "dumb guy" was also a common theme. A comment by Stewart on the difference between Bush and Kerry showed that, while Stewart was emphasizing the "frat guy" image of Bush, he was doing so in a way that indicated that Kerry had more intellectual standing and history of actually working on public issues. Thus, this characterization could be classified as either personal, substantive, or both: "Returning from Southeast Asia, Kerry further distanced himself from Bush by joining the antiwar movement . . . and he became a U.S. Senator instead of wondering around in an alcoholic haze until he was 40" (July 29, 2004).

The *Daily Show*'s main personality-based jokes were about the Democratic primary being generally uninteresting. They called the segments that covered this time period in the elections the "Race from the White House," which indicated that the Democrats were unlikely to win with their uninspiring candidates. There was also humor about the voters themselves being disengaged from the primary, and unable to name the candidates: "Everyone knows there's 'Necky' (Dean) . . . and 'Frown-o' (Kerry) . . . then there's the dude who looks like a gnome (Kucinich)" (September 9, 2003). A few days later, Stewart stated that, "Wesley Clark's announcement brings to 10 the number of Democrats running for president that most Americans can't name" (September 17, 2003). Later on, after the Primary was over, the "Kerry is boring" theme emerged. While talking to a group of bored-looking children and teachers about his education plan that would challenge "No Child Left Behind," Stewart said, "Kerry then unveiled his own education plan, 'No Child Left Awake'" (May 5, 2004). But mostly, what Democratic candidates were mentioned for was their looks and tone of voice, and they were not criticized in terms of policy positions.

Personality-based humor about both Bush and Kerry on *SNL* came together when they were "interacting" in a sketch which depicted what a meeting between them might have been like near the Yale campus in 1968. This sketch emphasized the elitist background of both of the candidates as belonging to an exclusive class that most Americans could not relate to. Both characterizations of "Bush-as-frat-guy" and John Kerry as the "stiff guy" emerged in this sketch:

**Bartender**: Got your diploma, George?

**George W. Bush**: Yes, sir. Listen to *this*: "This diploma defers upon George W. Bush . . ."—that's *me*—" . . . a Bachelor of Arts, with a major in Physical Education . . . And a minor in Partying!" I wrote that in myself!

[Bush sits next to Kerry] Hey, buddy, nice shirt. Are you missing your Cub Scout troop, or something?

**John Kerry**: No, actually, I'm a lieutenant in the United States Navy, on leave from active duty in Vietnam.

**George W. Bush**: Whoa! Son of a bee sting! I know you! You're John Kerry! You graduated two years ago—remember *me*? George Bush! I was the one who, uh . . . put the firecracker in that bulldog's butt at the Princeton game!

**John Kerry**: Oh, yes, I remember. A friend of mine explained to me that it was *humorous*—and that an appropriate response would have been *laughter*. ("Mike's Bar," December 14, 2004)

Kerry as "flip-flopper"—unable to make up his mind and taking several positions depending on which way the political wind was blowing—was another aspect of personality-based humor delivered against Kerry on *SNL*, especially in debate sketches: "Was it the right action to remove [Saddam] from power? No way. Was he in possession of weapons of mass destruction? Absolutely. Did he possess these weapons? No he did not. And that has always been my position" ("Presidential Debate," October 2, 2004). Earlier, during the primaries when Edwards was still running, he was characterized as shallow, and as someone who took advantage of his good looks. A parody political ad had him appearing in a towel to gain votes over Kerry ("Meet the Press, March 6, 2004). They showed Howard Dean as emotionally unstable, excessively cursing while on the phone ("Howard Dean Headquarters," January 17, 2004), finally culminating in a parody of the "Dean Scream" incident ("Weekend Update," February 7, 2004).

Later in the 2004 race, there were a handful of incidents where the candidates Kerry and Edwards rather overtly mentioned that Vice President Cheney's daughter was a lesbian. During the real final Presidential Debate, Kerry stated, "If you were to talk to Dick Cheney's daughter, who is a lesbian, she would tell you that she's being who she was, she's being who she was born as." The purpose of mentioning her sexual orientation was to point out the hypocrisy of the Republican Party's platform against marriage equality, but it came off as political opportunism. *SNL* satirized this as the candidates seeming unable to stop casually dropping the information at every opportunity during the debates. Kerry made several mentions of Cheney's daughter's sexual orientation, bringing it into answers to questions to which it had no relevance in an *SNL* "Presidential Debate" sketch, on October 23, 2004: "Jim, I think if you were to ask Mary Cheney, Vice President Cheney's daughter, who is a lesbian, I'm sure she would tell you one, that she's being who she is. And two, that we went into Iraq the wrong way." Although these largely irrelevant interjections spoke to the character of the Democratic ticket, they were not particularly critical of their competency for office, and did not concentrate on their policy positions. However, other jokes, mainly on the *Daily Show*, addressed these issues. And the *Post* and the *Times* began to take more notice when they did.

## SUBSTANTIVE HUMOR BEGINS TO GAIN MOMENTUM

If any substantive humor about the Democrats existed at all on the *Daily Show*, it came when Kerry tried to act like a "working class"–sympathizing candidate. One of the things that George W. Bush was often mocked for in late-night comedy was his emphasis on, and exaggeration of, a Southern accent, when his birthplace was Connecticut and his educational background was Yale. Kerry shared this tendency with Bush and occasionally fell into the appearance of inauthenticity: "And as I stand here in my borrowed work jacket in front of a sign that says 'The Real Deal,' I say to you there is no irony in these statements. None! None at all! No Irony!" (February 11, 2004). The lack of difference between Bush and Kerry's backgrounds was a major talking point of this election. Acting like a "regular guy" was something Bush tried to do all along, so would not be a particularly substantive criticism of him; but for Kerry to try to follow in this mode of expression made him seem incompetent.

Stewart pointed out that the Bush administration's mishandling of the aftermath of the Iraq invasion allowed terrorists to gain the weapons that Saddam Hussein used to control.

> **Stewart**: The President said that if John Kerry had been in office, we wouldn't have even had a war to argue about.
>
> **Bush**: If Senator Kerry had his way, we would still be taking our global test, Saddam Hussein would still be in power, he would control all those weapons and explosives, and could have shared them with our terrorist enemies.
>
> **Stewart**: Our terrorist enemies have them now. That's the whole point.
>
> (Pretends to stick pen in his eye) (October 28, 2004)

A segment with then-*Daily Show* correspondent Stephen Colbert points out the hypocrisy of Zell Miller's statement at the RNC in 2004:

> **Zell Miller**: Today's Democratic leaders see America as an occupier, not a liberator. And nothing makes this Marine madder than someone calling American Troops occupiers rather than liberators!
>
> **Colbert**: Well, there Miller was right. No one who equates our military action in Iraq with an occupation is fit to lead our troops.

**Stewart**: But the President said the same thing—look at this!

[Clip of Bush] The people of Iraq do not support an indefinite occupation. They're not happy they're occupied. I wouldn't be happy if I was occupied either.

**Colbert**: OK, Jon, I see your game. Showing the hypocrisy of Miller's statement by turning his own words against him, thus undermining the very premise if my and his entire analysis. (September 2, 2004)

Substantive humor on *SNL* was mostly limited to George W. Bush, and mainly focuses on the mishandling of the War on Terror. After the initial victories, including taking over Baghdad, the administration did not have a solid plan in place to deal with a potential insurgency. "Terrorist confidence and morale have never been higher . . . uh . . . we're still working on Phase Three" ("Presidential Debate," October 2, 2004).

> As of yesterday, the Bush administration said they still haven't found the source of the White House leak that outed a woman as a CIA operative. So, just to recap, here are the things President Bush can't find: The White House leak, Weapons of mass destruction in Iraq, Saddam Hussein, Osama Bin Laden, A link between Saddam Hussein and Osama Bin Laden, the guy who sent the anthrax through the mail, and his own butt, with two hands and a flashlight. ("Weekend Update," October 3, 2003)

After months go by, and it became apparent that no Weapons of Mass Destruction were to be found (the ostensible reason that Iraq was invaded in the first place), late-night comedy programs began to mock the administration mercilessly, particularly about the cost of rebuilding: "Because, partly that's the point of a blank check. And, in all honesty, it'd just be a guess, anyway!" ("A Message from the President of the United States," November 1, 2003). Other than commentary about the war, substantive humor against the Democratic field on *SNL* generally mocked them for being ideologically fragmented, their infighting, and being indecisive on policy positions. Lieberman was an easy target. The shows satirized him as being out of touch and inauthentic: "I am a hardcore, hip-hop, rock 'n roll candidate. I bring in the noise, and provided that it is fiscally responsible, I shall bring in the funk as well. And that, my fellow Americans, is fo' shizzle" ("Hardball," December 13, 2003).

*SNL* joked about the scandal about Bush going AWOL from the Texas Air National Guard, (which brought Dan Rather's career at the CBS Evening News to an end): "The White House Tuesday defended President Bush against Democratic accusations that he was absent without leave . . . A spokesman labeled the claims 'shameful,' and 'the worst of election year politics,' and 'completely true'" ("Weekend Update," February 7, 2004). The SwiftBoat ad campaign against John Kerry was something that *SNL* came out completely against. The show characterized the idea that Kerry did not do all he claimed in Vietnam as a lie. Even though the ad campaign was not funded by the Bush campaign, Bush did not completely decry it, and connections were made between a Florida campaign office and the efforts to diminish Kerry's military service.[2] *SNL* carried the absurd claims made in the ads to their logical conclusion by inflating them, but only slightly. Men like the ones that appeared in the ad were satirized in a sketch on October 2, 2004.

> **Steve Cordier**: We happened upon two Viet Cong soldiers, and everyone thought it was an ambush. John Kerry jumped off the boat and chased after them. Within minutes, he returned to the boat with the soldiers and said, "These men are in love." And he conducted a gay marriage ceremony. To honor, obey, and love you long time. It made us all sick. ("Swift Boat Veterans for Truth")

In one segment, Stewart criticized an assertion by Robert Novak, who refuted the fact that John Kerry's SwiftBoat shipmates stood with him at the DNC. "Because in this country, when a scurrilous charge is made against you by people, you're guilty unless you prove otherwise, that's how it works!" (August 10, 2004). According to Stewart, the election was polluted by outside groups trying to exert influence through personal attacks, while the official campaigns did not have to get their hands dirty.


## THE RISE OF THE *DAILY SHOW* AND THE INFLUENCE OF STEWART ON MAINSTREAM POLITICAL DISCOURSE

The *Times* and the *Post* often quoted the Pew study to back up their statements about the influence of late-night political comedy. The positive effects of people increasingly getting their news from late-night comedy were also given as proof that the papers were correct in praising them.

> As one of many young voters who say they get most of their campaign news from the irreverent "Indecision 2004" segment on "The Daily Show," on the Comedy Channel, Jeff Leek, 22, a statistics major at the University of Washington, said politics were a big topic this year among his friends. "There's less cynicism, less of this 'oh, it doesn't matter.'" (Timothy Egan, "Vote Drives Gain Avid Attention of Youth In '04," *New York Times*, September 15, 2004)

This praise was especially evident when it came to the shows helping the campaign of John Kerry over George W. Bush: "the convention coverage, seeping through the filter of late-night monologues or quickly scanned headlines, can nonetheless help plant a positive image of Mr. Kerry in the minds of these voters" ("A Stage for Candor," *Washington Post*, July 26, 2004). Not all the writers saw the influence of political humor in other areas of the public sphere as positive.

> Television is increasingly awash in fake anchors delivering fake news, some of them far more trenchant than real anchors delivering real news . . . This phenomenon has been good news for the Bush administration . . . Of late it has gone so far as to field its own pair of Jayson Blairs, hired at taxpayers' expense: Karen Ryan and Alberto Garcia, the "reporters" who appeared in TV "news" videos distributed by the Department of Health and Human Services to local news shows around the country . . . Back at Comedy Central, Jon Stewart was ambivalent about the government's foray into his own specialty, musing aloud about whether he should be outraged or flattered. One of his faux correspondents, though, was outright faux despondent. "They created a whole new category of fake news—infoganda," Rob Corddry said. "We'll never be able to keep up!" But Mr. Corddry's joke is not really a joke. The more real journalism declines, the easier it is for such government infoganda to fill the vacuum. (Frank Rich, "Operation Iraqi Infoganda," *New York Times*, March 28, 2004)

> But by now comedy has become such a standard tool for politicians that candidates for high office like Arnold Schwarzenegger and John Edwards have announced their intentions to television hosts like Jay Leno and Jon Stewart . . . The point is that if comedy has long been a critical weapon used by commentators against politicians it is now also a standard political tool used by politicians to defuse criticism and to court voters. (Bruce Weber, "Strategy and Spin Are Cool, But Voters Like to Laugh," *New York Times*, March 8, 2004)

However, the "infoganda" model was something that the *Daily Show* in specific continually called out, and many programs often mocked politicians for feeble attempts at humor. The official political sphere may occasionally use the same humorous methods, but they did not often succeed.

One area in which there was broad agreement was the fact that the *Daily Show* was critical of other television news and political media that covered the election. The writers that highlighted the *Daily Show*'s criticism of the media simultaneously bolstered their own arguments and placed themselves above the polluted sphere of television news. Why did the criticism contributed by the *Daily Show* stand out? The *Times* used the show's attitude toward television news' coverage of the Democratic National Convention as evidence of it being shallow. It stood out from the other late-night programs in that it "zeroed in on the television journalists who chose to snub the convention as they covered it [and] lampooned those who deplored the slick, synthetic packaging of events, then grew indignant when Al Sharpton diverged from the script" (Alessandra, Stanley, "What We Missed in Boston," *New York Times*, August 1, 2004).

Another area in which the *Daily Show* was said to be more thorough was in its criticism of the invasion of Iraq. The *Post* called it "the year's best news and information program . . . [and] the only one early on to ask the tough questions about the decision to invade Iraq. Of course, it was for humorous effect, but at least they were asking" (Lisa de Moraes, "CBS Clocks Out on Airing Reagan's Convention Speech," *Washington Post*, July 20, 2004). In comparison to other late-night comedy, the *Daily Show* was superior, in particular to Jay Leno: "Never risking an original perception, his topical jokes are gag recyclings of the conventional wisdom, making him indistinguishable at times from a Republican Party shill" (Tom Carson, "Last Comic Standing," *New York Times*, October 3, 2004). Although 2008 would bring an interesting confrontation between David Letterman and Republican nominee John McCain, the political comedy of the talk-show format programs would not rise to the level of pure critical commentary that the *Daily Show* established. Ratings for basic cable programs were not subject to the same kind of pressures as network TV, and thus could take more risks. But the newspaper commentary was more focused on blaming the talk show host specifically for not being more original or willing to stand up for the truth, even if it went against "conventional wisdom."

One incident that resulted in the acceptance of Jon Stewart in particular as an influential political and media commentator was the infamous *Crossfire* incident, when Jon Stewart appeared on the old version of CNN program on October 15, 2004, and criticized it as harmful to America—"He said the program is 'hurting America' by encouraging partisans to yell at each other" (Howard Kurtz, "The Campaign of a Comedian; Jon Stewart's Fake Journalism Enjoys Real Political Impact," *Washington Post*, October 23, 2004)—as it had, in recent years, devolved into a shouting match between the "Conservative" host Tucker Carlson, and the "Liberal" host, Paul Begala. The president of CNN, Jonathan Klein, attributed the show's cancelation after twenty-three years in part to Stewart's critique in a *Times* article: "'I agree wholeheartedly with Jon Stewart's overall premise.' He said he believed that especially after the terror attacks on 9/11, viewers are interested in information, not opinion" (Bill Carter, "CNN Will Cancel 'Crossfire' And Cut Ties to Commentator," *New York Times*, January 6, 2005). One exceptional thing that the *Times* and the *Post* noted about the *Daily Show* was that it was highly critical of cable news. This was especially true of Fox News, which proposed that they create a "Truth Squad" to get to the bottom of what's really going on in the election in a non-partisan way. The first question in this "new era" was asked of John Sununu by Fox News host Chris Wallace:

**Wallace**: Tell me the three worst things about John Kerry's economic policies.

**Stewart**: You know it's questions like that that almost make a man lose his faith in Fox News Truth Squads. (April 7, 2004).

However, Stewart did not restrict his criticism to the right-leaning Fox, as was seen in the *Crossfire* incident, and this quote, which pointed out that none of the cable news outlets ask adequate follow-up questions. When various Republican commentators (Like RNC Chairman Ed Gillespie), speaking on CNN and MSNBC, as well as Fox, call John Kerry and John Edwards the most liberal Senators in history, despite the dubiousness of this claim based on their voting records, on, Fox, etc., Stewart called it out: "And while we don't have any idea what that means or where those rankings come from or how they were arrived at or whether it's even true . . . I don't like the sounds of it . . . Talking Points—they're true because they're said a lot" (July 14, 2004). Stewart criticized CNN especially in its placement of profit motive over information, in its airing of a debate which Stewart regarded as shallow: "Last night, CNN aired 'America Rocks the Vote,' a 90-minute pander . . . I'm sorry, special" (November 5, 2003). Stewart's appearance and impact on *Crossfire* highlights the importance that the *Daily Show* was beginning to have during the 2004 election cycle. The show was no longer just a substantive satire of the political process, but also of the media, which had become inextricably linked to it. If the quality of television media coverage specifically was not good, the public will not make informed decisions. This was the meaning of Stewart's "hurting America" comment: rational public debate was being sidelined by meaningless shouting matches where the loudest one wins. The fact that the *Daily Show* had become the alternative, and that Stewart was the voice of informed reason, did not sit well with him, which will be discussed later. As Darrel West, a Brown political scientist and author puts it, "The 'Crossfire' conflict supports the charge that the line between television news and entertainment was blurred beyond all recognition . . . [Tucker Carlson] wasn't wanting commentary, he wanted entertainment" (Damien Cave, "If You Interview Kissinger, Are You Still a Comedian?," *New York Times*, October 24, 2004). The two hosts publicly criticized Stewart for being "sanctimonious," but Stewart returned the criticism:

But he is fed up with a process in which "people who are giving talking points come on these shows and are questioned by people on the other talking-pointed side. 'Crossfire' is the crack cocaine, the purest distillation of it." Some journalists have rallied to his defense. "Jon Stewart never said he was going to renounce his standing as a smart guy who went to William and Mary and as a sharp social critic," says NBC anchor Brian Williams, a past "Daily Show" guest. "Sure he has an impact. The din of our media has reached the point where we could use a have-you-no-sense-of-decency-sir-at-long-last moment." (Howard Kurtz, "The Campaign of a Comedian; Jon Stewart's Fake Journalism Enjoys Real Political Impact," *Washington Post*, October 23, 2004)

This last comment by Brian Williams, contextualizing Stewart's remarks in terms of the end of the McCarthy era, genuinely elevated his discourse to the level of historical importance. Many commentators in the papers were quite happy with how the incident played out, as if they wanted to say the same thing themselves for a long time:

> Jon Stewart could not resist a last dig at CNN's "Crossfire" during his mono-
> logue on Comedy Central on Monday night. "They said I wasn't being funny
> . . . And I said to them: 'I know that. But tomorrow I will go back to being
> funny'" . . . that is why his surprise attack on the hosts of CNN's "Crossfire"
> was so satisfying . . . he told Paul Begala and Tucker Carlson that they were
> partisan hacks and that their pro-wrestling approach to political discourse was
> "hurting America." . . . Real anger is as rare on television as real discussion.
> (Alessandra Stanley, "No Jokes or Spin. It's Time (Gasp) to Talk," *New York
> Times*, October 20, 2004)

Stewart was uneasy with his position as the voice of reason: "Asked whether he worried about reports that young viewers get most of their political news from late-night TV programs, he responded, 'Every day, sir.'" However, he knew that an alternative was necessary. Speaking on the "relatively atrocious" nature of cable news, he said, "It's not that we shouldn't know when someone is kidnapped, it's that we should not have to wait until they come back to see other news" (Lisa de Moraes, "Ted Nugent's Preemptive Strike," *Washington Post*, January 10, 2004). Stewart's place as an alternative voice opened him up to criticism from the traditional news sources he had mocked. This caused him to try to distance himself from his newly crowned title: "he hotly denies allegations that he has become a 'pundit' or, as Newsweek recently put it, 'He's starting to be taken seriously as a political force.' 'I've made wonk? Very exciting . . . We're in worse shape than I thought'" (Staff, "Jon Stewart, the Immoderator," *Washington Post*, January 22, 2004).

The focus that the *Times* and the *Post* placed on this entire dialogue showed that they wanted to position themselves on Stewart's side in opposition to the polluted cable and network news that he disparaged. "'When I listen to Jon, he really is profoundly concerned and angry about real issues,' Koppel says. "He is to television news what a really great editorial cartoonist is to a newspaper'" (Howard Kurtz, "The Campaign of a Comedian; Jon Stewart's Fake Journalism Enjoys Real Political Impact," *Washington Post*, October 23, 2004). "Sorry, Jon, but you can't interview Bill Clinton, Richard Clarke, Bill O'Reilly, Bob Dole, etc., etc., and still say you're just a comedian" (Damien Cave, "If You Interview Kissinger, Are You Still a Comedian?" *New York Times*, October 24, 2004). However, perhaps sensing that they might be fighting a losing battle, "Television news programs, trying to court this audience, routinely run clips of Jay Leno, David Letterman and Stewart" (Howard Kurtz, "39% See Bias in Reporting on Campaign; Nontraditional Media Gain Ground, Poll Finds," *Washington Post*, January 12, 2004).

## THE SHOWS SET THE TONE FOR DISCUSSION OF BUSH'S INADEQUACIES

One of the most common ways the writers in the papers spoke of the comedy programs was to use quotes from them as a proxy for opinions they already had. Although this occurs with many of the programs, again, it was mostly about the *Daily Show*, which shows that it was a richer narrative resource. Criticism of President Bush was a frequent topic: "The debate tomorrow should not seek to discover which candidate would be more fun to have a beer with. As Jon Stewart of the 'The Daily Show' nicely put in 2000, 'I want my president to be the designated driver'" (Al Gore, "How to Debate George Bush," *New York Times*, September 29, 2004). Bush's intelligence, as well as his seriousness as a candidate, was addressed in this way: "Stewart made a serious remark that goes to the heart of what has been Bush's problem. He referred to the president's nonexistent 'learning curve,' which is indeed troubling . . . Bush has shown little growth" (Richard Cohen, "The President Vanishes," *Washington Post*, October 15, 2004) with Stewart also calling Bush "thickly muddled" in his debate performances. These were substantive critiques of Bush's ability to be president. Compare this to Jay Leno's (and *SNL*'s) frequent jabs at Bush's reputation of a former "frat guy" which were not particularly critical in a real way: "For two years and four months, America waited, patiently, for this moment: the day George W. Bush's old fraternity brothers would party at the White House . . . 'Boy, that is every C-student's dream come true . . . ,' Jay Leno marveled . . . 'Go back to your class reunion as president'" (Dana Milbank, "At Bush Bash, The Dekes Come In Like a Lamb; President's '68 Frat Brothers Party Hardly at White House," *Washington Post*, May 30, 2003). Letterman, possibly taking a cue from the more substantive *Daily Show*, was quoted as saying that Bush "is asking Congress for $80 billion to help rebuild Iraq . . . And when you make out that check, remember there are two L's in 'Halliburton'" (Brian Faler, "Letterman Jibe Takes on Life as Political Ad," *Washington Post*, September 19, 2003). This joke had an interesting impact on political discourse:

> The Democratic-leaning activist group American Family Voices uses the line in a spot accusing the administration of cronyism and Halliburton of profiteering. "Billions of tax dollars going directly to Halliburton through sweetheart,

no-bid government contracts," the announcer in the ad says, after quoting the Letterman joke. ("A Stage for Candor," *Washington Post*, September 19, 2003)

Bush was not the only target of substantive jokes, especially on the *Daily Show*. Paper columnists used Stewart's words to express their own displeasure about the lack of real differences between Bush and Kerry, and the empty rhetoric that they perceived the candidates would often use:

> Stewart pinpointed the differences between the two candidates in October's GQ: "One is making America stronger and safer and is looking out for you, the hard-working American voter. The other has made strong decisions for a safe America, so that hard-working Americans can be stronger and safer." (Peter Carlson, "Election Uncoverage, From the Wheel Deal to the Abstinent Voter," *Washington Post*, October 26, 2004)

This lack of difference emerged especially when Stewart criticized the overly centrist-to-conservative policy positions of former vice presidential candidate Joe Lieberman (an accurate assessment given future debates on the Affordable Care Act): "Rival campaigns dismissed [Lieberman] as too conservative, deriding him as 'Bush Lite.' At one point . . . Jon Stewart satirized him as 'the candidate for people who want to vote for George Bush but don't find [Bush] Jewish enough'" (Paul Farhi and Lisa Rein, "Connecticut Senator Quits Race After Weak Second in 'First State,'" *Washington Post*, February 4, 2004).

## THE CANDIDATES ON THE *DAILY SHOW* AND *SNL*: INCREASINGLY SUBSTANTIVE CRITICISM

Going on programs like *SNL* or the *Daily Show* was increasingly used in this election year as a tool for the candidates to improve their image as a method of damage control, especially in the case of Howard Dean, or to simply make them seem more likeable, especially in the case of the rather wooden Kerry. The candidates appeared on late-night comedy programs to appear more "real," but this tactic was often regarded as ineffective. Ben Karlin, executive producer of the *Daily Show*, said:

> "There's almost nothing genuine about a politician appearing on our show, including those we like. We're being used to bring them some associative hipness—so they can say, look at us, our guy can laugh at himself. We have no illusions about it. We're just another part of the media strategy." Indeed, such a media strategy could be seen most clearly at work after the Dean "scream," when the candidate immediately made himself available to do a self-deprecating

"Top Ten" list on Letterman, if only with the hope that that new tape loop might replace the one of his Iowa yelp on cable and network news. (It was not to be; Dr. Dean trying to be funny was not as funny as Dr. Dean's improvised Iowa peroration.) (Frank Rich, "Paar to Leno, J.F.K. to J.F.K.," *New York Times*, February 8, 2004)

However, as the *Times* noted, "Even before Monday night, opponents were trying to portray Dr. Dean as the angriest man in politics, prompting 'Saturday Night Live' last weekend to depict him as a cursing egomaniac" (Jim Rutenberg, "A Concession Rattles the Rafters [and Some Dean Supporters]," *New York Times*, January 21, 2004). There was a two-way effect here: shows with more personality-driven comedy like *SNL* or Leno's took cues from the prevailing media image of the person in question, thus amplifying and reifying the image. At the same time, the candidates tried to use the shows, as well as the more substantive *Daily Show*, to change the direction of public opinion, as Ben Karlin stated, above. As Charles Krauthammer put it, "When the late-night comics call you . . . 'the Incredible Hulk' (Conan O'Brien) and 'Mr. Rogers with rabies' (Jay Leno), you've got trouble. The most difficult thing to recover from in politics is ridicule" (Charles Krauthammer, "Paradise Lost," *Washington Post*, January 23, 2004). Conversely, "the same media that played the 'I Have a Scream' speech time and again also gave him the opportunity to come back on the David Letterman show" (Howard Kurtz, "Trailing in the Media Primary, Too; Dean's Hot-and-Cold Press Coverage Sparks Debate Over Objectivity," *Washington Post*, January 29, 2004).

The way that narratives built upon one another, with the assistance of late-night comedy programs, was demonstrated in the following *Post* quote: "By yesterday, every new development [about Kerry] was being reported with a sinking-ship tone . . . Things hit a new low when Kerry did the 'Tonight Show' and a foulmouthed puppet—Triumph the Insult Comic Dog—made fun of him" (Howard Kurtz, "Howard Dean's Media Landslide; Pundits Call a Winner, a Bit Prematurely," *Washington Post*, November 13, 2003). Kerry's attempt to seem like a "real" person by appearing on the *Tonight Show* backfired when the joke was on him rather than about him. Bush's campaign had become wise to this mechanism in ways that Kerry's did not. Tobe Berkovitz of Boston University's communications school said: "Bush needs to show he is the commander in chief of substance, and you don't do that with David Letterman or Jon Stewart or Jay Leno" (Howard Kurtz, "Bush to Defend Record on TV; Talk Shows Have Garnered Key Role in Presidential Politics," *Washington Post*, February 6, 2004). Bush would not have stood a chance on these shows because of all the easy targets about his personality that he provided over the years. He did not have the problem of not seeming "real," and thus did not need to use the shows as the Democratic candidates did. Although he made himself a target for seeming too unserious (see Stewart quote above about wishing for a "designated driver"), Bush did not make the situation worse by trying to augment his "realness" by relying on late-night comedy. The result was (at least in part) his victory in the 2004 election.

When the papers did have extended commentary on shows other than the *Daily Show*, they tended to focus on how the programs satirized the candidates' personalities, rather than their commentary on substantive issues.

> The nation's late-night comedians still haven't quite pegged him. They haven't completed the ritual of turning a presidential candidate into a stock character like Bush the Dumb Frat Boy, Gore the Know-It-All Stiff, Clinton the Gluttonous Lecher or Reagan the Amiable Dunce. Comedians have tried the Rich Guy . . . They've also tried the War Bore, as depicted in jokes about Mr. Kerry's frequent references to his Vietnam service. There's also Kerry the Waffler on issues . . . The most popular persona so far seems to be Killjoy Kerry, as depicted in the many jokes about his long face and dour demeanor. (John Tierney, "Political Points: Kerry Missing Late-Night Peg," *New York Times*, March 14, 2004)

The lack of difference between the candidates' backgrounds was also a topic on other programs, although not in a particularly substantive way: "As Jay Leno noted, the choices in the presidential election range all the way from a rich, white guy from Yale to a rich, white guy from Yale" (John Tierney, "How Blue and Red Emerged from Old Blue," *New York Times*, March 21, 2004). Late-night comedians poking fun at Kerry's choice of hobbies was also a topic of discussion in the papers: "David Letterman mocked him for windsurfing instead of campaigning. Jay Leno played the flip-flop card, quipping that even Mr. Kerry's hobby depends on which way the wind blows" (Kate Zernike, "Who Among Us Does Not Love Windsurfing?," *New York Times*, September 5, 2004). Charles Krauthammer managed to transmute a rather meaningless comment by Jay Leno into an indictment about Kerry's stance on the substantive issue of Iraq, but it came off as a bit of a stretch:

> When Kerry went off windsurfing during the Republican convention, Jay Leno noted that even Kerry's hobbies depend on wind direction. Kerry on the war has become an object not only of derision but of irreconcilable suspicion. What kind of man, aspiring to the presidency, does not know his own mind about the most serious issue of our time? (Charles Krauthammer, "Nowhere Left to Flop," *Washington Post*, September 17, 2004)

Even Tina Fey, who would become a solid force for substantive parody in the 2008 election cycle, merely made fun of Bush's jumpsuit when discussing the infamous "Mission Accomplished" landing on the aircraft carrier, when there were so many other possible avenues. The *Times* missed this point entirely:

"On 'Saturday Night Live,' Tina Fey subjected the photographic record of his getup to close scrutiny and wondered if he had stuffed 'socks down the front of the jump suit'" (Frank Rich, "The Jerry Bruckheimer White House," *New York Times*, May 11, 2004). *SNL*'s lack of substantive humor confused those writers in the *Post* and the *Times* who liked to lump all late-night comedy together. Those who paid more specific attention to the *Daily Show* did not fall into this narrative mode.

At this point, it was clear that *SNL* was not taking on the candidates in a substantive way. Writers in the *Post* and the *Times* discussed *SNL* in much the same way that they discussed Leno, etc. There were personality-driven caricatures and no expectations that *SNL*'s commentary would be any different from the regular talk show hosts, other than being perhaps a bit more elaborate in execution. However, at this point, even though the writers occasionally wrote about the distinction between substantive and personality-based humor, they didn't fully embrace that there was a distinction, often lumping Jon Stewart in with the other late-night comedians. This was in spite of the fact that they often singled him out for particular praise or, in the case of Tom Shales, particular derision. This confusion was typified by a piece in the *Post* which discussed a Center for Media and Public Affairs study about political humor on television.

> George Bush still wears a dunce cap. And John Kerry is one strange-looking dude . . . But this is one contest where winning amounts to losing: 94 percent of the jokes about intelligence, and 89 percent about honesty, involved the president. Kerry drew nearly half the cracks aimed at a candidate's appearance . . . Bush's other vulnerabilities at that hour, according to the report: his military service and his credibility on Iraq . . . Kerry gets needled on his wealth and reputation for flip-flopping. (Howard Kurtz, "Bush and Kerry, a Running Gag on Late Night," *Washington Post*, March 22, 2004)

What was not done in this article was to make a distinction between who was making what kinds of jokes, only a numerical count of the targets of the humor, which was what the study reported.

## CONCLUSION

The writers in the *Post* and the *Times* highlighted the differences between Jon Stewart's and the *Daily Show*'s sort of comedy, and the personality-based humor of *SNL*. This was a time when jokes about candidates' looks or speech patterns were a detriment to the type of issue-based humor that was necessary, and by contrast, made *SNL* look like a form of comedy that belonged firmly in the twentieth century, and the comedy of the *Daily Show* in the twenty-first. In 2008, *SNL* would get the message, and catch up. A specific reflection of this trend of the *Daily Show* taking one and issue and doing substantive humor about it, while *SNL* did personal humor about the same thing, was the way they portrayed Bush's intelligence. *SNL* made it seem as if there wasn't too much of a difference between Bush and Kerry, "the stiff guy vs. the dumb guy." Both went to Yale, were wealthy, etc. But the *Daily Show* wasn't merely mocking his mannerism, malapropisms, or background, they were questioning whether or not he was fit to be the president in the first place, using his bad decisions and questionable judgments about the need to go to war as a backdrop. Thus, there really was a difference between the candidates because Kerry would likely not have had the same policies.

Appearing on the late-night comedy programs had become another important aspect to campaigns, and even though politicians did find it necessary to appear on them in the past in order to seem like a "regular person," the growing realization that the shows were where a large portion of the younger voting public got their news made it even more necessary than before (Feldman and Young 2008; Young and Tisinger 2006; Young 2006). The papers noted that Bush didn't appear on them, and it could be inferred then that he didn't need to, because he was not going to get that part of the electorate anyway. In the 2004 election cycle, mainly Democratic candidates appeared on them; in 2008, it would shift to an almost equal representation. Going on the shows could (and in 2008, did) backfire for the candidates who may seem as if they were failing to perform authenticity of being "real" and merely using the shows as cover (Larson and Porpora 2011; Alexander 2010). But not going on them would miss a vital audience. In previous years, this concern was not as great, and in this year, the discourse by some journalists about appearing on the shows taking away from the gravitas of the candidates has disappeared. In fact, rather than criticize comedy programs for being shallow and taking away from the seriousness of political narratives in general, the journalists were now more likely to characterize mainstream media coverage of the election as narrow and largely uncritical. The aftermath of 9/11 made it more necessary than ever that journalism be willing to question the official policies of the president and his administration, but instead they went on the opposite direction, opening up a space of opportunity for a new way of discussing politics to come about (Calavita 2004).This contribution enhanced the vibrancy of civil society (Alexander and Smith 2005; Alexander 2006). The newspaper writers, while reflecting on this need, did not simultaneously reflect on their own complicity with it. Instead, they spent time writing about things like Jon Stewart's impact on cable news, particularly his criticisms of the partisanship of Fox, and the shallowness of CNN, exemplified by his role in getting *Crossfire* to be canceled (Jacobs and Michaud Wild 2013).

Historically, when a television program would be so up front about criticizing the president's policies, they risked getting taken off the air, as happened to the Smothers Brothers in the prior century (Bianculli 2009). Unlike the talk show format programs with a monologue that often featured political jokes, the *Daily Show* dealt with substantive issued head-on, while still retaining some of the personality-based humor of the past. This made the show more accessible to viewers, and softened some of the harsher criticism. Additionally, the show was not fully partisan, calling out Democrats when their policies were less than progressive. The show's propensity to use politicians' own words against them by going through archival footage and seeing when they contradicted themselves made it an invaluable resource for journalists, both in newspapers and on television, who could simply lift the segments or transcripts of them verbatim to demonstrate a point.

A number of new narratives in the media coverage about political comedy on television emerged in the 2004 election cycle. In 2000, Jon Stewart was still an unknown quantity. So much changed from that election cycle to this one, because of the September 11 attacks, the wars in Iraq and Afghanistan, and the lack of criticism of the Bush administration in mainstream journalism (as well as its complicity in spreading false information). The role of "serious journalist" was one that Stewart wanted to reject, making himself out to be "just a comedian." When writers and citizens began to realize that his voice was one of the only major ones in the public sphere that fostered dissent and questioning of the official Republican Party line, the contrast became starker between "comedy" and substantive satirical criticism. Journalists had to point it out. The fact that Stewart was rejecting his serious role, even as it was growing, shows that he was not attempting to usurp or assume this role, but that it happened organically. Writers in the *Post* and the *Times*, who had not questioned the wars as much as perhaps they believed they ought to have, were now open to finding any voice that agreed with them, in order to try to prevent Bush from being reelected. Although this failed, the structural propensity for the journalists to use satirical comedy narratives as a resource would continue to stay in place, into the next election cycle and beyond.

## NOTES

1. http://www.people-press.org/2004/01/11/cable-and-internet-loom-large-in-fragmented-political-news-universe/.

2. http://www.usatoday.com/news/politicselections/nation/president/2004-08-20-swift-boat-flier_x.htm.

## Chapter Five

# The 2008 Election

## *Authenticity (Or Lack Thereof)*

Humor in the 2008 election cycle early on was characterized by its remarks about the extremism of the Republican primary candidates, and the infighting between Barack Obama and Hillary Clinton being harmful to the party on the Democratic side. Later, when the nominees had been selected, it shifted to criticism of John McCain's pick of Sarah Palin as his running mate, and mockery of how the media and Republicans were trying to demonize Barack Obama for his perceived racial and religious otherness. Newspaper commentary was especially engaged with *Saturday Night Live*'s portrayal of Sarah Palin as dangerously incompetent. Two main areas stand out in journalistic commentary on the 2008 election cycle; first, writers were focused on how well or how poorly candidates appearing on the shows performed. Obama was ranked most competent, with Clinton behind him; McCain made some major mistakes (namely the Letterman appearance fiasco), while Palin was both the most scrutinized and least able to portray herself as a genuine, authentic politician. The second area was the discussion by journalists of the place that political comedy had now firmly occupied, that of a substantive, critical perspective that television news had increasingly failed to live up to in the 2000s thus far. Two other areas, that of journalists relying on the shows' words to express their opinions, and the relevance of the topics on the shows being worthy of paying attention to, were by this election cycle taken for granted, and couched in terms of the other two areas. This election cycle also saw the addition of the *Colbert Report* to the late-night comedy landscape. I considered the duration of the 2008 election to last from April 26, 2007, to November 4, 2008. I identified sixty-three total *Daily Show* segments, fifty *Colbert Report* segments, and ninety-seven *SNL* sketches and "Weekend Update" jokes.

Issues that entered into this campaign that had not previously been anywhere near as relevant in any other were race and religion. Barack Obama,
being biracial, was the catalyst for several different negative, racially charged
narratives emerging in the campaign, which the *Daily Show* addressed. Jon
Stewart did many segments throughout the campaign titled "Baracknophobia"
(complete with a graphic of Obama mixed with a spider). Indeed, his race
brought out a lot of hidden fears among some parts of the voting population.

> There's one emerging fear that trumps all others—Baracknophobia! It is defined
> as the irrational fear of hope. The irrational fear that behind the mild-mannered
> façade, Barack Obama is intent on enslaving the white race . . . it's true, wake
> up white people! The sickness manifests itself mostly through rumor, often in
> the form of the only email your grandmother has ever been able to successfully
> forward. (June 16, 2008)

The "wake up white people" phrase is one often used by White Supremacists
to try to galvanize support. The usage of it associated the criticisms of Obama
with those who would be radically racist. Stewart called out cable news here:
on one hand, they condemned it, but on the other helped to spread the rumors
(like asking if he took the oath of office on the Koran).

Discussions of the cover of the *New Yorker* in July of 2008, which depicted Michelle and Barack Obama as terrorists, or black power supporters,
drew controversy—while it was meant to satirize the media narratives, some
thought it went too far, and actually reinforced them.[1] But Stewart pointed out
that Obama not getting upset about it proved he wasn't an Islamic extremist,
because getting upset over cartoons is something that they have historically
done, according to specific incidents, as well as stereotypes about Muslims.
Both Stewart and Colbert did not have as much to say about Sarah Palin as
*SNL* did, possibly because she was so obviously incompetent, and *SNL* was
providing such a devastating satire of her, that they may have felt their time
was better spent on other issues. Their satire of her focused on her statements
(or lack thereof) on Russia, climate change, and the Bush Doctrine. The *Daily
Show* made specific reference to the parody, but in the context of a substantive critique of how Republicans dealt with the poor economic situation.

> **Sean Hannity**: Senator Barack Obama yesterday was attacking Senator McCain
> for saying that the fundamentals of the economy are strong.
>
> **Stewart**: HE DID WHAT. Go on.
>
> . . .
>
> **Palin (interview on campaign trail)**: Did you watch Tina Fey on Saturday
> Night Live?

I watched with the volume all the way down. It was hilarious. Again, didn't hear a word she said. But the visual, spot on.

**Stewart**: Yah, the way she was pretty with glasses? Hilarious. (September 18, 2008)

A majority of *Daily Show* segments were slanted toward Democrats (52.38 percent), while another significant segment had no slant (39.68 percent); only 7.98 percent were slanted toward Republicans in criticism of Democratic candidates and policies (Table 5.1). The percentages were similar for the *Colbert Report*, with a slightly greater edge toward Democrats (Table 5.2).

**Table 5.1.   Slant Toward?** *DS*

|  | None | Democrats | Republicans |
|---|---|---|---|
| 2008, Whole Election Cycle (63) | 25 (39.68%) | 33 (52.38%) | 5 (7.98%) |

**Table 5.2.   Slant Toward?** *Colbert Report*

|  | None | Democrats | Republicans |
|---|---|---|---|
| 2008, Whole Election Cycle (50) | 16 (32%) | 33 (66%) | 1 (2%) |

The slant on *SNL* in 2008 was more complex than on the *Daily Show* or *Colbert*. There was mostly no slant at all; and a lot of the slant toward Democrats took place after Palin entered the race (Table 5.3).

**Table 5.3.   Slant Toward?** *SNL*

|  | None | Democrats | Progressive | Republicans |
|---|---|---|---|---|
| 2008, Whole Election Cycle (97) | 58 (59.8%) | 32 (33%) | 3 (3.1%) | 4 (4.1%) |

The *Daily Show*'s humor had slightly more substantive jokes (44.44 percent) with most of them aimed at Republicans (Table 5.4). Colbert's humor was 60 percent personal, and both personal and substantive humor mostly favored Democrats (Table 5.5).

**Table 5.4.   Personal or Substantive?** *DS*

|                                                  | Both      | Personal   | Substantive |
|--------------------------------------------------|-----------|------------|-------------|
| 2008, Whole Election Cycle (63)                  | 12        | 23         | 28          |
|                                                  | (19.05%)  | (36.51%)   | (44.44%)    |
| 2008, Whole Election Cycle, Republicans (5)      | 0         | 4          | 1           |
|                                                  | (0%)      | (80%)      | (20%)       |
| 2008, Whole Election Cycle, Democrats (33)       | 7         | 7          | 19          |
|                                                  | (21.21%)  | (21.21%)   | (57.58%)    |
| 2008, Whole Election Cycle, No Slant (25)        | 5         | 12         | 8           |
|                                                  | (25%)     | (48%)      | (32%)       |

**Table 5.5.   Personal or Substantive?** *Colbert Report*

|                                                  | Both      | Personal   | Substantive |
|--------------------------------------------------|-----------|------------|-------------|
| 2008, Whole Election Cycle (50)                  | 3         | 30         | 17          |
|                                                  | (6%)      | (60%)      | (34%)       |
| 2008, Whole Election Cycle, Republicans (1)      | 0         | 1          | 0           |
|                                                  | (0%)      | (100%)     | (0%)        |
| 2008, Whole Election Cycle, Democrats (33)       | 2         | 17         | 14          |
|                                                  | (6.1%)    | (51.5%)    | (42.4%)     |
| 2008, Whole Election Cycle, No Slant (16)        | 1         | 12         | 3           |
|                                                  | (6.3%)    | (75%)      | (18.7%)     |

*SNL*'s humor was fairly equal between personal and substantive overall. But there was a strong pro-Democrat substantive bias; most substantive jokes favored Democrats, and were against Republicans, mainly because of the anti-Palin tone that took place later on (Table 5.6).

**Table 5.6.   Personal or Substantive?** *SNL*

|                                                  | Both      | Personal   | Substantive |
|--------------------------------------------------|-----------|------------|-------------|
| 2008, Whole Election Cycle (97)                  | 10        | 47         | 40          |
|                                                  | (10.3%)   | (48.5%)    | (41.2%)     |
| 2008, Whole Election Cycle, Republicans (4)      | 2         | 1          | 1           |
|                                                  | (50%)     | (25%)      | (25%)       |
| 2008, Whole Election Cycle, Democrats (32)       | 3         | 5          | 24          |
|                                                  | (9.4%)    | (15.6%)    | (75%)       |
| 2008, Whole Election Cycle, Progressive (3)      | 0         | 0          | 3           |
|                                                  | (0%)      | (0%)       | (3%)        |
| 2008, Whole Election Cycle, No Slant (58)        | 5         | 41         | 12          |
|                                                  | (8.6%)    | (70.7%)    | (20.7%)     |

The prominence of the *Daily Show* that began in 2000, and became strongly entrenched in 2004, was deepened in 2008, for two reasons: the increasing tendency for journalists to realize that what Stewart was doing was informed more by substantive policy or competency concerns about the candidates; and the debut of the *Colbert Report*, which, although different in form than the *Daily Show*, was similar in function. Colbert was another, similar voice that could counteract both the Republican echo chamber of Fox News, but also continue to challenge the capableness of cable news in general, as it worked as a direct parody of it at times. Another influential factor on journalists' discourse in the *Post* and the *Times* during this cycle was *SNL*, specifically Tina Fey's impression of vice presidential candidate Sarah Palin. It was widely studied in communications literature as potentially having influenced voters through what researchers called the "Fey Effect"—those who saw the parody of her poorly performed network television interviews were likely to have a low opinion of her (Baumgartner, Morris, and Walth 2012; Esralew and Young 2012; Young 2011). However, this study demonstrates that mainstream journalists in the public sphere were just as, if not more, influenced by the parody, and suggests that the so-called Fey Effect could have also been amplified by these intermediaries (Alexander 2004; Jacobs and Townsley 2011).

## PERSONAL HUMOR IN 2008 CONCENTRATED AT BEGINNING OF ELECTION

Early on in the election cycle, there was an equally lazy, non-substantive treatment of most of the primary candidates from both parties on *SNL*. The show characterized the Republicans as anti-science and superstitious religious zealots with strange beliefs. This included Mitt Romney as well as the Republican field in general: "Presidential candidate Mitt Romney told 60 Minutes this week that he can't imagine anything more awful then polygamy, except having only one wife" ("Weekend Update" May 12, 2007); "During last week's Republican debate, 3 of the 10 candidates said they did not believe in evolution, including Kansas senator, Sam Brownback, who said he would defend his conviction, one side of the Earth to the other" ("Weekend Update" May 12, 2007). Democratic candidates did not fare much better, and many were featured in a sketch that featured former Alaska Senator Mike Gravel and Chris Dodd lamenting about the advantages that Bill Richardson had because he was "half Mexican":

**Dodd**: Nobody would dare argue with you because you're half Mexican. You know unless they are three quarters Mexican or full on Mexican.

**Gravel**: I wish I was half Mexican

The sketch later on went to explore Gravel's supposed mental instability. Gravel's campaign was most well-known for bizarre, difficult-to-interpret campaign videos, practically no positive polling numbers, and strange statements in the media.

> **Gravel**: All right, you guys probably won't like this idea, but I think we should kidnap her . . . I'm serious, when she gets here, a couple of us grab her while the others chloroform her and tie her up.
>
> **Edwards**: Wait a second, do any of us even have rope and chloroform?
>
> **Gravel**: I do, in my car. ("Democratic Nominees Backstage," November 3, 2007)

Personality-driven humor on *SNL* characterized McCain as very old, and unable to win votes from any part of the electorate except a dwindling number of those voters who were very old themselves, in a fairly mean way: "Senator John McCain addressed his supporters, saying, 'Stand up with me, my friends. Stand up and fight for America.' To which his supporters responded, 'We can't!' [picture of people in wheelchairs is shown]" ("Weekend Update," March 8, 2008).

> **Brian Williams**: NBC News has obtained a copy of McCain's birth certificate that appears to confirm that he is not only old, but very old. The kind of old that makes you not really trust him with scissors. Due to the potentially damaging nature of these allegations, we've invited Sen. McCain to be on the program . . . Here's a surveillance photo of you, Senator, walking into Bob Evans to take advantage of their buffet.
>
> **Sen. John McCain**: Yes, I was having dinner. I don't see how that's relevant.
>
> **Brian Williams**: Can you see the time stamp on that photo, Senator? It says 4:30 in the afternoon. ("NBC Special Report," March 15, 2008)

Race was an issue in the election, and was treated more substantively later on, but was also the subject of non-substantive, personality-based humor on *SNL*. Some people claimed that Barack Obama had an advantage because he was biracial; no one would want to be seen criticizing him, lest they be perceived as racist. This was clearly a ridiculous assertion, due to lingering racist societal attitudes, and to their credit, *SNL* used it to emphasize the absurd tone that the campaign often took:

> **Jesse Jackson**: Mr. Obama, you a smoker, so it's fine to partake of a cigarette here and there . . .
>
> **Rev. Al Sharpton**: But if it's a whole pack of Newport menthols—

**Together**: They take it away!!

**Jesse Jackson**: It's fine to have the media talk to women from your past . . .

**Rev. Al Sharpton**: But if they dig up ONE baby mama . . . ("Weekend Update," May 17, 2008)

Obama had to contend with issues that no other major candidate ever had to before: namely the intersection of his race and his rumored religion. Because Obama is biracial, his blackness was emphasized by racially insensitive commentators, while at the same time being called into question due to his white mother. In addition, the fact that his father was Muslim overshadowed the fact that he was a Christian. At the same time, his particular brand of Christianity was criticized, because of the comments of the pastor at his former church, Rev. Jeremiah Wright, who was often perceived as expressing too much black anger for the comfort of some audiences. *SNL* mainly contended with the race and Islam issues: "On Wednesday, Barack Obama danced live, via satellite, for the Ellen DeGeneres show, in an attempt to prove that he's not a Muslim but, rather, very, very white" ("Weekend Update" October 25, 2008). In contrast, the main personal attribute that Hillary Clinton was mocked for was her association with her husband. "Hillary Clinton's campaign, on Friday, released her joint tax returns, showing $109 million in income over the last seven years. Though most of that comes from Bill Clinton's speaking engagements, book royalties, and stud fees" ("Weekend Update," April 5, 2008). Her gender was not an issue in the same way or to the extent that Obama's race and religion was. But the more unpleasant aspects of Bill Clinton's legacy remained to taint her campaign; the assumption was that if she were to become president, there may be some influence from him in her administration the same way that she influenced his. Although his presidency was functionally more positive than negative, he will never be able to escape being the subject of jokes about his checkered past (Alexander, Giesen, and Mast 2006).

## SUBSTANTIVE HUMOR: TERRORISM AND THE ECONOMY

Major substantive issues that all three programs discussed included foreign policy and the economy. Regarding foreign policy issues, the primary topics were the wars in Iraq and Afghanistan, specifically comparisons to the Bush administration's actions and policies. Earlier in the election cycle, when the Republican field had not yet been narrowed down to John McCain and debates were occurring with frequency, it was easy for the *Daily Show* to demonstrate that not only were the current candidates likely to continue Bush's interventionist policies, but would also escalate them. When asked a question about what could be done about Iraq's nuclear program, candidate Rep. Duncan Hunter said:

> I would authorize the use of tactical nuclear weapons if there was no other way to preempt those particular centrifuges . . .

> **Stewart**: (looking very shocked) Nuclear weapons to take out a centrifuge. Mm. Yes, last night's debate gave Republican candidates the opportunity to distance themselves from President Bush and his moderate policies. Although many still agreed with Bush's most important decision . . . [referring to starting the Iraq war] (June 6, 2007)

Stewart went on to discuss the candidates' positions on the justifications for the War in Iraq. When asked about going into Iraq, even knowing that there were no weapons of mass destruction, they all still said it was the right thing to do. Stewart said this was "the first documented cases of 20/20 hind blindness" (June 6, 2007). Later in the election cycle, Republicans caught on that they had too much in common with the Bush administration, and that Obama's slogan "Change You Can Believe In" was actually resonating with the voters. However, because of these early debates where they seemed to not only want to go the same hawkish way as the Bush administration, but to actually push further in that direction, any sort of attempt at painting themselves as different became inherently laughable. Stewart picked up on this easily, when they Republicans decided they needed to rebrand their image: "'The Change You Deserve' [on Republican website GOP.gov] is actually a slogan that's already taken. But not by a political party, but by Effexor, a powerful antidepressant medication which I can only assume after the past 7 years, you're already taking" (May 15, 2008). But candidates paradoxically needed to align themselves with Bush in order to retain the Republican base, while at the same time having to appeal to those who were weary of the previous eight years. Ultimately this was a losing battle.

McCain and Bush once had a confrontation in 2000 about McCain being mentally unstable and having post-traumatic stress disorder after his imprisonment in Vietnam. After Bush won the nomination, McCain was able to put all that behind him. Bush is shown giving McCain a half-hearted endorsement on the *Daily Show*: "all right so, no explicit endorsement from George W. Bush, although on the plus side, no explicit endorsement from George W. Bush" (March 6, 2008). It seemed that Hillary Clinton may also have been too hawkish for Stewart, as he took the opportunity to criticize her as well. Discussing the minor discrepancies between their foreign policy ideas,

Obama believed it was unwise to not communicate with foreign leaders we disagreed with, as that was a continuation of old policies that did not work, while Clinton just wouldn't "commit" to meet with them in her first year in office, Stewart had this to say:

> How would Obama counter this statement to highlight his campaign's narrative of Hillary as an inside the beltway hack tainted by fifteen years in Washington (shows picture of Cheney with Hillary's head). Here's what Obama would do:
>
> **Obama**: I don't want a continuation of Bush/Cheney. I don't want Bush/Cheney light.
>
> Oh, he would call her that directly. (August 2, 2007)

This can be perceived one of two ways: either Stewart was disagreeing with Obama, citing this as a slight against her, or he was using it to in fact call Hillary Clinton "Bush/Cheney light," meaning that her policies were uncomfortably close to the previous administrations'. In this way, the *Daily Show* took a firm stance against the continuation or escalation of the use of force, making it an unambiguous narrative source for journalists to use when doing the same. This would be especially important later on in the election cycle, when Sarah Palin and her views on the Bush Doctrine came up.

Besides foreign policy, domestic economic problems were similarly dominant in public sphere debates during the 2008 election cycle. Candidates who demonstrated a lack of understanding about how serious the financial crisis was becoming also were portrayed as unrealistic in their views (which would also come up later in reference to Palin). Many media figures had initially been excited for Fred Thompson's debut. When he did appear, he was stilted, and said he did not believe the economy was in a downturn. Stewart said, "It turns out Fred Thompson, though a skilled actor, not so hot at improv, despite his many years in the Uptight Citizens Brigade" (October 10, 2007). Although at first glance this seemed like a shot at Thompson's stiffness, it shows that he was easily criticized for not being able to come up with an adequate response to questions about the economy; therefore, he wouldn't be able to improve it, if he did not even understand it. Giving bad interviews was a performative failure that increasingly received attention in this election cycle (Alexander 2010). Colbert exclusively criticized Republicans throughout the entire campaign. During Primary season, a frequent target for him was Fred Thompson as well, whom he also mocked for not believing there was an economic downturn in the first place (October 16, 2008). Thompson was also subject to personality-based humor about his age from Colbert: "The Fred Thompson Presidential juggernaut keeps languidly creaking forward. I originally thought Thompson's trademark laziness was an asset in the campaign.

After all, if slow and steady wins the race, then imagine what stationary and half-asleep could do" (October 4, 2007).

Colbert said other Republicans were like Teddy Roosevelt, in that they had big, boisterous personalities, while Democrats were more like FDR, in that they offered specific solutions to the problems at hand (September 25, 2008). Republicans had no ideas of their own, and were only able to react and unsuccessfully make fun of the Democrats. Failed humor was almost worse than irrationality; Colbert mocked the McCain campaign for handing out "Barack Obama Energy Plan" tire gauges, a poor attempt at satirical criticism: "You see, it's a great way to drive home what a ridiculous plan this is. Plus it's an easy way to check your tire pressure. And that can save you a lot of money" (August 5, 2008). When asked about corruption, Republicans would deflect questions with talk about rebuilding the family structure, relying upon old tropes of culture wars which had worked in the past, but were no longer relevant (May 7, 2007). And the only things they could tout as victories were things like when Mitt Romney bragged he won elections in the Primaries in states where he lived: "It's the same sense of victory when I came home at night, and my wife has not changed the locks on our house" (February 6, 2008).

On September 24, 2008, the Republican nominee John McCain suspended his presidential campaign, for what he explained at the time was to deal with the economic crisis that had fractured the U.S. economy (and would continue to do so for years to come). This was met with derision but pundits and comedians alike, as an odd move that was only meant to gain publicity, and would be largely ineffective with actually helping with the problems at hand. Stewart discussed the incident, saying he "blew off his interview with David Letterman" to basically rush around giving other interviews, trying to explain how suspending his campaign could possibly help the financial crisis.

> Because of the grave condition of this situation, returned for a possible Senate vote for the first time since April 6th. And as his plane landed in Washington, D.C., a mere 22 hours after his initial New York announcement . . . I mean for god's sakes, you could have walked there in that time! . . . (But they'd all reached an agreement before he got there.) So to sum up: the net effect of John McCain suspending his campaign: angering David Letterman. (September 25, 2008)

*SNL* discussed the Republican candidate's economic policies as if they were a joke in and of themselves from then on. A serious substantive issue, the economic crisis was used as a way to expose McCain as the wrong choice to deal with the mess as president. Additionally, a sketch that made fun of that issue also hinted at another main way that *SNL* (and all comedians) portrayed McCain—as so old, he's senile. This is reminiscent of the way that Reagan was characterized in the 1980s. Finally, the sketch also incorporated a third element: "Joe the Plumber." Samuel Joseph Wurzelbacher gained the nickname when he became an ally of the McCain/Palin campaign as a voice for conservative taxpayers.

> **Sen. John McCain**: The fact is, Senator, only one of us has a record of fighting wasteful government spending, and it's me. As President, I would go after the bloated budgets with a GIANT hatchet, and THEN use a scalpel. Or I might take the advice of my friend, Joe the Plumber, and use a plunger.
>
> **Sen. Barack Obama**: A— a—a plunger? I don't understand.
>
> **Sen. John McCain**: Obviously, Senator. It's not an ordinary plunger. It's a magical plunger.
>
> **Sen. Barack Obama**: So, your friend "Joe the Plumber" has a "magical plunger"?
>
> **Sen. John McCain**: That's correct.
>
> **Sen. Barack Obama**: Would your friend Joe, be, by any chance, uhhh—an "imaginary friend?" ("Presidential Debate," October 16, 2008)

Much of the press and comedians did not take him seriously, and he was often invoked as a meme to demonstrate the facetiousness of the Republican campaign.

One of the most identifiable themes of the 2008 election (as well as obviously 2004) was that, in the post 9/11-era, fear, terrorism, and the emphasis on foreign threats were used as narrative devices, especially by the Republican candidates. Colbert, not having been on in the previous cycle, was now able to highlight these as excessive and overused. Early on in the election, he commented that all of the candidates represented "a potentially disastrous fuck up," interestingly on the sixth anniversary of the attacks (September 11, 2007). Could the American people be trusted to elect a leader who would keep us safe? Dire warnings of Republican candidates that the Democrats couldn't be trusted to do this implied that death would result from their election, and Colbert mocked the idea of running a fear-based campaign in general. To do appeal to this is irrational and ultimately anti-Democratic (Alexander 2006). Specifically, Republicans conflated terrorism directly with Islam, a tactic the Democrats tended to avoid. And the quote by Joe Biden during a debate in October 2007, that Giuliani only ever said in speeches "a noun, and a verb, and 9/11" was echoed by Colbert: "Rudy Giuliani Has used the words 'Islamic Terrorism' so many times, 'September 11' is starting to get jealous" (August 9, 2007). The Democrats did not use the words "Islamic Terrorism" but they talked about al-Qaeda frequently, as well as other specific threats: "That's four different enemies. They make it sound like we're in the middle of a complex, nuanced struggle requiring deep understanding of the differences between politically and religiously diverse groups. How are you gonna fit that on a bumper sticker?" (*Colbert Report*, August 9, 2007). It would seem that the wars in Iraq and Afghanistan would be a major topic for substantive comedy, but it did not get brought up very frequently on *SNL*. There are a few brief mentions of foreign policy positions, but comedy about it is mostly contained to Palin's lack of foreign policy experience, which I will discuss later in this chapter.

## INFIGHTING BETWEEN DEMOCRATIC
## FRONTRUNNERS LEADS TO CRITICISM

In a lighter moment earlier in the election cycle, when John Kerry endorsed Obama, Colbert said, "I don't agree with anything he said, or anything he stood for, but he did not deserve that" (January 10, 2008). But later, and by far, the vast majority of the humor on Colbert about the Democrats was directed at the Clinton campaign's negativity toward the Obama campaign. Thus, this humor was almost entirely pro-Obama, and was not slanted toward Republicans. Why was there such strife between the two primary frontrunners? It appeared that heading into the 2008 convention, neither candidate would have enough delegates to easily clinch the nomination, necessitating a brokered convention. This was seen as potentially harmful to the party. Initially, it looked as if Hillary Clinton was going to fight the exclusion of the delegates from Michigan and Florida. These two states had held their primaries earlier than they were to be allowed, thus Clinton being the only candidate on the ballot. The Obama campaign argued then that they were not fair contests. A compromise was reached wherein each delegate would count for half. Although contested, this compromise eventually stood, and Barack Obama's momentum picked up before the convention.

But before this was all settled, Clinton seemed to be prepared to fight all the way to the convention floor. Just when things would look resolved, she would offer resistance. Colbert was highly critical of these tactics, saying things like, "Nothing brings closure to a campaign like opening it up again" (August 11, 2008). Going back and forth and being indecisive, and that being harmful to the party, was the major source of Colbert's criticism of her. He spoke of Clinton as being inconsistent about what states should count when she agreed not to argue the point, and was hyperbolic, comparing her struggle to civil rights arguments about voting, stating, "she's being remarkably consistent in saying whatever it takes to win" (May 29, 2008). He even went so far as to allude to her tactics as being similar to Karl Rove's, who had tried to offer her advice on dealing with a brokered convention. Colbert remarked,

"If you set the rules, it is almost impossible to lose" (May 6, 2008). This is still more of a comment about Rove, but it shows that Colbert was making substantive commentary and allusion to her employing the same sort of dirty tricks. When it was said that blogger Matt Drudge got a photo from the Clinton campaign of Obama dressed in traditional Somali clothing (including wearing a turban), Colbert commented on this. To counter accusations of drumming up race-based or anti-Islamic feelings against her opponent, the Clinton campaign manager criticized the Obama campaign for suggesting the photo of him in the clothing was divisive. Colbert sarcastically commented that "it brings the nation together in the belief that Barack Obama is a terrorist" (February 26, 2008).

Additionally, there were several jokes and sketches on *SNL* that mocked Clinton for doing everything necessary to gain the upper hand on Obama, even if it was pointless or unethical. They characterized Clinton as overly aggressive and a sore loser:

> **Clinton**: All right energy policy. The big oil companies are quite happy with the status quo. They are earning record profits and pretty speeches are not going to make them give up power. It's going to take a fighter, not a talker—someone who is aggressive enough and relentless enough and demanding enough to take them on. Someone so annoying, so pushy, so grating, so bossy, and shrill with a personality so unpleasant that at the end of the day, the special interests will have to go, "Enough! We give up! Life is too short to deal with this awful woman! Just give her what she wants so she'll shut up and leave us in peace." And I think the American people will agree that someone is me. ("Democratic Debate," March 1, 2008)

"Hillary Clinton, on Tuesday, said she is not a quitter, and compared herself to Rocky Balboa—the washed-up, over-the-hill, white contender, who, despite a herculean effort, is soundly beaten by the charismatic black guy!" ("Weekend Update," April 5, 2008).

Even Bill Clinton, while campaigning for Hillary, made anti-Obama statements that Stewart believed he otherwise would not have made. When Bill Clinton called Barack Obama's campaign a "fairytale," Stewart retorted, "Your campaign slogan was 'A Place Called Hope.' ... If his wife wasn't running, he'd be all over Obama" (January 28, 2008). When the Clinton campaign compared Obama's tactic of "winning" to taking pages out of "Karl Rove's playbook," Stewart portrayed this as tremendously ridiculous. In one segment, he got out a very old book that, when opened, ghosts appeared to come out. He criticized this turn of phrase, saying, "Slightly misstating someone's position on trade doesn't appear to be in there" (February 26, 2008). But even so, Hillary Clinton was not as divisive as the Republicans had been regarding any of the substantive issues at hand. So, when Clinton went onto several Sunday morning talk shows, and tried to prove her humanity, she seemed overly chipper, laughing more maniacally each time she's asked the same questions again and again. Stewart mocks her, saying, "'I'm joyful!'" Was this laughter spontaneous? In some instances, it did seem justified, as when she goes on Fox news, and they ask her why she's so "hyper partisan"—and she really laughs, genuinely. "OK, I get it, you go on Fox news, and they ask you why you're so partisan. That's funny" (September 25, 2007).

> **Hillary**: First: I am a sore loser. If, and when, I am the nominee, I know, as do the superdelegates, that Sen. Obama will work his heart out for my election. If, on the other hand, Sen. Obama is chosen, I will probably refuse to campaign for him! Or, if I do so, it will be in a resentful, half-hearted way, thus ensuring his defeat—so that I can run again in 2012. You see, unlike my opponent, I am just not going to lose gracefully. It's not a criticism of Sen. Obama . . . it's just a fact! . . . Now, to those of who that worry, if my opponent is denied the nomination, that African-Americans might simply stay home, I remind you: a. until Sen. Obama shockingly, and, might I add, rudely and selfishly, won the Iowa caucuses, most African-Americans supported me; b. my husband was the first Black president; and, c. in the days ahead, we expect to receive the endorsement of America's preeminent African-American leader, Rev. Jeremiah Wright. ("A Message from the Next President of the United States," May 10, 2008)

When Hillary Clinton was on the show, Stewart addressed this directly. When she appeared on his show on March 3, 2008, he aired to her a clip of her giving a speech in Ohio where she said they need a president who's going to care about the working people, and referred to them as the "salt of the earth."

> **Stewart**: I always feel bad for Ohio, and I'll tell you why. It seems like every four years, people fly in and they crisscross the state, and they go, "Ohio, you are the salt of the earth, you are the blue-collar people, and then the election is over and they disappear, and nobody in Ohio gets to hear from them. How do you convince people that have been in this abusive relationship with politicians for this long, how do you convince them of the sincerity of what's going on there?

> (Hillary is laughing)

> **Hillary**: I got up this morning and went out to the shift change at 5:30 at one of the big auto plants in Toledo . . . I'm just trying to be there with people and let them know that I care about what goes on in their lives and I know that they've got a lot of tough challenges . . . it can't just be about the speeches . . . you're right, when that's all over they're still gonna be losing jobs and healthcare . . . we need a president who gets up every day and cares about the American people, what a novel idea.

She more or less deflected his questions, and went on to talk about coalitions needed to get universal healthcare, etc.

## MAINSTREAM MEDIA A TARGET
## FOR LATE-NIGHT COMEDY

The way that the mainstream media—especially cable news—narrated the campaign was a major source of commentary by the *Daily Show*; it highlighted contradictory statements most of all. The program often showed cable news commentators saying the campaign should be covered one way, and then showing clips of them doing the opposite of what they said should be done. For example, Stewart joked that Obama shouldn't be upset about the *New Yorker* cartoon depicting him as a Muslim extremist, because he was not one, and that was what actual extremists were likely to do:

> **Chris Matthews**: It's offensive, say both the Obama and McCain Campaigns, and I agree.
>
> Tacky, outrageous, offensive . . .
>
> Good for you, media! You should be outraged! How dare the New Yorker Magazine present horrible misperceptions of Barack Obama without clearly stating whether or not the allegations are true. That is so your job. (July 15, 2008)

The amount of time spent rehashing the same discussions and essentially filling time by talking about nothing with any substance was another criticism of cable news: "you might be thinking that just the very nature of having to kill six hours dissecting 43 separate results that would ultimately lead to no resolution would be the very definition of tedium! Well you my friend would be wrong" (February 6, 2008). People on news programs discussed how complex, interesting, and fascinating and exciting the campaign was. But then they would say simplistic things like "voters like to vote for who they like." Stewart replied to this by saying, "I'm the same way with the foods I eat and the stuff I do" (October 31, 2007). Media figures had early on declared Hillary the winner and unbeatable. However, they contradicted themselves by saying Obama was up to the challenge of proving himself in the debate: "But wait. You just told me it was over. Now it's apparently the fight of the century? Wow, what a manufactured showdown" (January 9, 2008). Talking about Hillary Clinton's defeat by Obama in the New Hampshire primary, the media used hyperbolic popular culture references:

> What kind of references are these? Friday the 13th, Empire Strikes Back, and The Abyss. Decent movies. But this is a big primary, does anybody have a struggle analogy that's a little more epic?
>
> **Chris Matthews**: Hillary Clinton's campaign, is not, to use the parlance we all use, positioned well. If you remember in the great movie, Lawrence of Arabia . . .

Oh, sweet Jesus.

**Chris Matthews**: . . . where the Turks aimed all their guns at the sea, and the Arab revolt came in from the desert . . . this latter-day Lawrence, Barack Obama, crossed the Nefud, and came behind the Clintons, into their own base . . .

[Stewart is shown with head on his desk in frustration]

And that's what happened in New Hampshire! But of course, I was wrong two minutes ago! [Mocking Chris Matthews:] That guy is insane. (January 9, 2008)

*SNL* satirized Barack Obama's popularity (compared to both Clinton and later McCain). With Clinton, there was a sense that the media was not being tough enough on Obama, and that he could do no wrong. In response to this criticism, they actually did become tougher on him after certain sketches aired that criticized their lack of scrutiny (which got a great deal of attention in the press, discussed below).

Like nearly everyone in the news media, the three of us are totally "in the tank" for Senator Obama. We will make every effort tonight to keep these biases hidden, but should it become obvious, please remember we're only human. I, myself, have been clinically diagnosed as an Oba-maniac! While my associate, John King, just last week suffered his third Barack-Attack . . . Now, let's meet the candidates. Just four years ago, Barack Obama was known only as a brilliant, charismatic, and universally admired member of the Illinois State Senate. Today, he is one of our nation's truly visionary leaders, and, soon—knock on wood—the first Black President of the United States. Senator Barack Obama. In 1992, Hillary Clinton's husband, William Jefferson Clinton, became the 42nd President of the United States. A few years after that, he cheated on her again, and she was able to ride the ensuing wave of sympathy into the U.S. Senate, against a weak Republican opponent in an overwhelmingly Democratic state. In the Senate, she is widely known as a good listener, with an excellent attendance record. ("CNN Univision Democratic Debate," February 23, 2008)

Colbert, like Jon Stewart, was also apt to denigrate cable news for playing into the simplistic media narratives that the Republicans (and to a lesser extent the Clinton campaign) were trying to make the main story of the election, instead of policy. Fox News kept bringing up Obama's middle name, Hussein, while other media was almost unthinkingly very pro-Obama, and the contrast was jarring (July 21, 2008); a theme that *SNL* would explore and which the newspaper writers would take great notice of. Barack Obama's "fist bump" incident was one of these things—what the viewer interpreted it as revealed more about them, and potentially racist views: "Terrorist fist jab" Fox News called it, and Colbert said of it, the fist bump "is like a Rorschach test" (June 10, 2008). Colbert portrayed the tactics of cable pundits as backfiring, and he turned out to be right: "The media has hammered Obama over the Reverend's comments, putting the Senator on the defensive, and backing him into a corner. A corner with five cameras, eight flags, two microphones, and thirty minutes of uninterrupted airtime, right where Obama's at his weakest" (March 18, 2008). Making irrational statements, and then giving Obama the perfect opportunity to demonstrate his rationality in light of them, was a very counterproductive strategy. The functioning of democracy was put squarely in the corner of the Democratic Party, when Colbert highlighted situations as described above, as well as pointing out that conservative pundits, like George Will, said that they wanted "quality" voters, not quantity, because young voters were more likely to vote for Obama. Their choice to vote was criticized because it went against the outcome Republicans desired (October 1, 2008). By the time the campaign had reached the point where McCain had become the nominee, and the antics involving Sarah Palin and ancillary characters like Joe the Plumber had started, it was almost as if Colbert was letting the people speak for themselves. Most of the narrative satirical work had been done for him. "Clearly, the McCain Campaign is targeting its most important voter: Joe the McCarthy" (October 28, 2008).

Was Obama a radical, sympathetic to the causes of the Weather Underground or the Black Panthers? Certainly, the vague association with William Ayres fueled these fires, specifically because of comments by Sarah Palin. Her commentary about "palling around with terrorists" got a lot of media attention, but ultimately backfired because of its irrationality. Obama really did not know Ayres well and only served on the board of directors of the Woods Fund of Chicago at the same time as he did, for three years. In one segment, Palin was shown as saying "it's time we met the real Obama" in an interview. Stewart responds: "Paling around is a pretty serious accusation. What kind of crazy source do you get that kind of information from?" It then emerges that the source was the *New York Times* (October 7, 2008). Members of the media talked about Obama "playing the race card" because he said, "So what they're saying is, we know we're not very good, but you can't risk electing Obama. He's new, he doesn't look like the other presidents on the currency." Stewart characterized this very small comment as playing the race card, and more of a comment about the Republicans' making racial commentary in their ads. But he did say Obama took the bait. Everything in the media is a "card" of some kind—gender, class, etc. (August 4, 2008). Obama's race and rumored religious affiliation with Islam was a source of mockery as well. Inclusion of jokes about these issues further highlighted the extremely negative personal tone that the election took against him: "On Wednesday, Barack Obama danced live, via satellite, for the Ellen DeGeneres show, in an attempt to prove that he's not a Muslim but, rather, very, very white" ("Weekend Update," October 25, 2008). On October 10, 2008 at a McCain rally, a woman asked John McCain about Obama being an "Arab," which he handled in a polite, but firm manner, correcting the misidentification. Despite this, the video of the exchange made McCain's supporters seem out of touch with reality and racist. A parody of the "Crazy old lady" from the campaign rally took shape.

> **Crazy McCain Supporter**: I gotta ask you a question. About Obama . . . I can't trust him. Obama.
>
> **Seth Meyers**: Why—why can't you trust Obama?
>
> **Crazy McCain Supporter**: I read about him . . . and he's a . . . he's a . . . he's a . . . he's a Arab.
>
> **Seth Meyers**: No. No, ma'am, he's not an Arab. ("Weekend Update," October 16, 2008)

Gender was also an issue; the fact that no matter if Hillary Clinton won the nomination or Barack Obama did, there would be a major party nominee for president that was not a white male for the first time in history. Some people saw this as a historic step toward progress and equality in general, but the contentious campaign between the two frontrunners highlighted the question many were afraid to ask: would it be better to have the first woman president, or the first non-white one? On *SNL*, Tina Fey spoke for Hillary Clinton:

> I think what bothers me the most is when people say that Hillary is a bitch. And, let me say something about that: Yeah, she is! And so am I! . . . You know what? Bitches get stuff done. . . . So, I'm saying it's not too late, Texas and Ohio! Get on board! Bitch is the new black! ("Weekend Update," February 23, 2008)

Meanwhile, a few weeks later, outspoken black comedian Tracy Morgan took Obama's side, while mocking some harmful stereotypes:

> Why is it every time a black man in this country gets too good at something, there's always someone to come around and remind us that he's black? . . . I got a theory about that. It's a little complicated, but, basically, it goes like this: We are a racist country. The end! . . . People say he's not a fighter. Let me tell you something, he's gangster. He's from Chicago! Barack is not just winning because he's a black man. If that were the case, I would be winning. And I'm WAY blacker than him! I used to smoke Newports and drink Old English! I grew up on government cheese! I prefer it . . . In conclusion, three weeks ago, my girl, Tina Fey—she came on this show, and she declared that "Bitch is the new Black." And you know I love you, Tina. You know you're my girl. But I have something to say: Bitch may be the new Black . . . but Black is the new president . . . bitch! ("Weekend Update," March 15, 2008)

For both Democrats and Republicans, religion was a topic that the *Daily Show* characterized in different ways; primarily, it was used to call out hypocrisy by the Republican party. The pastor at Obama's former church, Jeremiah Wright, was used as a wedge issue by the Republicans to try to paint Obama as somehow "un-American"; however, one of McCain's supporters, John Hagee—pastor of Cornerstone Church in San Antonio, Texas, a non-denominational megachurch, had said a lot of negative things about Muslims, and compared Catholics to Hitler. John McCain said he was glad to have his support, and Stewart pointed out that Obama was being raked over the coals about Wright, while no one said anything to McCain about these statements (April 24, 2008). Another major incident involving religion during the campaign was the statement by Obama about Pennsylvania, that "You go into some of these small towns in Pennsylvania . . . the jobs have been gone now for 25 years . . . they get bitter or they cling to guns or religion . . . or antipathy towards people who aren't like them . . . anti-immigrant sentiment . . . " (Obama Fundraiser, April 6, 2008). Stewart characterized the backlash against this as overblown, saying, "That is outrageous, sir, outrageous! These people do not turn to god and guns and mistrust of foreigners because of a downturn in the economy . . . those are the very foundations those towns are built on, sir" (April 14, 2008).

Later, the same ideas that had been applied to Hillary Clinton during the primary—bound to lose, did unethical things in the campaign, or allowed them to happen—were applied to the Obama vs. McCain contest: "A woman in Pennsylvania who claimed that a man attacked her and carved a 'B' on her face when he saw her McCain bumper sticker, admitted Friday that she made the story up. Still unanswered: Who did this to John McCain? [image: McCain with "Obama 'Hearts' Ayers" tattoo on his arm]" ("Weekend Update," October 25, 2008).

> **Bob Schieffer**: Gentlemen, over the last few weeks, the tone of this campaign has become increasingly nasty. Senator Obama, in describing your opponent, your campaign has used words like "erratic," "out of touch," "lying," "losing his bearings," "senile," "dementia," "nursing home," "decrepit," and "at death's door." Senator McCain, your ads have featured terms such as "disrespectful," "dangerous," "foreign," "sleeper agent," and "uncircumcised." Are you both comfortable with this level of discourse? ("Presidential Debate," October 16, 2008)

## FEY'S PARODY OF PALIN

The dialogue on the first sketch about Palin on *SNL* centered on the three main subjects discussed in the papers: Russia, climate change, and the Bush Doctrine.

**Clinton**: I believe that diplomacy should be the cornerstone of *any* foreign policy.

**Palin**: And I can see Russia from my house!

**Clinton**: I believe that global warming is caused by man.

**Palin**: And I believe it's just God hugging us closer!

**Clinton**: I *don't* agree with the Bush Doctrine.

**Palin**: [laughs] I don't know what that is! ("A Non-Partisan Message from Sarah Palin & Hillary Clinton," September 13, 2008)

The comments about "keeping an eye on Russia" Palin made in the original interview were simplified into the absurd claim "I can see Russia from my house," which she never directly stated. But it is this slight departure from what was actually said that pushed the reality into the realm of absurdity, and made Palin appear foolish. This sketch was conversation between Hillary Clinton played by Amy Poehler, and Palin played by Fey. It was clearly meant to highlight the differences between the two female candidates; later, writers in the newspapers would make comments about how the choice of Palin was a cynical attempt to pull disillusioned Hillary Clinton voters from voting for Obama, and if that was indeed the case, it backfired tremendously.

Stewart was more likely to let her own words speak for themselves: He commented on the Charlie Gibson interview, where she was being questioned about the Bush Doctrine: "She doesn't need to know what the Bush Doctrine is, she is the Bush Doctrine. Her foreign policy experience consists of being able to see Russia from an island in Alaska" (September 15, 2008). Stewart talked about her primarily in terms of how other media figures were hypocritical when it came to glossing over her many faults. He pointed out the incongruity of Karl Rove lauding Palin for her experience, being the mayor of Wasilla, Alaska (population 3,000) and its governor, while criticizing Obama's possible pick of Tim Kaine (whose experience was being Mayor of Richmond and Governor of Virginia). Additionally, Bill O'Reilly was shown making contradictory statements about celebrity Jaime Lynn Spears' pregnancy and Sarah Palin's daughter's (*Daily Show*, September 3, 2008). Colbert highlighted the absurdity of the McCain/Palin's constant use of the word "maverick," and how it was essentially meaningless; reflexively going against rules for no rational reason other than to appear different: "John McCain and Sarah Palin are going to win this election. Why? Because they are mavericks" (November 3, 2008). Ultimately, he appeared confident that Obama would win, and didn't need to do a lot of the narrative work, but let the situation speak for itself, as the *Daily Show* also did, to a lesser extent.

Heck, gosh, me and Todd, you betcha, we're just average, working-class, salt-of-the-earth Governor and snow machine champions. Governor Palin gets up every morning and puts on her governin' overalls and goes down to put in an 8-hour shift over to the executive branch factory . . . How can a woman who spent more on clothing in six weeks than most Americans make in two years, show that she can still relate to the common folk? (She is shown greeting a crowd lauding their Carhart overalls and steel toed boots.) (October 22, 2008)

Palin appearing on *SNL* came too late to do anything about her image. One sketch involved the candidate (portrayed by Fey) at a press conference:

**Reporter**: Yeah, at a rally in North Carolina this week, you said that you like to visit the "pro-America parts of the country." Are there parts of the country that you consider un-American?

**Palin**: Oh, you know, that was just my lame attempt at a joke. But, um, yes—New York, New Jersey, Massachusetts, Connecticut, Delaware and California. But, then, also, too, you have states like Ohio and Pennsylvania and Florida, which could be real, real anti-American or real, real pro-American. It's up to them (she winks). And now, I'd like to entertain everybody with some fancy pageant walkin'. ("Palin Press Conference," October 18, 2008)

The last part was a reference to her having been in beauty pageants in the past. After this exchange, they camera cuts to a location backstage, where the real Palin is watching with *SNL* producer, Lorne Michaels, and later, Fey's co-star on the show "30 Rock," Alec Baldwin:

**Michaels**: I really wish, uh, that that had been you. . . . (the night's guest, actor Mark Wahlberg, appears briefly and storms off angrily)

**Michaels**: He didn't like the impression we did of him on the show.

**Palin**: Tell me about it.

**Alec Baldwin**: Hey, Lorne. Hey, Tina. Lorne, I need to talk to you. You can't let Tina go out there with that woman. She goes against everything we stand for. I mean, good Lord, Lorne, they call her . . . what's that name they call her? Cari . . . Cari . . . What do they call her again, Tina?

**Palin**: Uh, that'd be Caribou Barbie.

**Alec Baldwin**: Caribou Barbie! Thank you, Tina. I mean, this is the most important election in our nation's history. And you want her—our Tina—to go out there and stand there with that horrible woman. What do you have to say for yourself?

**Michaels**: Alec, this is Governor Palin.

As writers in the *Times* and the *Post* would later note, Palin appeared a bit too genuinely angry, and the attempt to appear able to laugh at herself seems to have gone awry.

Later, right before the election, after it seemed like McCain would almost certainly lose, he appeared on *SNL* himself, alongside Fey as Palin. It took the form of them basically having an end-of-campaign fire sale on the home shopping channel, QVC. First, they made fun of her expensive wardrobe scandal:

> **Sen. John McCain**: The final days of any election are the most essential. This past Wednesday, Barack Obama purchased airtime on three major networks. We, however, can only afford QVC.
>
> **Gov. Sarah Palin**: These campaigns sure are expensive! (she strokes her jacket lapel)
>
> **Sen. John McCain**: They sure are. They sure are. ("A Special Message from Sen. John McCain & Gov. Sarah Palin," November 1, 2008)

Other topics, that played like a "greatest hits" of the controversies and scandals, included mentions of Joe the Plumber, the association the McCain/Palin campaign made with William Ayres (and what busy hockey mom wouldn't want to freshen up her home with Sarah Palin's "Ayers Fresheners"? You plug these into the wall when something doesn't quite smell quite right.). At the end of the sketch, Palin turns to a different camera and whispers:

> Okay, listen up everybody, I am goin' rogue right now, so keep your voices down. [she holds up a "Palin 2012" t-shirt ] Available now, we got a buncha' these "Palin in 2012" T-shirts. Just try and wait until after Tuesday to wear 'em, okay? Because I am not goin' anywhere! And I'm certainly not goin' back to Alaska! If I'm not goin' to the White House, I'm either runnin' in four years or I'm gonna be a white Oprah, so . . . you know, I'm good either way! ("A Special Message from Sen. John McCain & Gov. Sarah Palin," November 1, 2008)

This sketch was a perfect send-off to the campaign, complete with a resigned McCain, and the satire of what many people had come to believe at this time—that Palin was squeezing everything she could get out of the opportunity, because it was unlikely that, given her poor performance, it would ever happen again.

## PERFORMATIVE SUCCESSES AND
## FAILURES DISCUSSED IN THE PAPERS

Most notably in 2008, the parody of Sarah Palin by Tina Fey became recognizable shorthand for the way journalists talked about the candidate, showing that a satirical portrayal of the candidate was taken just as seriously as any facet of mainstream journalism would be. Journalists saw her opinions, interviews, and policy positions through the lens of the parody of them. The parody was scrutinized far more than the actual interviews. Because of this, there was greater focus on her than any other candidate, influencing the overall public sphere dialogue about her more than anything else. The fact that commentary from the cultural sphere had such an impact on the sphere of news journalism in this election cycle clearly demonstrates a directional flow of influence of the opinion leaders of comedy, namely Jon Stewart, Stephen Colbert, Tina Fey, and all the associated shows' writers, that shaped the narratives in the newspapers, and in turn public opinion (Katz and Lazarsfeld 1955). The satire on the programs was a relatively autonomous, influencing variable in this election. The trend toward this had been building over time, but in 2008, it was fully realized.

The papers remarked upon Clinton's appearances on *SNL* and the *Daily Show*, but did not analyze them in any great depth, saying, "Her appearances on 'Saturday Night Live' and 'The Daily Show with Jon Stewart' were also generally well received last week and . . . presaged a big comeback at the polls" (Mark Leibovich, "A Scorecard on Conventional Wisdom," *New York Times*, March 9, 2008). The appearance on the *Daily Show*, where she was asked many important questions about the substance of her campaign and policies, was glossed over, and represented an important opening for the newspapers to truly engage with where her message was lacking:

> Among the events on her schedule are an interactive town hall meeting Monday night and a satellite appearance on Comedy Central's "Daily Show with Jon Stewart." Over the weekend, she flew to New York for a surprise appearance on NBC's "Saturday Night Live," part of a frenetic late push to revive her candidacy. (Anne E. Kornblut and Shailagh Murray, "Democratic Candidates Trade Gibes Across Ohio; Obama Takes On Clinton on Foreign Policy," *Washington Post*, March 3, 2008)

Why did she need to revive it in the first place? Obama appeared much more at ease on the programs than she did, more easily mocking himself (such as when he appeared in an *SNL* skit in November, 2007, wearing a mask of his own face). The only negative about him that was not race or religion based (and therefore not mockable, because that would be perceived as racism or Islamophobia) was his "elitism." This was not easy for him to counter directly, mainly because of his speech patterns and occasional "stiffness," despite his greater ease with humor. But his wife, Michelle, did not have any of these personality characteristics, real or imagined, and her appearance on *Colbert* helped to dispel some of these images and make him more relatable. It wasn't so much what she said, but how she "was," in that she speaks in a much more down-to-earth and warm manner than her husband. Maureen Dowd's comments in the *Times* represented the superficial-level perception of Obama that summed up the facile commentary about him the public sphere, but even she found that Michelle Obama was able to do something to counter the negative perception:

> Obama did not grow up in cosseted circumstances . . . But his exclusive Hawaiian prep school and years in the Ivy League made him a charter member of the elite, along with the academic experts he loves to have in the room . . . Michelle did her best on "The Colbert Report" Tuesday to shoo away the aroma of elitism. (Maureen Dowd, "Eggheads and Cheese Balls," *New York Times*, April 16, 2008)

Hillary Clinton would not have had the same advantage if her husband had appeared on any of the shows. His tainted personal image from his presidency at that time would have worked against her, in terms of her relationship with him, which would have overshadowed any of the positive feelings that had built about his actual presidency since he left office.

John McCain appeared on *SNL*, but his more famous appearance—or initial lack thereof—was on the *Late Show* with David Letterman. When the financial crisis hit, McCain "suspended" his campaign, and went back to Washington; he said it was to deal with the problems that had arisen, but many saw it as a cynical attempt to distract voters from the fact that his campaign was going down the drain after his pick of Palin as a running mate. One way that he handled this situation very poorly was when he was scheduled to appear on David Letterman's show, and cancelled at the last minute, even though he *did* manage to make it to the "CBS Evening News" studio to be interviewed by Katie Couric.

> It all started last month when the GOP candidate backed out of an appearance on the show, telling the late-night host personally that the economy was in such a state of crisis that he was suspending his political campaign and had to rush back to Washington . . . That first night, when McCain canceled, Letterman threw up the CBS in-house video feed showing the senator from Arizona getting his makeup touched up pre-Couric chat. (Lisa de Moraes, "Will Gloves Come Off When McCain Faces Letterman?" *Washington Post*, October 16, 2008)

Eventually, McCain was forced to go on the show and apologize, after Letterman did not let up on him in the slightest, often including him in the "Top Ten" segment, and growing increasingly critical of his very trustworthiness.

> John McCain, so pugnacious in his encounters with his Democratic rival, folded like a tent when confronted last night by late-night host David Letterman, whom

McCain stood up last month. "I screwed up," McCain said of his last-minute decision to cancel his appearance on CBS's "Late Show" last month, forcing Letterman to scramble to find a replacement guest . . . "Can you stay?" [Letterman] asked, dripping cynicism . . . The candidate admitted he "screwed up" but bravely tried to suggest he'd done Letterman a favor by backing out of his previous date . . . "I haven't had so much fun since my last interrogation," said McCain, a Vietnam War POW. (Lisa de Moraes, "Last Debate Is Not a Winner, In the Ratings," *Washington Post*, October 17, 2008)

However, nothing in any election cycle compared to the dislike in the mainstream press of Sarah Palin. And *SNL* gave writers the perfect framework from which to discuss exactly what substantive issues were most worrying about her.

In the *Times*, Columnist Gail Collins wrote an op-ed that criticized McCain for picking an inexperienced extremist Evangelical Christian to try to play up to women voters and his base, and said Palin's "guard stands as our last best defense against possible attack by the resurgent Russian menace across the Bering Strait" (Gail Collins, "McCain's Baked Alaska," *New York Times*, August 30, 2008). Considering that Palin stated this later on in the ABC *World News* interview conducted by Charlie Gibson on September 11, 2008, this was an eerily far-seeing comment. After the failed Palin interviews, and the *SNL* parodies of them, and after McCain had to apologize to David Letterman, it appeared that the McCain/Palin campaign was doing more damage control than campaigning. Polling showed this, as well as Palin's actions. When Palin went on *SNL*, she was trying to prove that she had a sense of humor about herself; but she did not succeed at counteracting the parody of her: "The 'SNL' skits gave Ms. Palin the last word in every joke . . . the strategy . . . looked a bit odd . . . her performance did little to assuage the concerns that have troubled many Republican and independent voters" (Alessandra Stanley, "On 'SNL' It's the Real Sarah Palin, Looking Like a Real Entertainer," *New York Times*, October 20, 2008). Palin appeared to disdain Tina Fey and was uncomfortable. She was put on the show by the campaign to be more "real" and display authenticity by being able to laugh at herself, but the performance looked contrived. Palin's appearance on *SNL* on October 18, 2008, had an effect on polling data, as voters liked her more before the interviews and the impression. Palin had "become a drag on the GOP ticket: 52 percent of voters said McCain's selection of her makes them doubt the types of decisions he would make as president, a reversal from a Post-ABC poll following the nominating conventions" (Jon Cohen and Dan Balz, "Democrat Remains Well Ahead," *Washington Post*, October 21, 2008).

There was not much known about Palin before the interviews with Katie Couric and Charlie Gibson that Tina Fey parodied, and journalists used the parody to criticize Palin. Although some writers claimed that this may have affected how the voters thought about her, and ultimately McCain (Baumgartner, Morris, and Walth 2012), writers in the *Times* and *Post* derided Palin after *SNL* showed the parody, and it was mentioned in nineteen articles in the *Post* and twenty-seven articles in the *Times* thereafter. Three issues—Palin not knowing the meaning of the "Bush Doctrine," climate change, Alaska's nearness to Russia as a substitute for foreign policy experience—were the main topics writers discussed. About Palin's confusion over the "Bush Doctrine,"[2] Columnist Bob Herbert in the *Times* wrote, "I've gotten the scary feeling, for the first time in my life, that dimwittedness is not just on the march in the U.S., but that it might actually prevail" (Bob Herbert, "She's Not Ready," *New York Times*, September 13, 2008). These comments were made *before* Tina Fey's satire on *Saturday Night Live*. What happened *afterward* demonstrated an influence on the official journalistic sphere by the cultural/aesthetic public sphere (Jacobs 2012).

After the first sketch, most of the journalists in the *Post* and the *Times* saw her from then on as an incompetent exaggerator of her own qualifications. "Palin was halting, repetitive and occasionally stumped on basic questions. And the worst moments [of the Couric interview]—boasting again, Tina Fey-like, of Alaska's proximity to Russia—have been endlessly replayed on other networks and the Web" (Howard Kurtz, "'Substantive' Press Is Taken for a Spin," *Washington Post*, September 29, 2008); "Some of Palin's occasionally rambling responses to Couric have been used verbatim in Tina Fey's 'Saturday Night Live' send-up" (Rob Jewell, "Biden and Palin—Better than Baseball," *Washington Post*, October 2, 2008).

> Palin tends to "slip back to her talking points," as CBS's Katie Couric recently put it. John McCain is a maverick. Lots of things need some shakin' up . . . "Forgive me, Mrs. Palin," faux Katie Couric said to faux Sarah Palin on last week's "Saturday Night Live," "but it seems to me that when cornered you become increasingly adorable." (Libby Copeland, "Shooting From the Hip, With a Smile to Boot," *Washington Post*, October 1, 2008)

Ultimately, because of her poor performance and how *SNL* emphasized it, there was a low bar set for her to succeed in the debate between her and Joe Biden: "The criteria for success for Palin was, don't sound like Tina Fey and don't get into a situation in which it appears you're incredibly intellectually shallow. She did that, and everyone's saying it was a triumph" (Howard Kurtz, "A Political Debate with Two Scorecards," *Washington Post*, October 4, 2008). Instead of showing political competency against Biden, "The debate . . . was between the dueling images of the Alaska governor: the fuzzy-minded amateur parodied—with her own words—by Tina Fey" (Alessandra

Stanley, "A Candidate Recaptures Her Image," *New York Times*, October 3, 2008). After the representation of Palin as ridiculous caught on, it did not go away. She did not talk to the media for a period of time after the nomination. This gave the impression that the campaign had something to hide: "Ms. Fey's take on Ms. Palin has all but defined the candidate, who has resisted media coverage" (Bill Carter, "An Election to Laugh About," *New York Times*, October 9, 2008).

This description of Palin's comments in the vice presidential debate about the state of the economy was totally colored by the impression:

> "We're gonna ask ourselves what would a maverick do in this situation, and then ya know, we'll do that." . . . Oh, wait a minute. That wasn't Gov. Sarah Palin in the debate. That was Tina Fey doing her impression of Sarah Palin . . . an impersonation . . . so resonant, it almost displaced Ms. Palin's own performance as herself. . . . At times there has even been some ambiguity about where reality ends and caricature begins. (Edward Rothstein, "The Power of Political Pratfalls," *New York Times*, October 13, 2008)

Republicans as well as Democrats began to have serious reservations about her: "Her performance in the interview sparked serious heebie-jeebies among Republicans" (Mark Leibovitch, "Laugh, or the World Laughs at You," *New York Times*, October 5, 2008). The McCain campaign wanted Palin to appeal to women voters, especially Independents and those who might have wanted Hillary Clinton to win. Her lack of experience was marketed as a positive quality, because she would "shake things up" and not be a "Washington insider"—ironic because McCain had been in Washington for so long. These were two key components of the McCain campaign's strategy that were taken apart by the parodies of the interviews. Regarding the former, Fey's characterization of Palin made people think she was picked more for her looks than acuity (the "fancy pageant walkin'" line, above, demonstrates that, pointing to her past in beauty pageants) and would be a poor second compared to Clinton. The fact that Clinton and Fey were shown in a sketch together emphasized the differences side-by-side. The parody also highlighted Palin's ignorance on important issues: "Voters were about evenly divided on [the question of Palin's experience] a month and a half ago, but toward the end of September a clear majority said she was not qualified. In the new poll, 58 percent said she is insufficiently experienced" (Jon Cohen and Jennifer Agiesta, "Perceptions of Palin Grow Increasingly Negative, Poll Says," *Washington Post*, October 25, 2008). As the election date drew closer, this trend continued: "The polls also suggest that Sarah Palin has, in two short months, managed to scare the pants off large portions of the population" (Gail Collins, "America's Election Whopper," *New York Times*, November 1, 2008). Palin's own words increased opposition to her; voters subsequently wanted Obama to win even more. Preventing Palin from becoming vice president became an important goal and contributions to Obama's campaign increased.

One of the major parts of this anti-Palin movement of the electorate was that it helped fix the inter-party rupture created by the primary campaign between Obama and Clinton, summed up in a *Post* article, where they interviewed women voters who had previously supported Hillary:

> The Hillary voter has come home . . . "Palin—God forbid! Where did they find her?" Evelyn Fruman exclaimed Monday before a Clinton speech at a Jewish community center here . . . Nearby, Rina Jampolsky was wearing a "Hillary Sent Me" button . . . "I thought I wouldn't vote at all when Hillary left the race," she said. "But as soon as McCain selected Sarah Palin, my decision was made." (Dana Milbank, "An Unwitting Assist from the Hockey Mom," *Washington Post*, October 14, 2008)

Even comments about Palin that once had a completely positive connotation—such as the fact that she "energized" the McCain campaign—became clouded by her inadequacies. "Though she initially transformed the race with her energizing presence and a fiery convention speech . . . after weeks of intensive coverage and several perceived missteps, the shine has diminished" (Jon Cohen and Jennifer Agiesta, "Skepticism of Palin Growing, Poll Finds," *Washington Post*, October 2, 2008). The *Post* wrote about male voters talking in Virginia, in a conversation that spoke volumes about Palin's failed performance as a competent politician: "'But Sarah Palin is great, even though she's not so keen on foreign policy,' [the first man] said. 'She's not keen on anything,' [the second man] retorted. 'John McCain could keel over and have a heart attack, and we'd be left with a dingbat'" (Brigid Schulte, "Winchester Still Waiting and Wondering," *Washington Post*, November 2, 2008).

## JOURNALISTS RECOGNIZE GREATER
## SUBSTANTIVE HUMOR CONTENT

In the 2008 election cycle, journalists were unequivocal about the influence that late-night comedy programs were having on the public dialogue about the election. They discussed the fact that many people got their information from them and the shows' direct impacts on the media. They recognized that that the programs favored Democratic candidates, and they were "an underrated factor in this campaign, and an undeniable advantage for Obama [who] . . . has basically joked and danced his way through such appearances . . . Jon Stewart asked him about 'the whole socialism/Marxist thing'" (Howard

Kurtz, "Softer Shows Hard on McCain," *Washington Post*, November 3, 2008). By contrast, previous election cycles were not as tailor made for the more critical satire that was now being recognized: "Eight years of George W. Bush really weren't a great boon to the show; he seemed hard to satirize . . . Bush turned out to be his own best parody, a self-satirizing figure who seemed to thwart friendly spoofing" (Tom Shales, "Early Returns Are Promising In 'SNL's' Thursday Campaign," *Washington Post*, October 10). Due to the confluence of the transformation of the shows, in response to the overly complacent media environment after 9/11, and the specific personalities of this election cycle's candidates, the programs had the opportunity to be more influential, an opportunity that they specifically took.

One of the biggest influences that *SNL* had on campaign coverage was its jokes about how the media was very critical of Hillary Clinton, but willing to let Barack Obama off the hook on practically every issue. Several sketches were devoted to this. In another example of newspapers taking advantage of every opportunity to criticize network and cable news (perhaps to make themselves look better in comparison), journalists often spoke of this supposed influence. In fact, the "characterization [was] stoked nearly every day since by Mrs. Clinton and her aides" (Jacques Stenberg, "On The Press Bus, Some Questions Over Favoritism," *New York Times*, March 1, 2008) as fuel to the fire that the media was treating her unfairly. In turn, campaign coverage on television shifted, and many commentators directly discussed the skits as the primary reason why: "It took many months and the mockery of 'Saturday Night Live' to make it happen, but the lumbering beast that is the press corps finally roused itself from its slumber Monday and greeted Barack Obama with a menacing growl" (Dana Milbank, "Ask Tough Questions? Yes, They Can!," *Washington Post*, March 4, 2008). Multiple times, the papers stated that "the tone of the Democratic contest seems to have shifted, with Senator Hillary Rodham Clinton's campaign more buoyant and Senator Barack Obama's more defensive," and attributed it to "the 'Saturday Night Live' show on Feb. 23, when . . . it mocked the news media for treating Mr. Obama more gently than it treated Mrs. Clinton press" (Katharine Q. Seelye, "News Coverage Changes . . . ," *New York Times*, March 5, 2008). Further, the Clinton campaign was able to use that narrative, both in a debate and in confrontations with the "Why did it take a skit on 'Saturday Night Live' to change the tone of TV news operations' Democratic primary coverage? . . . [critics] pointed out how [Barack] Obama was getting the softballs, while Hillary [Clinton] was getting the knock-down pitches'" (Lisa de Moraes, "CNN, 'SNL' and TV Critics' Primary Concerns," *Washington Post*, July 12, 2008).

The Wright story initially erupted in March, shortly after journalists were stung by a pair of "Saturday Night Live" skits that portrayed them as in the tank for

Obama . . . [Afterward] the press was no longer giving him the benefit of the doubt. Minor incidents—Obama throwing gutter balls or refusing to indulge in high-calorie foods—were trumpeted as evidence that he is an out-of-touch Harvard elitist. (Howard Kurtz, "Obama's Chilly Spring; Once-Cordial Press Coverage Turns Decidedly Cool," *Washington Post*, May 5, 2008)

This was one of the most direct influences that a comedy program had on the way that journalists covered a presidential campaign.

As in previous years, journalists revisited the idea that many people, especially younger voters, were getting their information about politics from the late-night comedy shows. When the shows went off the air due to the writers' strike, "hundreds of thousands of American citizens lost contact with what's going on in the outside world. The recourse to vintage episodes of 'The Colbert Report' immediately disconnected voters—at least the ones too young to remember the '70s—from the nation's unfolding political drama" (Staff, "Beware Reality," *New York Times*, November 9, 2007).

It is no secret that late-night comedians have become quasi news anchors, especially to under-30 voters—about half of whom say they at least sometimes learn about the campaign from programs like "Saturday Night Live" and "The Daily Show" (compared with about a quarter of people ages 30 to 49), a 2004 Pew Research Center survey found. (Adam Nagourney, "A Year Still to Go and Presidential Politics Have Shifted Already," *New York Times*, November 4, 2007)

Journalists saw this as benefitting the Democrats. The Center for Media and Public affairs conducts regular studies on which party or candidates are the targets of late-night humor. Even though the Democratic candidates have more jokes aimed at them, according to their study from January 1, 2008, to October 10, 2008, it was fairly obvious that the more substantive ones, aimed at Republicans, were what was resonating with journalists. But the number of jokes and who they were aimed at was not the only thing that journalists paid attention to. For the first time, in this election cycle, they began to acknowledge that it wasn't just exposure to the jokes that was having an influence; it was the critical qualities of them:

Following 9/11 and the invasion of Iraq, the show focused more closely not just on politics, but also on the machinery of policy making and the White House's efforts to manage the news media. Mr. Stewart's comedic gifts—his high-frequency radar for hypocrisy, his talent for excavating ur-narratives from mountains of information, his ability, in Ms. Corn's words, "to name things that don't seem to have a name"—proved to be perfect tools for explicating and parsing the foibles of an administration known for its secrecy, ideological certainty and impatience with dissenting viewpoints. (Michiko Kakutani, "The Most Trusted Man in America?" *New York Times*, August 17, 2008)

In fact, this article observed (without the advantage of having a great deal of specific empirical data to back up the assertion) the same phenomenon that this book has shown—that the *Daily Show* in particular went from personality-based humor to emphasizing the substantive problems with the Bush Administration, and by extension, subsequent Republican candidates:

> Over time, the show's deconstructions grew increasingly sophisticated. Its fascination with language, for instance, evolved from chuckles over the president's verbal gaffes . . . to ferocious exposes of the administration's Orwellian manipulations: from its efforts to redefine the meaning of the word "torture" to its talk about troop withdrawals from Iraq based on "time horizons" (a strategy, Mr. Stewart noted, "named after some-thing that no matter how long you head towards it, you never quite reach it"). For all its eviscerations of the administration, "The Daily Show" is animated not by partisanship but by a deep mistrust of all ideology. A sane voice in a noisy red-blue echo chamber, Mr. Stewart displays an impatience with the platitudes of both the right and the left and a disdain for commentators who, as he made clear in a famous 2004 appearance on CNN's "Crossfire," parrot party-line talking points and engage in knee-jerk shouting matches.

This was the first election cycle in which Stephen Colbert's show was on, and it was also recognized as a major force unto its own, even though it was a part of the overall landscape of political satire. His "character," a more direct satire of both conservative politics in general, and conservative media commentators in specific, was a unique response to the post-9/11 media landscape: "As Mr. Colbert demonstrated on Sunday morning [on "Meet the Press"], it isn't that he finds the Beltway's folkways amusing, he finds them appalling" (David Carr, "The Gospel According to Mr. Colbert," *New York Times*, October 22, 2007). Finally, there had been a recognition that what Stewart and Colbert were doing was qualitatively different from what had been done in the past, and late-night monologues were still doing even at the same time:

> John McCain is a doddering fossil. Hillary is pathological ambition poured into a frigid pantsuit. And Barack—well, Barack Hussein Obama's mere name is mined for cheap yuks because comedically, he's proved about as hard to pin back as a pair of protruding ears. Those are one-note caricatures perpetuated weeknightly largely by broadcast TV's late-night chat hosts, who are paid to multiply audiences by the lowest comedic denominator. And because of this political shtick, Peterson, the author and University of Iowa academic, accuses Leno and Letterman and Conan and company of practicing only "pseudo-satire."

True satirists, Peterson contends, are genuine critics . . . Which is why he believes the likes of Stewart and Colbert are healthy contributors to the election's national conversation—whether they themselves subscribe to such influence or not . . . once satire takes hold, perhaps its greatest influence is encouraging critical thought. (Michael Cavna, "Comedians of Clout; In a Funny Way, Satirical Takes Can Color Perceptions of the Presidential Contenders," *Washington Post*, June 12, 2008)

The critically satirical shows were not only "real" satire, but often times *real news*: "Next to such 'real' news from CBS, the 'fake' news at the network's corporate sibling Comedy Central was, not for the first time, more trustworthy. Rob Riggle, a 'Daily Show' correspondent who also serves in the Marine Reserve, invited American troops in Iraq to speak candidly about the Iraqi Parliament's vacation" (Frank Rich, "As the Iraqis Stand Down, We'll Stand Up," *New York Times*, September 9, 2007) which was something not seen anywhere else. Journalists also took note of how military leaders overemphasized the progress in Iraq in the past, and compared to how they spoke of it in the present, where they now criticized the president: "The before-and-after videos didn't air on CNN or MSNBC or ABC. Instead, the revealing sound bites ran back to back on 'The Daily Show With Jon Stewart.' The satiric Comedy Central program regularly unearths telling footage ignored or overlooked by the real news guys" (Paul Farhi, "It's Funny How Funny Just the Facts Can Be; 'Daily Show' Staffer Mines News for Laughs," *Washington Post*, April 30, 2008). Stewart, even though he continued to downplay his role in the public sphere as "just a comedian," never held back when it came to pronouncing his disdain for television news: "'Obama could cure cancer and [Fox news would] figure out a way to frame it as an economic disaster' . . . Stewart . . . declared his love for newspapers as a better source of political coverage but said they are fighting 'a losing battle because they're getting overshadowed'" (Howard Kurtz, "No Joke: Jon Stewart Takes Aim At 24-Hour Cable News 'Beast,'" *Washington Post*, August 26, 2008). However, television was not the only thing he criticized, saying that newspapers were better, but not without problems when it came to staying outside the political influence machine (and this kind of criticism of "access" journalism has come under intense criticism from media analysts during the Trump era). He apparently "touched a nerve when he criticized journalists for having off-the-record dinners with politicians . . . 'That colors your vision of them so clearly and so profoundly . . . the more you get sucked into it, the more you become part of that machinery.'" Although it is important that this was mentioned, there was not much reflexivity about it on the part of newspaper journalists.

## CONCLUSION: THE TRANSFORMATION
## AND ITS CONCRETIZATION

The 2008 election cycle shows the transformation that started taking place when the *Daily Show* premiered in 2000—not only a shift from personality-based humor to substantive satire, but also the journalists who wrote about it actively pointing it out and discussing how important it was to political discourse in general (Schudson 2011). Gone are the days of writers lamenting that people were getting their news from these sources. Early on, journalists acknowledged that (according to Pew and other studies) voters, especially younger ones, were increasingly receiving their news this way (Cao 2008, 2010). But that trend was always accompanied by ambivalence about the effect on democracy it could have (Jacobs 2012). Now, they worried that these same citizens would not be adequately informed when the shows suffered because of the writers' strike that made it difficult to produce the shows (Fox, Koloen, and Sahin 2007).

The humor on the programs started off with more personal jokes. But there was a transition from personal humor early on (mostly with respect to wide range of primary candidates) to more substantive jokes after that. Even the personality-based humor during the Primary phase of the election cycle was laced with substantive undertones. Regarding the economy, the splash that Fred Thompson made at first was quashed by jokes about him not understanding the seriousness of the economic problems the country was facing; this underlied the satire about him being an actor, old, not serious, and unintelligent. McCain managed to give all comedians an opening to mock him regarding the economy with the campaign suspension fiasco, and his snub of David Letterman. His campaign mishandled the response to economic crisis. The tactic failed to appear serious, and seemed as if it was a substitute for real action. Sarah Palin failed to perform legitimate, authoritative, knowledgeable political authenticity, both on and off the comedy programs. The parodies of her provided ample openings for journalists to hold up as an example of why she would not make a competent vice president, in both personal and substantive ways. More substantive humor throughout the campaign focused both on the economy, and the direction the country should take regarding terrorist threats and the wars. Stephen Colbert and Jon Stewart were likely to favor Obama, because he was the least hawkish of all the candidates, having not supported the War in Iraq in the first place. In this way, among others, they were able to shape political debates (Couldry 2006; Hesmondhalgh 2007). Here also, McCain failed to convey that his presidency would take the country in a different direction. And the early Republican Primary candidates were going against public opinion that the wars should be reined in, not expanded.

With respect to Hillary Clinton, personality-based humor focused more on her husband's former indiscretions, and not her directly. While there were few times her gender was attacked, Obama's perceived religious background and middle name were openly called into question. John McCain was being more rational than Sarah Palin; during a press conference, a woman asked him if Obama was an Arab, which demonstrated that the paranoia about his ethnic background was out in the open. However, he dealt with this situation in a prudent way. Yet at the same time, Palin was free to make all the insinuations about "palling around with terrorists" that she wanted. These racist dogwhistles were effective only to an extent; satire on the shows was easily able to call them out (Jones 2009, 2010). Journalists amplified the humor, and were able to use the characterization of Obama as un-American as irrational. Generally, the shows did not criticize Obama's policy positions, and only lightly mocked the way he talked or other relatively meaningless things. When he appeared on the programs, he was genuinely funny, but Clinton was a little defensive. Palin, when she appeared on *SNL*, did not seem genuine (Alexander 2010; Moy, Xenos, and Hess 2006).

Most critical humor about Clinton was directed at the conflict between her and Obama regarding the fight for the Democratic nomination. Journalists were concerned that this would hurt the party as a whole in the long run, and were able to use the criticisms that (especially Colbert and Stewart) were making about the way her campaign was acting, comparing the tactics to that of Karl Rove. Further, journalists were able to utilize the jokes on all the programs, especially *SNL*, about how the cable and network television news media was "in the tank" for Obama, thus making themselves look more reasonable. Even though Stewart made some specific criticisms that even newspaper journalists were too inside the system themselves, the writers in the *Post* and the *Times* were either able to gloss over them or ignore them completely, even though they had the opportunity to do otherwise (Borden and Tew 2007). Even after the failures of prominent newspaper journalism after 9/11 (McClennen 2012), journalists generally lacked the capacity to be reflexive about their own failings (Jacobs and Michaud Wild 2013).

While journalists once denigrated *SNL* as being vicious and essentially without substantive content, in 2008 they listen to it for narrative cues, and lauded Stewart and Colbert as being more competent political speakers than those on most television news. Peterson and Kern's (1996) concept of "cultural omnivorousness" is demonstrated in the journalists' developing attitudes about political comedy on television. This change can be attributed to several factors; that as new cohorts of journalists come into the forefront of deciding what is relevant political speech, they are bringing with them a liking for forms of culture that are not commonly considered meaningful in earlier periods; that the newer groups of people are "gentrify[ing] elements of popular culture and incorporat[ing] them into the dominant status-group culture" (906); and that forms of speech previously associated with "inferior" media, like late-night television comedy, are no longer so stigmatized as political sensibilities change. This idea can be linked to Katz and Lazarsfeld's (1955) analysis of opinion leaders. Sometimes, the new experts (like Stewart or Colbert) do not come from elite backgrounds, and open up the public sphere to alternative voices. This process really began in 2000, but solidified throughout the decade. Their contribution is necessary to expansion of public discourse, the kinds of voices who are allowed to speak, and ultimately increases the types of things that are allowed to be discussed. Katz and Lazarsfeld stated that one of their most important findings is that they found two types of influence:

> Formal media will influence mainly by representation or by indirect attraction . . . by what they tell. People, however, can influence both this way and by control. People can induce each other to a variety of activities as a result of their interpersonal relations and thus their influence goes far beyond the content of their communications. This is probably the most important reason why we have found the impact of personal contact to be greater than the impact of formal media. (185)

There are two main reasons why this may have changed. One is that direct, face-to-face, personal associations may have decreased, and may have been replaced by solitary media consumption (Putnam 2001). The second is that they really were too early to look at the influence of television, which may have a greater influence than print media or radio, at the very least since people's time engaged with that medium continues to increase. This is why voters need not have seen the Palin parody, for example, to have been influenced but it, and why the "Fey Effect" studies are unable to draw out the more interesting parts of how the political comedy/cultural sphere acts as a semi-autonomous, independent variable on the sphere of serious news journalism. There is evidence presented here for a direct influence of satire on television on journalists, and thus on the public sphere as well.

## NOTES

1. PBS NewsHour. 2008. "New Yorker Cover Satirizing Obama Raises Controversy." July 14. http://www.pbs.org/newshour/bb/politics-july-dec08-obamacover _07-14/.

2. Conservative *Washington Post* columnist Charles Krauthammer was the first to use this phrase in 2001 to refer to a number of things, including defensive first strike war and Bush's desire to "spread Democracy" in the Middle East and North Africa as a means to combat presumed Muslim extremism. He challenged Gibson's questioning of Palin about it, and even his understanding of it, in a *Post* article titled "Charlie Gibson's Gaffe," September 13, 2008. But whether or not Gibson understood it was not as important as whether or not Palin agreed with, or even understood the policy. This is what other journalists, and *SNL*, soon focused on.

# Conclusion

## The Structural Transformation
## of Political Humor

The research areas that this analysis addressed can be categorized into three main areas. The first is the question of how has political comedy on television in the United States changed over time; *SNL* has been a narrative force that has run through all of the political life of the United States since 1974. Perhaps being born in the Watergate era, arguably the most inherently ironic and satirizable political scandal of the twentieth century, set it on that path. The inclusion of a segment specifically for the mocking of the news of the day, and the fact that they continued that tradition, was the basis for later programs like the *Daily Show* and the *Colbert Report. SNL* was the only such semi-weekly place where this sort of direct news-desk style satire occurred. Academics and journalists wrote about the monologues of late-night talk shows as setting the tone for how Americans discussed politics, but often the hosts were only taking advantage of popular sentiment. *SNL* sketches allowed the actors on the show to specifically parody politicians. Yet there was a general divide between the two types of humor: sketches largely played on the personal characteristics of the figures and did not delve much into their policies, and "Weekend Update" jokes were often at least somewhat more substantive in content. And this is the way that political satire remained until the *Daily Show* came along.

There was equilibrium throughout the 1980s and 1990s where *SNL* in some ways helped maintain the political status quo. However, changes in the television industry provided a space for a more focused, substantive political satire that could be on four nights a week (at first for a half an hour, and then for an hour after the premier of *Colbert*). A few-minutes long "Weekend Update" segment during the normal season of *SNL* was no longer adequate. Right-wing talk radio and Fox News, which came to prominence during the

Clinton administration, did not have any kind of comparable left-wing response. The terrorist attacks and subsequent wars in 2001, when journalism seemed to abdicate its responsibility to provide adequate investigation and an alternative voice to what the presidential administration was saying, solidified the *Daily Show*'s place as an important place where citizens could see their own viewpoints represented, who were not seeing it many other places in the mainstream media. The *Colbert Report* brought this concept full circle, as a more direct parody of conservative cable news "talking heads" like Bill O'Reilly. *SNL* might have faded into irrelevance if it were not for the 2008 parody of Sarah Palin, which was much more substantive, as it directly addressed her lack of knowledge and questionable policy positions, as well as her more mockable personality characteristics.

The second question this work addressed was, what does exposure to political comedy do to journalism, and in turn, what effect does that have on citizens, voters, and politics? Initially, journalists broke into two separate camps regarding how they regarded the increasing influence of political comedy on discourse about elections. On one hand, there was a tendency to worry that entertainment and politics were becoming more alike, and that this would be damaging to the seriousness of the political process and democracy in general. On the other hand, this analysis revealed that many writers used the criticisms of the show when what they really wanted to say was too polemical or perhaps unprofessional; a direct quote from the comedian or sketch would often substitute for their own voice. In the earlier election cycles, journalists worried that jokes about a candidate's age, or potentially misleading representations of their earlier years as drug or alcohol users, or womanizers, would have an unfair impact on how voters perceived that candidate. However, this concern was largely unfounded, as the comedy was usually just going with the prevailing winds of public sentiment. Later, when the more substantive comedy emerged, the fears of getting informed from political comedy evaporated when it became apparent that what the shows were doing was often more hard-hitting and elucidating than what network and cable news accomplished throughout the 2000s (Jones 2004; Jacobs and Michaud Wild 2013). Even though Jon Stewart and Stephen Colbert in particular criticized newspaper journalism along the same lines, writers glossed over these issues and were not self-reflexive about their own complicities in this problem. They continue to largely ignore the criticisms levied against them, even after the 2016 election.

Although there were several studies that attempted to show the direct impact of Tina Fey's impression of Sarah Palin on *SNL* on the campaign (Baumgartner et al. 2012; Young 2011; Esralew and Young 2012; Young and Flowers 2010), and ultimately John McCain's loss, the results of them were often mixed and inconclusive. A more nuanced narrative analysis of newspaper commentary here shows that journalists were very influenced by it, and often used it as a shorthand for referring to the vice presidential candidate. It is difficult to measure the full effects of the Fey impression, but it appears that it had a diffuse and far-reaching influence. The male voters quoted talking about her in 2008 in the *Washington Post* may or may not have regarded her as a "dingbat" only from watching her poorly performed interviews. One effect of political comedy that empirical research shows is that people who watch are as informed as those who watch traditional news sources, and are those who are more informed are more politically engaged (Baumgartner and Morris 2006, 2007; Cao 2010; Cao and Brewer 2008; Cao 2008). This different way of talking about politics is more accessible to viewers, especially younger ones. The transformation of political comedy from sometimes lighthearted, sometimes relatively vicious personality-based jokes, into a resource for journalists and voters to call upon, to be better informed by, and to inject a dose of skepticism about candidates' claims and competencies, is evident in this analysis.

The third area that this study addressed is the question of why was the increase and discussion of critical perspectives in political comedy on television an important sociological issue. It is relevant because of what the discourse can and has contributed to civil society. As mentioned, the general failure of traditional journalism to fully inform the public and present alternate viewpoints after September 11, 2001, opened up a space in the public sphere that has been occupied by political comedy ever since. Criticizing, or even questioning, the Bush administration's policies in a "time of war" was seen as unpatriotic. Satire is not held to the same social norms as any other form of discourse; it can "get away with" things that serious discussions of politics cannot (Jones 2010). Ultimately, presenting differing viewpoints in a democratic society works in favor of rationality, and the silencing of them, whether overt or tacit, will eventually be seen as bad for civil society (Alexander 2006). Journalists certainly made these clams directly about the *Daily Show* and the *Colbert Report*.

Previous studies of political humor on television have focused on media effects and content analysis. Media effects have been regarded as either negative (mass distraction) or positive (increasing knowledge and civic engagement). The negative approaches have tended to be more theoretical than empirical, and were conducted at a time when the ways in which audiences gained political information (and acted on it) were in a state of transformation (R. L. Peterson 2008; Postman 1985), or focused more narrowly in the narratives of certain segments of a show rather than all of them taken as a whole (Day 2012; Shoemaker and Weinstein 1999). Now that the change over from getting political information from the trusted anchor on network news in the pre-deregulation era, to getting information from the more fractured and polarized landscape of talk radio, cable news, internet, and late-night political comedy programs had completed, a new study of how political comedy has permeated the narratives was necessary. More positive effects studies have tried to prove things like the "Fey Effect," where voters who watched Tina Fey's parody of Sarah Palin on *SNL* were shown to be slightly less likely to vote for her and had somewhat contradictory findings (Young and Flowers 2010; Baumgartner et al. 2012; Young 2011; Esralew and Young 2012). However, the effects were minimal, and did not take into account the influential outside judgments of opinion leaders in prestigious newspapers like the *Post* and the *Times* (Katz and Lazarsfeld 1955). If they were exposed to the parody, they passed it along to their readers who, in turn, need not have watched Fey's performance at all. Content analyses have centered on the idea of an intersubjective culture where all the media narratives collide (Jenkins 2008) and have positive effects on civic engagement (Jones 2004, 2010; Gray, Jones, and Thompson 2009); however, the process by which this occurs has not been shown prior to this study. In order to demonstrate empirically that the programs have had an intersubjective influence, there needed to be a close examination of the codes and narratives of the shows over time, and where and when their effects showed in the other sphere of mainstream journalism. In this way, there is a comprehensive and integrated look of the programs' salience increasing.

Three main areas of analysis of *SNL*, the *Daily Show*, and the *Colbert Report* show where the narratives became influential on mainstream journalism over time: what are the main codes in each election cycle; do the narratives become more substantive over the years, and if so, who do they mostly target; and how does *SNL* compare overall to the *Daily Show* and the *Colbert Report*. Generally, personal humor mostly targeted Democrats, while substantive mostly targeted Republicans. This can explain a great deal about why journalists took satirical commentary seriously after they began to recognize these trends and use them. As time went on, the shows transformed into more rational carriers of democratic codes than television news often did, and writers in the *Post* and *Times* were able to draw boundaries between themselves and network and cable news using the shows' increasingly critical satire (Jacobs 2012; Jacobs and Michaud Wild 2013). How, specifically, did these changes take place from 1980 to 2008?

The 1980 election cycle appeared more critical of Jimmy Carter; however, after Reagan had been in office for eight years, and even going forward in to 1988 when George H. W. Bush was running, *SNL* was more critical of the Republican candidates. This may have been a general trend of going after the incumbent party. In general, though, they mocked personality characteristics, with each election cycle being the majority of jokes that way, with 1984 having the greatest minority percentage of substantive jokes. Dan Quayle was the hallmark of 1980s *SNL* satire, being easily mocked for his verbal gaffes. When Ferraro ran, *SNL* only made jokes about her gender, and did not discuss her policy positions. The volume of political jokes increased dramatically from 1984 to 1988. Satire slanted in each year toward the Democrats; Republicans were held as being out of touch, and holding the best interests of the rich. The news media was satirized as being inept, dull, and gimmicky. The years of 1992 and 1996 were relatively similar to both each other and the previous cycles, in that jokes were also mostly personal and mostly favored Democrats; however the amount of jokes and sketches again increased from the 1980s. These years were focused on the style of the comedians delivering the jokes; Kevin Nealon's deadpan style and Norm MacDonald's over-the-top personal attacks (which eventually got him fired, even though they were often incisive) made the years reflect their unique voices. Jokes about voters being confused or uninformed entered the narrative. Iran-Contra and other scandals, as well as the infamous government shutdown were mentioned, but only briefly. The economy was the main topic of substantive humor, as the country recovered from the 1980s-era recessions, and *SNL* directly blamed Republican policies. Personal humor, about Dole's age, Ross Perot's strangeness, Quayle's culture wars attacks, and Bill Clinton's personal life, were the most memorable topics. All in all during these years, *SNL* did not particularly take sides. The anti-incumbency tone was gone, as Clinton had done a fairly good job in his first term. Late-night comedy on television during the 1992 and 1996 election cycles was characterized by a noticeable reliance upon personality-based humor at the expense of jokes about substantive issues. If the 1980s was typified by jokes about Ronald Reagan's age, that theme was repeated and greatly amplified in the 1990s by jokes about Bob Dole's age. The tawdriness of jokes about Bill Clinton's presumed sexual improprieties crept in as well (and this was before the Clinton/Lewinsky scandal). Newspaper commentary in the *New York Times* and the *Washington Post* often focused on the trend toward the occasionally vicious personal humor on the shows. This era included *SNL*, David Letterman, newcomer Conan O'Brien, the departure of Johnny Carson, and the rise of Jay Leno. But at the same time, journalists also began to take note of the public's increasing attention to these shows as a source of news. However, the journalists who wrote about it were unable or unwilling to understand why this change was beginning to occur; it was a trend that would only increase as time went on. The writers in the papers saw the comedy as boring, formulaic, and safe, which was not an entirely unfair assessment. In 1992, jokes about Dan Quayle's intelligence would be seen as hurting the Bush campaign (a foreshadowing of what happened with Sarah Palin in 2008). In 1996, journalists saw the constant harping on Bob Dole's age as hurting his campaign. Once his poll numbers began to slip, the jokes about him intensified. The jokes about Clinton's moral character, however, were seen as something he could more easily brush off, especially in the 1996 election cycle, since the economy was doing well.

The focus of political comedy on television really began to change in 2000, due to a three main factors; one, the shift on *SNL* away from the single comedy personality at the "Weekend Update" segment to a more gender diverse two-person delivery; two, the debut of the *Daily Show*, which quickly became an "alternative" news source for young voters; and three, the election dispute debacle, which made them all seem to take politics much more seriously, when it looked like corruption and cronyism would decide the outcome. Humor both increasingly began to favor the Democrats and become more substantive after this, and this trend would only advance after 9/11. On *SNL*, humor went from not really favoring any party, to favoring Democrats. Before the election dispute, *SNL* was most notable for the impression that Will Ferrell did of George W. Bush. His misstatements and garbled words became the go-to way of parodying him, but the satire was not critical or substantive enough to address his policies; thus journalists did not latch on to it as a narrative resource to criticize him in a meaningful way. His characterization as a "partier" in college was part of the past, and did not speak to his present competency. Bush was caricatures as the "dumb guy" and Gore as the "stiff guy," and neither were a particularly good choice. They were both wealthy and came from privileged educational backgrounds. The show even called back Dana Carvey, who had done the impression of the previous President Bush on *SNL*, a parody that was enjoyed by the man himself; thus, it did not elucidate any real concerns about his presidency. On the *Daily Show*, Bush was portrayed as unpleasant and petty, pointing out his appearance on Letterman's show as sarcastic and mean to the host who had recently had heart surgery. In terms of substantive concerns, Bush was shown as being confused about foreign policy and world leaders, and being hawkish, while Gore was satirized as having a confusing, jargon-laden, and overly simplistic economic policy.

After the election dispute, although it was a short period, *SNL* in particular moved from more personal to more substantive satire, which was critical of both the poorly handled resolution to the election, as well as a greater focus on how Bush's policies would affect the country if the election was decided in his favor. His intelligence was portrayed less as bumbling but harmless, to more of a serious detriment on his ability to govern effectively. The *Daily Show* utilized its technique of showing a politician speaking on several programs, and sticking to their talking points, by showing Gore going on several shows after the election and not being forceful enough in calling out the poor way that the resolution to the dispute was being handled. Overall, both shows made remarks about the serious problems that having the Supreme Court decide the election, rather than the voters, might have on democracy itself. A critical mass of substantive satire was achieved in the 2004 election cycle; the issues that were most prevalent on most network and cable news were also prevalent on political comedy shows, namely the questionable evidence that led the United States into war, the further escalation of it, the interminable length of the Primary, the negative rumors about Bush's time in the Air National Guard, the "Swiftboat" attacks against John Kerry, his reputation as indecisive, and both Bush and Kerry's past education at Yale. The latter was a point which all comedy programs took as the candidates failing to perform authenticity, including Bush's exaggeration of his Southern accent. There was also a great deal of infighting among the Democrats, portrayed by the comedy programs as hurting the party, a theme which would reemerge in 2008 (and again in 2016). There was a widening of the gap between substantive humor aimed at Republicans, and personal humor aimed at Democrats. Although it had a larger amount of jokes aimed at Democrats, there was an even stronger division along those lines on the *Daily Show*, which was further entrenched as a source of reliable political information.

By 2008, the *Daily Show* was in a position to set the tone for the way that many journalists talked about politics; later, after the nomination of Sarah Palin, *SNL* became a significant part of this process as well. The addition of Stephen Colbert's show to the way politics was discussed added to the importance of the programs—after the 2006 White House Correspondents' Dinner, where he, in a satirical manner, openly criticized George W. Bush's foreign policy in front of him, Colbert began to be taken very seriously. His satire also focused on being critical of the media and its failings, as the character he was playing was a direct parody of conservative Fox News pundits such as Bill O'Reilly. The addition of Colbert's parody of him and people like him highlighted the absurdity of conservative media "talking heads" who were more bluster than substance. Humor on the *Daily Show* and *Colbert* in 2008 was more strongly polemical, favoring Democrats, then on *SNL* which was slightly more neutral, until Sarah Palin was selected. On all the shows, substantive humor was mostly directed against the Republicans. Personal humor was most evident in the beginning of the election, and was directed against both parties' candidates, since there was a large, open field of candidates, many of whom had very pro-war beliefs (on the Republican side) or were unlikely to gain a lot of popular support (on the Democratic side).

Later, after Barack Obama and Hillary Clinton became Democratic frontrunners, humor focused on race, religion, and gender, issues that were specifically treated one-dimensionally by the news media, which the shows additionally made fun of. Cable and network news journalists were parodied, specifically on SNL, as being uncritical of Obama, while going after Clinton, and once they did enough jokes and sketches about this, television news journalists responded to that criticism; newspaper journalists then pointed to the irony of a comedy program giving the more polluted sphere of television news a wake-up call. Infighting between the Democratic candidates, which almost led to a contested Primary, was especially satirized on *Colbert*. Later, criticism of how Republicans treated Obama's race and religion were critically parodied on the shows, making evident the racism that underlied them. On the Republican side, the two most substantive issues discussed were foreign policy, as all the shows firmly came out against escalating the wars, which the Republican candidates wanted to do, and the economy, especially later on. John McCain's decision to "suspend his campaign" was viciously mocked as a campaign tactic, rather than an honest attempt to do anything that might help, and hurt his performance as a competent politician. The choice of Sarah Palin also hurt his image, as she was clearly not ready to take on the second most powerful role in the government. The Republicans were portrayed on the comedy shows as making emotional, rather than rational appeals to win the campaign.

In order to demonstrate how the shows' narratives became influential on the journalistic public sphere, this analysis looked at how cultural performances by speakers in the cultural sphere, using the method of writing and on television programs, directly influenced thought in spheres outside of them. As demonstrated above, the "democratic code" (Alexander and Smith 2005) is seen in political communication in the public sphere of late-night television political comedy. "The resulting binary codes mark out and classify the world, defining and evaluating in terms of the sacred and the profane the motivations, relationships, and institutions that are to be sought out, or avoided" (14). Debates about whether or not the political actors and their policies and performances were believable and genuine were sparked, furthered, and enhanced by the shows. The things the programs and the speakers on them discussed, parodied, and satirized, show the "struggles for inclusion and legitimacy [which] involve efforts to claim rational status, and efforts to discredit and debunk others depend upon the application of labels from a negatively coded list of psychological attributes" (15), such as competency, authenticity, and rationality. In the analyses of the changing way this was discussed in the sphere of serious news journalism, it is evident that it has shaped the discourse of civil society. The next section discusses the specific ways in which this has occurred over the years.

## JOURNALISTS' EVOLVING NOTIONS
## OF TELEVISION POLITICAL COMEDY

This study deals with specific cases in each election cycle that show how late-night comedy has become a meaningful force in contemporary political discourse. It has demonstrated this change in four specific areas in how it is discussed in the larger public sphere: journalists' increasing tendency to refer back to the incidents, people, or policies parodies or discussed on the comedy programs as relevant topics of discussion; journalists' increasing reliance on the perspectives presented on the shows to stand in for their own opinions; discussions of the increase in candidates appearing on the programs and the need for them to successfully perform political competency while at the same time being able to laugh at themselves; and the transformation of a more personality-based way of being critical about the candidates to a more substantive way of contending with them, and journalists' recognition of this phenomenon as important. The change demonstrates that the programs are in line with the "democratic code" of rational, evidence-based judgments that can help shape opinion, and thus cultural autonomy, enabling the actors on the programs "to play a key role in the determination of political outcomes" (Alexander and Smith 2005).

This realization builds slowly over these eight election cycles. Starting in 1980, there was a centrality of Johnny Carson's monologue as a "bellwether" for what the citizens and voters were most likely to be most concerned with that the time. *SNL* was not considered by journalists to be on the same level. It was discussed as being crude and unnecessarily mean, and was said to potentially have an overall negative impact on younger reporters who were more likely to be attracted to it, rather than the more mature and staid comedy of Carson, in comparison. *SNL* was said to portray candidates in an undignified way. In 1984, Carson was a little off the mark about Reagan, who Carson seemed to find uninspiring, but who won in a landslide; however, journalists were also wrong, because they largely agreed with him. The people were not as willing to accept any portrayal of Reagan as old and forgetful, and this year saw a general disconnect between the journalists' appraisal of the shows, and what the voters actually did. A more rich resource of candidates in both parties that could be mocked for things that journalists and the public more readily accepted came in 1988, now that the field was open after Reagan could no longer be reelected. Dan Quayle became the standard by which *SNL* and late-night talk show hosts could mock someone for not being very smart, and not because they were just getting old. Gary Hart's indiscretions and Joe Biden being accused of plagiarism and dissembling about his accomplishments were things that the comedy could easily satirize, and journalists could readily utilize these narratives. Journalists began to realize that once a negative satirical portrayal caught on, it was difficult to shake off, in the modern media landscape where so many people would see it and discuss it with one another. But this force was not in this decade regarded by journalists as a major factor in the success or failure of a candidate, but rather only a contributing one. The election cycle of 1992, with respect to political comedy, was almost entirely overshadowed by third-party candidate Ross Perot. Journalists latched on to *SNL*'s portrayal of him as changeable and generally bizarre, and his running mate as old and confused. Dan Quayle remained as a prime target, with his spelling gaffe and strange criticisms of popular culture. Journalists began to realize that people were gaining more knowledge about political campaigns from the monologues and sketches, but they did not do much more than recognize the growing phenomenon. The 1996 election cycle saw a return to more traditional and nearly exclusive attacks on Republican candidates, a phenomenon that would continue into the next century, and be one which journalists would have a greater reliance upon using as a narrative resource. In particular, Norm MacDonald's parody of Dole on *SNL* was seen more in terms of his temper, rather than in terms of making fun of him for his age, as in the prior case of Reagan. Clinton's alleged sexual proclivities, "draft-dodging," and drug use were also satirized, but journalists focused on them less, a theme that would recur when journalists did not buy into the show's humor about George W. Bush along similar lines. In 1996, journalists mentioned for the first time a Pew Research poll that gave empirical data about how many voters were getting their news from late-night comedy. They would continue to mention such polls in future election cycles as evidence that entertainment and news were converging; later, they would use such data as evidence that the shows were having a positive effect on democracy by informing parts of the public who might not get information otherwise.

A change takes place in 2000. There is a continuation of the tendency for journalists to place greater importance on television comedy's impact on the narratives about the candidates and the elections, but they were not certain or unified about what that impact is or how great it was. There was still a focus on *SNL* and late-night talk show hosts' monologues, but they did not particularly include the new *Daily Show* as much of a part of this. There was lamentation about the confluence of news and entertainment on one hand, and recognition of the possibility that greater engagement with politics through a more accessible medium like comedy could be good for civic engagement on the other; one has to be at least a little informed in order to get the jokes, after all. Journalists quoted political campaigns who said they believed political comedy's influence was growing. This was the general tone throughout most the election cycle; however, the stakes changed after the election was disputed and went to the Supreme Court, and journalists recognized that the comedy programs were uniquely positioned to highlight the absurdity of it all. After other events in this decade, this new niche for political comedy would only deepen. By 2004, the divide in the country was deep, and the comedy shows reflected it. In particular, the *Daily Show* was increasingly critical of not just politics, but of the media's role in it. Satire had taken up the role of calling out the administration where mainstream news failed; newspaper writers pointed to this, while at the same time failing to recognize their complicity in it. They focused instead on things like the infamous *Crossfire* appearance by Jon Stewart, where he said the poor quality of debate had harmed America and democracy. Instead of complaining that Americans were getting their news from the programs, there was recognition that it was better than the one-sided, generally pro-administration viewpoint people were getting from television and cable news. Young voters were leaving the traditional media sourced behind, reflected in new 2004 Pew numbers. Stewart as the new Cronkite did not sit well with the comedian, but it did with most of the journalists. By the time of the 2008 presidential election, there was little concern on the part of journalists that that political comedy could have any negative effects on democracy. The *Daily Show* was seen as more reliable than mainstream television news; it had its own agenda, which was one of exposing falsehoods and making connections between the various things politicians said at one moment versus the things that they might say in another, to serve their own interests rather than be honest. Gone was the ambivalence of journalists toward political comedy; it had proven itself as an important informational resource, and a new moral compass. Journalists worried that the writers' strike could disrupt this.

Another way in which the shows had an influence on the public sphere, and journalism in particular, is when writers over the years have used direct or paraphrased quotes from the programs to represent their own opinions; this was the especially the case when their views were polemical, controversial, or reflected their critical views of television news. As with every other interpretation of what was happening with political comedy on late-night television, this factor evolved over the years from a few brief mentions to an all-out usage of a satirical portrayal as shorthand for the writers to use. Going back to the 1980 election cycle, there was still a favoring of Carson over anything else. Perhaps because of Carson's respected place in popular culture, writers privileged his views about then-candidate Ronald Reagan and failed to see how popular he was with so many voters. In 1984, Carson was once again prescient, and the journalists had stayed with him as a predictor of how elections might go, as Carson essentially predicted that Gary Hart would win the New Hampshire Primary over Walter Mondale; but even so, this was a minor thing, considering Mondale would go on to win the nomination. Carson's opinions were no longer in line with the electorate, and this provided an opening for other late-night programs, like *SNL*, to replace him as a bellwether. And this proved to be the case; journalists were more likely to quote more varied sources after this election cycle, including David Letterman and *SNL*. Jokes about the competency of Dan Quayle (which would be echoed later in journalists utilizing *SNL* as a narrative resource about Sarah Palin) where the writers quoted comedians were frequent in 1988. These were typically ways that the journalists could get away with making remarks about the personal characteristics of the candidates however, and more substantive criticisms would occur later. But in 1988, besides Quayle, it was all about the appearances of the candidates as competent political actors. On the Republican side, there was George H. W. Bush's "wimp factor" which shows mocked, and on the Democratic side, there was Dukakis trying to appear tough by riding a tank which backfired, and his "boringness" which the shows mocked and the writers picked up on. Dan Quayle continued to be a subject from which journalists drew direct quotes from the satires of him. By this time, he'd had his "potato" spelling gaffe incident, as well as his ridiculous escalation of the culture wars by criticizing the life choices of a fictional television character. The election was close, and Bush's campaign could not afford such negative publicity. Journalists who didn't want them to win had extra ammunition provided by Quayle, and enhanced by ready-made commentary on the comedy shows. Additionally, the 1996 election cycle saw many quotations about the extremism of Pat Buchanan from the late-night shows.

The next three election cycles marked a turning point with the relationship between journalism and the late-night comedy programs. The *Daily Show* premiered, and although in 2000, journalists were skeptical of how normatively positive its influence was, they recognized it; but they were slow to adopt it as an important source to quote, still relying more on the talk show format programs and *SNL*. Even at this time, though, cable and network news programs were using clips of it; it is likely that the journalists did not want to align themselves with the more polluted format of television. By 2004, the reluctance to use observations from Jon Stewart had decreased dramatically, due to the disputed election and the terrorist attacks and subsequent wars. There emerged a strong division between the kind of commentary that the *Daily Show* did, which was a substantive, utilizable source of criticism, and the type of things that other late-night comedians did, which tended to be more personal in nature. For Stewart, Bush was untrustworthy and lied about events occurring in the Middle East in order to get the country into a war. Many were of the opinion by this time that Bush was not smart enough to be president, and the humor about him shifted from just making fun of the way he talked, to the fear that he was unqualified to be president. This marked a distinction for journalists in the type of humor talk show hosts like Leno would use, compared to the more substantive *Daily Show*. By the 2008 election cycle, journalists in the *Post* and the *Times* were frequently as concerned as Stewart, Colbert, and possibly the writers on *SNL* that if Republicans won, the country would become more hawkish, and later displayed worry that if McCain won, the unqualified Sarah Palin would be second in line for the presidency, echoing former concerns about Bush. The way that *SNL* portrayed Palin became the stand-in for the way that the journalists discussed her, almost as if they were relieved another area of the public sphere was finally seeing the things they were, and the voting public was actually listening.

Politicians went from hardly ever appearing on late-night talk shows and *SNL* in the 1980s, to appearing on them regularly in 2008. Third-party candidate John Anderson's appearance on *SNL* was met with mixed feelings; when Jesse Jackson appeared in 1984, it was discussed, but there was not much impact associated with it. Generally it was not seen as necessary to gain exposure, and was regarded as part of the cheapening of democracy that came with the conflation of entertainment and politics (especially by Tom Shales in the 1990s, although even he came around to seeing it as necessary). Sometimes, the wives of the candidates would go on the shows for them, as Elizabeth Dole did on 1996 when she went on Leno's and Letterman's shows to make Bob Dole seem like a more relatable person; and as Michelle Obama did in 2008 on the *Colbert Report* to counter Barack Obama's image as too serious or elitist. This option was not available to Hillary Clinton, as jokes about her husband were still a staple of the shows. Candidates throughout the 1980s and 1990s election cycles went on the shows to seem more down-to-earth, but these appearances created the precedent that it was necessary to do so, and part of the overall performance of competency as a politicians and potential leader; after all, if they couldn't take some good-natured ribbing on *SNL* or a talk show couch, how well would they perform under the pressures of the presidency?

On such example of a failure was in the 2000 election, when George W. Bush appeared on Letterman's show, and seemed to insult him. He appeared mean-spirited and unfunny. He recovered, appearing on Leno later on, but the subsequent appearance was analyzed in comparison with his past failure. Even though it did not cost him the election, he did not appear on any of the programs in 2004 when he was running for reelection. Overall, though, appearances on late-night comedy programs were beginning to be seen by the journalists as a part of the fabric of the campaign, and becoming unremarkable and even mundane. There was risk in appearing foolish, but greater risk in appearing unable to be in on the joke; but for the writers, it meant that the shows were becoming co-opted at the same time. As the *Daily Show* became more accepted and "hip," the appearance of the self-deprecating candidate became a known quantity. Still, the candidate as "real" was epitomized in 2008 by Barack Obama; although it gave his critics an opening to call him a mere celebrity, it had an overall positive effect. More stiff or "wooden" candidates like Kerry, Gore, and McCain were at a distinct disadvantage, recognized by the journalists (a factor which contributed to Trump's success). Bush never even attempted to take up the Stewart challenge, and the papers pointed this out in 2004. In 2008, late-night comedy show appearances were influential and arguably as important as news program interviews. Hillary Clinton's appearance on the *Daily Show* then was said to have revived her primary candidacy, at least temporarily. Notable failures that journalists discussed in 2008 included Sarah Palin appearing on *SNL*, and not looking comfortable about it; but John McCain's failure to appear on Letterman's show, lying about why he had to cancel, and then later going on to apologize after David Letterman mocked him mercilessly showed how powerful these appearances could be.

The transformation from personal to substantive humor on late-night comedy has been thoroughly demonstrated; journalists' recognition of it is a phenomenon that needed more close examination to understand how political comedy on television became more influential in the public sphere. In the 1980s, critical satire was almost nonexistent on television, most likely because of how it had failed to stay on network TV in the 1970s. The *Times* quoted satirists like Mort Sahl as describing its low point, following prevailing political winds rather than leading. Voters would take it as part of the general milieu of impressions of politicians' personalities, and would be unlikely to be influenced, only solidifying opinions they already held. Entertainment was polluting news. *SNL* was part of this process as well, mostly sticking to making fun of the candidates' personalities rather than addressing their policies. There was little change from this mode in the 1990s, as the shows reinforced certain images of candidates being sexually promiscuous (like Hart, Clinton, and Kennedy), not very intelligent (like Dan Quayle), mentally unstable (like Ross Perot or Jerry Brown), or angry (like Bob Dole). Journalists regarded these personality-based parodies and jokes as solidifying impressions that viewers already had about the candidates. Journalists in the *Post* and *Times* were either ambivalent about the state of political comedy on television, or downright hostile to it, not believing it was particularly funny. The 2000 election cycle was where this trend began to change; at first, the election went similarly to all the previous ones. The programs mocked the personality characteristics of the candidates; Gore was boring and Bush was the guy who mispronounced words, and journalists really didn't fully buy either representation.

There was some acknowledgment by journalists that the *Daily Show* was taking things in a different, more substantive direction. Only after the election was disputed in Florida did journalists begin to more frequently take note of the fact that the comedy programs pointing out how ridiculous the situation was, and acknowledge that politics had become so absurd, the only appropriate response to it was through humor; while at the same time, the shows became more substantive themselves, perhaps realizing what was at stake.

The next two election cycles, with journalists depending upon quotes and ideas from the shows (especially from Stewart and later Colbert), show the importance of the critical, substantive comedy on the public sphere. Remarks about Bush's intelligence were less likely to be about his old days a partier or his speech patterns, and more likely to be about his actual competency and seriousness as a leader who did not have good intelligence coming from his advisors. The divergence between the *Daily Show* and Jay Leno, for example was more and more apparent. Leno kept doing frat jokes, and Stewart (and Letterman) was calling into question the administration's connections with Halliburton. However, despite all of this, both the programs and the journalists saw little substantive difference between Bush, Kerry, and Lieberman, in terms of their rhetoric. Other shows simply focused on Kerry and Bush's similar Yale backgrounds, which were not as important; journalists characterized *SNL* as falling into the latter type of more personality-based jokes. There was a recognition that the *Daily Show* was making real issues accessible to viewers in ways that television news often did not, and in ways that other late-night programs did not attempt to do. Journalists also used the shows' critical satire of the television news media to make the point that cable and network news were more openly hard on Hillary Clinton and treated Barack Obama more delicately.

In 2008, journalists were even stronger about their opinions that people were getting better information from the shows than television news. Specifically, writers in the *Post* and the *Times* pointed to the fact that news media in general had failed to adequately question Republicans' claims in the wake of 9/11, and addressed that fact that the *Daily Show* and the *Colbert Report* were filling this role. Stewart and Colbert were pointing out hypocrisy. They recognized that the programs favored Obama over McCain, and Democrats over Republicans, specifically because they wanted to take the country away from war, and not toward it, as Republican candidates early on in the election cycle appeared to openly want to do. Further, journalists believed that the difference between Palin and Bush in previous election cycles was that Bush was difficult to satirize, because he was essentially self-parodying, whereas satire of Palin had to be carefully cultivated, and focused on critiques of her policy positions and competency rather than just her personality.

## SATIRE'S IMPACT AND AVENUES
## OF FUTURE RESEARCH

This study shows that the *Daily Show* may have had a direct impact on *SNL*, and it becoming more substantive in its criticism by 2008; the general direction of political comedy was undoubtedly pushed this way by Stewart's program. They raised the bar, even if they did not want to acknowledge that this was what they were doing. It is logical to assume that *SNL* risked becoming irrelevant if they did not do something different, judging by how negatively journalists saw the program in the 1980s and 1990s. The unfavorable tone reversed completely by the 2008 election, as journalists began to speak of comedians as meaningful political analysts. As discussed in the chapter about 2008, the programs, their writers, and their personalities had become opinion leaders to the journalists, thus directing the course of public opinion (Katz and Lazarsfeld 1955). Commentators criticized cable and network television after 9/11 and the crisis of the 2000 election, opening up opportunities for new avenues of information that were less formal and more culturally driven. Journalists eventually caught on to this and accepted it as part of the informative media landscape. They themselves followed the trend of cultural omnivorousness, which meant that once-denigrated forms of culture were now more acceptable for elite consumers to refer back to as relevant (Peterson and Kern 1996). These changes were driven in part by developments in the news media as an industry—a greater number of choices did not always increase its quality—and in part by broad cultural factors as outlined above. As a result, journalists transferred their dislike of the once-polluted category of late-night comedy on television, most evident throughout the 1980s and 1990s, to the sphere of cable and network news journalism. It may be fair to say that the sphere of entertainment/satirical news programs have transferred from a polluted category to a semi-polluted one (Jacobs 2012); where journalists once vilified it as being a totally corrupting force on rational debate, as Putnam (2001) would argue, they transformed their discussion of it to conform more to what Schudson (2011) would argue—that politics is everywhere, and the shows are following this general trend.

As the jokes began to be aimed at substantive issues like candidates' knowledge, policy issues, overall ability to be effective politicians, and their authenticity as performing real competency, in contrast to relatively meaningless personal characteristics, journalists recognized that the shows were often more rational than television news. Additionally, humor itself is more accessible than the often polemical and drier presentations of traditional news (O'Rourke III and Rodrigues 2004). The shows can thus direct narratives outside of their own sphere (Couldry 2006; Hesmondhalgh 2007). These non-traditional sources of deliberation carved a place for themselves in the contemporary public sphere that follow Habermasian critical-rational guidelines, but do not strictly adhere to them. This study used the *New York Times* and the *Washington Post* as indicators of mainstream journalism; however, during this time, cable and network news also used clips of the comedy programs to back up their points or demonstrate them in different ways. Future research could include a study of these instances on various television programs. Further, an Annenberg study showed that individuals who watched Colbert were better informed about an important substantive political issue, namely super PACS (Hardy et al. 2014); other issues could be studied in similar ways. With Stephen Colbert moving to take over the *Late Show* on CBS, and abandoning his Swift-esque character, a subsequent study could analyze this program in comparison to others like it. Some political figures are perhaps more susceptible to satire than others. Donald Trump for example was not a political figure before his election in 2016, and thus may not have been subject to the same kinds of processes that were effective in satirizing traditional politicians. Additionally, how does TV news contend with the fact that they are often being mocked on these programs, while simultaneously using their clips? Further, TV news reporters, such as NBC *Nightly News'* Brian Williams, often appeared on the *Daily Show*. How might this fit into the wider media landscape? Do the media figures themselves, who are often being criticized, need to be in on the joke as well?

# Methods

This book contains two main types of analysis looking at two main sources of data. The first is a content analysis of some late-night comedy programs during the presidential election cycles, and the second is a narrative analysis of journalistic commentary on political humor on television during the same time periods. "Election cycle" in this case is the dates between the date of the first televised primary to nominate a candidate, to the election (with the exception of the 2000 election; here, the election cycle extends to the date of Al Gore's concession). "Late-night political comedy on television" consists of all mentions of evening talk shows on broadcast or basic cable, in the tradition of Johnny Carson, as well as *SNL*, the *Daily Show*, and the *Colbert Report*. After the influence of substantive satire on the *Daily Show* and the *Colbert Report* became widespread and critically recognized, through prizes like the Peabody and Television Critics Association awards, airplay of clips on "serious" news sources such as the NBC *Nightly News*, and a great deal of commentary in "serious" newspapers such as the *Washington Post* and the *New York Times* (Jacobs and Michaud Wild 2013), even the once-simplistic parodies of *Saturday Night Live* and character-based humor on hosted shows such as *The Late Show with David Letterman* became much more bitingly satirical and influential themselves, and writers in the newspapers talked about this. The attention to analysis of the two major newspapers shows the development and progression over time where programs like *This Week* on ABC and news coverage of major events on CNN and HLN often include clips of late-night political comedy.

The content analysis section of the project focuses on three programs: *SNL*, the *Daily Show*, and the *Colbert Report*. There are a total of 146 original *SNL* episodes throughout all the campaign cycles. A simple keyword search was conducted to identify each sketch that has relevance to the ongoing presidential election for each cycle. There are three election cycles that the *Daily Show* was on the air in the midst of, totaling 642 episodes: 2000 (176 episodes), 2004 (238 episodes), and 2008 (227 episodes). Guest interview portions of these shows are excluded for the purposes of this analysis; doing so makes this program more comparable to *SNL*, which does not have guest interviews (as on the *Tonight Show* or the *Late Show*). In general, prior to the guest interview segment on the *Daily Show*, two to four stories are addressed in one or two segments. Each story segment is treated as a separate unit of analysis. This yields an approximate number of 2,000 potentially relevant segments about the election. Of course, not all items are pertinent to the election, but 175 relevant segments are included for analysis, or slightly less than 10 percent of the overall sample, through simple random sampling. Using a similar method for the *Colbert Report*, which broadcast 225 episodes during the 2008 election cycle (the first cycle it was being produced), 22 episodes are included in the sample, and 50 relevant segments.

The journalistic commentary portion included all available content on LexisNexis from the *New York Times* and the *Washington Post*. While there are some mentions of political comedy on television in other sources available in the database, such as from the *Christian Science Monitor*, and network and cable news sources, the vast majority of the commentary that provides any in-depth discussion at all is located in the two major newspapers. Additionally, these newspapers are arguably the most influential published news sources in the United States. Instances of journalistic commentary about late-night political comedy on television are included during each election cycle from 1980 to 2008. Previous research (Jacobs and Michaud Wild 2013) has shown that writers for the *New York Times* and the *Washington Post*, when they agree with the critical standpoints of the *Colbert Report* and the *Daily Show*, often use commentary and direct quotes to make or bolster a critical argument that may reflect their own viewpoint.

# Bibliography

Alexander, Jeffrey C. 2004. "Cultural Pragmatics: Social Performance between Ritual and Strategy." *Sociological Theory* 22 (4): 527–73.

———. 2006. *The Civil Sphere*. New York: Oxford University Press.

———. 2010. *The Performance of Politics: Obama's Victory and the Democratic Struggle for Power*. New York: Oxford University Press.

Alexander, Jeffrey C., Bernhard Giesen, and Jason L. Mast, eds. 2006. *Social Performance: Symbolic Action, Cultural Pragmatics, and Ritual*. Cambridge, England; New York: Cambridge University Press.

Alexander, Jeffrey C., and Philip Smith. 2005. *The Meanings of Social Life: A Cultural Sociology*. New York: Oxford University Press.

Back, Les, Andy Bennett, Laura Desfor Edles, David Inglis, Ronald N. Jacobs, and Ian Woodward. 2012. *Cultural Sociology: An Introduction*. Hoboken, NJ: Wiley-Blackwell.

Bakhtin, Mikhail. 1968. *Rabelais and His World*. Cambridge, MA: The MIT Press.

Baumgartner, Jody C., Jonathan S. Morris, and Nathan L. Walth. 2012. "The Fey Effect: Young Adults, Political Humor, and Perceptions of Sarah Palin in the 2008 Presidential Election Campaign." *Public Opinion Quarterly* 76 (1): 95–104.

Baumgartner, Jody, and Jonathan S. Morris. 2006. "The Daily Show Effect: Candidate Evaluations, Efficacy, and American Youth." *American Politics Research* 34 (3): 341–67.

———. 2007. *Laughing Matters: Humor and American Politics in the Media Age*. New York: Routledge.

Bianculli, David. 2009. *Dangerously Funny: The Uncensored Story of "The Smothers Brothers Comedy Hour."* New York: Touchstone.

Borden, Sandra L., and Chad Tew. 2007. "The Role of Journalist and the Performance of Journalism: Ethical Lessons From 'Fake' News (Seriously)." *Journal of Mass Media Ethics* 22: 300–14.

Calavita, Marco. 2004. "Idealization, Inspiration, Irony: Popular Communication Tastes and Practices in the Individual Political Development of Generation X'ers." *Popular Communication* 2: 129–51.

Cao, Xiaoxia. 2008. "Political Comedy Shows and Knowledge About Primary Campaigns: The Moderating Effects of Age and Education." *Mass Communication and Society* 11: 43–61.

———. 2010. "Hearing It from Jon Stewart: The Impact of the Daily Show on Public Attentiveness to Politics." *International Journal of Public Opinion Research* 22 (1): 26–46.

Cao, Xiaoxia, and Paul Brewer. 2008. "Political Comedy Shows and Public Participation in Politics." *International Journal of Public Opinion Research* 20 (1): 90–99.

Couldry, Nick. 2006a. *Listening Beyond the Echoes: Media, Ethics, and Agency in an Uncertain World*. Boulder, CO: Paradigm Publishers.

———. 2006b. *Listening Beyond the Echoes: Media, Ethics, and Agency in an Uncertain World*. Boulder, CO: Paradigm Publishers.

Dannagal G. Young. 2011. "Political Entertainment and the Press' Construction of Sarah Feylin." *Popular Communication* 9: 251–65.

Day, Amber. 2012. "Live From New York, It's the Fake News! Saturday Night Live and the (Non)Politics of Parody." *Popular Communication* 10: 170–82.

Delli Carpini, Michael, and Bruce Williams. 2001. "Let Us Infotain You: Politics in the New Media Age." *Departmental Papers (ASC)*, January. http://repository.upenn.edu/asc_papers/14.

Esralew, Sarah, and Dannagal Goldthwaite Young. 2012. "The Influence of Parodies on Mental Models: Exploring the Tina Fey–Sarah Palin Phenomenon." *Communication Quarterly* 60 (3): 338–52.

Feldman, Lauren. 2007. "The News about Comedy: Young Audiences, the Daily Show, and Evolving Notions of Journalism." *Journalism* 8 (4): 406–27.

Feldman, Lauren, and Dannagal Goldthwaite Young. 2008. "Late-Night Comedy as a Gateway to Traditional News: An Analysis of Time Trends in News Attention Among Late-Night Comedy Viewers During the 2004 Presidential Primaries." *Political Communication* 25 (4): 401–22.

Fox, Julia R., Glory Koloen, and Volkan Sahin. 2007. "No Joke: A Comparison of Substance in The Daily Show With Jon Stewart and Broadcast Network Television Coverage of the 2004 Presidential Election Campaign." *Journal of Broadcasting and Electronic Media* 51: 213–27.

Gray, Jonathan, Jeffrey P. Jones, and Ethan Thompson. 2009. *Satire TV: Politics and Comedy in the Post-Network Era*. New York: NYU Press.

Hardy, Bruce W., Jeffrey A. Gottfried, Kenneth M. Winneg, and Kathleen Hall Jamieson. 2014. "Stephen Colbert's Civics Lesson: How Colbert Super PAC Taught Viewers about Campaign Finance." *Mass Communication and Society* 17 (3): 329–53.

Hesmondhalgh, David. 2007. *The Cultural Industries*. Thousand Oaks, CA: Sage Publications Ltd.

Hewison, Robert. 1981. *Monty Python: The Case Against*. London: Methuen Publishing Ltd.

Hollander, Barry A. 2005. "Late-Night Learning: Do Entertainment Programs Increase Political Campaign Knowledge For Young Viewers?" *Journal of Broadcasting and Electronic Media* 49: 402–15.

Jacobs, Ronald N. 2012. "Entertainment Media and the Aesthetic Public Sphere." In *The Oxford Handbook of Cultural Sociology*, edited by Jeffrey C. Alexander, Ronald Jacobs, and Philip Smith. New York: Oxford University Press.

Jacobs, Ronald N., and Nickie Michaud Wild. 2013. "A Cultural Sociology of the Daily Show and the Colbert Report." *American Journal of Cultural Sociology* 1: 69–95.

Jacobs, Ronald N., and Eleanor Townsley. 2011. *The Space of Opinion: Media Intellectuals and the Public Sphere*. New York: Oxford University Press.

Jenkins, Henry. 2008. *Convergence Culture: Where Old and New Media Collide*. New York: NYU Press.

Jones, Jeffrey P. 2004. *Entertaining Politics: New Political Television and Civic Culture*. Lanham, MD: Rowman & Littlefield Publishing Group, Inc.

———. 2009. *Entertaining Politics: Satiric Television and Political Engagement*. Lanham, MD: Rowman & Littlefield Publishing Group, Inc.

———. 2010. "More than 'Fart Noises' and 'Funny Faces': The Daily Show's Coverage of the U.S. Recession." *Political Communication* 8: 165–69.

Katz, Elihu, and Paul F. Lazarsfeld. 1955. *Personal Influence: The Part Played by People in the Flow of Mass Communications*. New Brunswick, NJ: Transaction Publishers.

LaMarre, Heather L., Kristen D. Landreville, and Michael A. Beam. 2009. "The Irony of Satire: Political Ideology and the Motivation to See What You Want to See in the Colbert Report." *The International Journal of Press/Politics* 14 (2): 212–31.

Larson, Magali Sarfatti, and Douglas Porpora. 2011. "The Resistible Rise of Sarah Palin: Continuity and Paradox in the American Right Wing." *Sociological Forum* 26 (4): 754–78.

MacNaughton, Ian. 1974. "Mr. Neutron." *Monty Python's Flying Circus*. London: British Broadcasting Corporation.

McClennen, Sophia A. 2012. *Colbert's America: Satire and Democracy*. New York: Palgrave Macmillan.

Moy, Patricia, Michael A. Xenos, and Verena K. Hess. 2006. "Priming Effects of Late-Night Comedy." *International Journal of Public Opinion Research* 18 (2): 198–210.

Niven, Daniel, S. Robert Lichter, and Dan Amundson. 2003. "The Political Content of Late Night Comedy." *Harvard International Journal of Press/Politics* 8: 118–33.

O'Rourke III, Daniel J., and Pravin A. Rodrigues. 2004. "The Onion's Call for Healing." *Society* 42 (1): 19–27.

Ozersky, Josh. 2003. *Archie Bunker's America: TV in an Era of Change, 1968–1978*. Carbondale, IL: SIU Press.

Peterson, Richard A., and Roger M. Kern. 1996a. "Changing Highbrow Taste: From Snob to Omnivore." *American Sociological Review* 61 (5): 900–7.

———. 1996b. "Changing Highbrow Taste: From Snob to Omnivore." *American Sociological Review* 61: 900–7.

Peterson, Russell L. 2008. *Strange Bedfellows: How Late-Night Comedy Turns Democracy into a Joke*. New Brunswick, NJ: Rutgers University Press.

Postman, Neil. 1985. *Amusing Ourselves to Death: Public Discourse in the Age of Show Business*. New York: Penguin.

Provenza, Paul, and Dan Dion. 2010. *Satiristas: Comedians, Contrarians, Raconteurs & Vulgarians*. 1st ed. New York: Harper Collins.

Putnam, Robert D. 2001. *Bowling Alone: The Collapse and Revival of American Community*. New York: Simon & Schuster.

Schudson, Michael. 1998. *The Good Citizen: A History of American Civic Life*. New York: Free Press.

———. 2011a. *The Sociology of News*. New York: W. W. Norton & Co.

———. 2011b. *The Good Citizen: A History of American CIVIC Life*. Reprint edition. New York: Free Press.

Shoemaker, Michael, and Scott Weinstein. 1999. *SNL Presents The Clinton Years*. New York: TV Books.

Silverman, David S. 2007. *You Can't Air That: Four Cases of Controversy and Censorship in American Television Programming*. Syracuse, NY: Syracuse University Press.

True, Cynthia. 2002. *American Scream: The Bill Hicks Story*. New York: Harper Paperbacks.

Williams, Bruce A., and Michael X. Delli Carpini. 2011. *After Broadcast News: Media Regimes, Democracy, and the New Information Environment*. Cambridge, MA: Cambridge University Press.

Williams, Bruce, and Michael X. Delli Carpini. 2000. "Unchained Reaction: The Collapse of Media Gatekeeping and the Clinton–Lewinsky Scandal." *Journalism* 1: 61–85.

Young, Cory. L, and Arhlene A. Flowers. 2010. "Parodying Palin: How Tina Fey's Visual and Verbal Impersonations Revived a Comedy Show and Impacted the 2008 Election." *Journal of Visual Literacy* 29: 47–67.

Young, Dannagal G. 2004. "Late-Night Comedy in Election 2000: Its Influence on Candidate Trait Ratings and the Moderating Effects of Political Knowledge." *Journal of Broadcasting and Electronic Media* 48: 1–22.

———. 2006. "Late-Night Comedy and the Salience of the Candidates' Caricatured Traits in the 2000 Election." *Mass Communication and Society* 9: 339–66.

Young, Dannagal G., and Russell M. Tisinger. 2006. "Dispelling Late-Night Myths: News Consumption among Late-Night Comedy Viewers and the Predictors of Exposure to Various Late-Night Shows." *Harvard International Journal of Press/Politics* 11 (3): 113–34.

Zoglin, Richard. 2008. *Comedy at the Edge*. New York: Bloomsbury.

# Index

1980 election cycle, 19, 144, 151
1984 election cycle, 22
1988 election cycle, 20–21, 48
1992 election cycle, 34, 37, 42, 44, 49, 52
1996 election cycle, 35, 40, 44, 50, 146, 150, 152
2000 election cycle, 52, 55, 56, 59, 62, 70, 81; ballots, 67–69, 79; *The Daily Show* on, 52, 56, 59, 70, 81; "Decision 2000," 70, 72; Electoral College in, 56; and Florida election results, 56, 60, 65, 67–69, 79, 155; popular vote and, 56; and voter disenfranchisement, 70
2004 election cycle, 84, 87, 95, 102–3, 147; and Democratic infighting, 84, 91, 147; impact of 9/11 on, 84, 87, 95, 102–3; length of Primary, 147
2008 election cycle, 17, 100, 105, 113, 132, 137; candidate authenticity and, 105, 137; Democratic infighting and, 105, 116, 148; financial crisis, 5, 113–14, 128
9/11. *See* September 11, 2001

ABC, 8–9, 47, 129, 136, 159; parodied on late-night television, 18, 45
abortion, 10, 63

Afghanistan, 4, 103, 111, 116
al-Qaeda, 115
*The American President* (film), 43
*American Spectator*, 13
Anderson, John, 5, 12, 19, 24, 153
*The Arsenio Hall Show*, 5, 46

Baldwin, Alec, 125; portrayal of Donald Trump, 2
Begala, Paul, 94, 96
Biden, Joe, 23; accusations of plagiarism, 28, 149; Vice Presidential debates, 115, 130
Bin Laden, Osama, 91
Bosnia conflict, 36, 41—42
Bradley, Bill, 64
Brokaw, Tom, 47, 71–72
Brown, Jerry, 35, 38–39, 49, 154; "Governor Moonbeam," 39
Buchanan, Pat, 35, 40–41, 43, 45, 50–51, 152
Bush Administration (2000–2008), 2, 4, 90–91, 93, 103, 111–12, 135, 143
Bush, George H.W., 1, 10, 17, 27, 22, 35, 37, 39, 44, 60, 144, 152
Bush, George W.: appearance on *Late Night with David Letterman*, 61, 73, 77, 146, 153; and capital punishment,

55–56, 60; criticisms of hawkishness, 112, 146, 153; as governor of Texas, 60, 62, 73; and Halliburton, 97, 155; malapropisms, 2, 55, 75, 102; parodied as "dumb," 55, 61–62, 77, 87–88, 100, 102, 146; parodied as "frat guy," 87–88, 97, 100, 155; parodied as partier, 55, 59, 61, 77–78, 146, 155; Southern accent, 33, 90, 147; and Yale University, 63, 84, 88, 90, 100, 102, 147, 155

Bush, Jeb, 67, 69, 76

Bush, Laura, 62, 87

*Bush v. Gore*, 55–72; criticisms of conflict of interest, 69; Florida Supreme Court and, 69; Katherine Harris and, 67, 69; U.S. Supreme Court and, 56, 68–70, 78, 147, 151. *See also* 2000 election cycle

cable news, 11, 13, 81, 99, 142, 147, 151, 159–60; 24-hour cycle, 136; conservativism, 142; criticism of, 84, 94–96, 102, 106, 109, 119–21, 133, 156; ideological polarization of, 13, 57, 81, 144; in print journalism, 144, 156; as uncritical of Obama, 138, 148, 155; use of clips from late-night comedy, 11, 68, 152, 157

cable television, 2–4, 7, 13; increase of critical political humor on, 2, 4, 13, 156; niche programming, 4, 151

Carell, Steve, 65, 75

Carlin, George, 6–7

Carlson, Tucker, 94–96

Carson, Johnny, 1, 9, 11, 14n5, 16, 23–30, 35, 77, 145, 149, 159; criticism of Ronald Reagan, 149, 151–52; jokes about Joe Biden, 28, 149; journalistic assessment of, 16, 24–25, 30, 149, 151–52; as national bellwether, 24, 149, 152; as pundit, 24

Carter, Jimmy, 15–16, 18, 23–25, 144; communication style, 15

Carvey, Dana, 1, 10, 34–35, 60, 146

CBS, 5, 7, 10, 33, 47, 73, 91, 128–30, 136, 157

censorship, 2, 4, 7–10, 12

Center for Media and Public Affairs, 49, 77, 101, 134

Central Intelligence Agency (CIA), 33, 66, 91

Cheney, Dick, 55, 61, 89, 113; daughter, 89

CIA. *See* Central Intelligence Agency

Clinton, Hillary, 12, 105, 117, 119, 123, 131; and anti-Palin sentiment, 132; as Bill Clinton's wife, 42–43, 80; criticisms of hawkishness, 112–13; effect of Bill Clinton's legacy on presidential campaign, 111, 120, 128, 138, 153; and gender, 122, 124, 147; harsh treatment by journalists, 133, 135, 155; parodied as sore loser, 118; performing humanity, 118; political infighting and, 105, 116; portrayal by Amy Poehler, 124

Clinton, Bill: and anti-Obama actions, 117; appearance on *The Arsenio Hall Show*, 5; approval of, 51; economy under, 35, 45, 64, 145–46; "first Black president," 118; as Hillary Clinton's husband, 43, 51, 80, 111; impeachment hearings, 63; parodied as draft-dodger, 38–39, 51, 150; parodied as drug user, 38–39, 42, 51, 142, 150; parodied as glutton, 41, 50; portrayal by Darrell Hammond, 1, 43, 63; scandals, 63, 145; sexual proclivities of, 35, 50, 80, 145; Whitewater, 42–43

CNN, 5, 45, 64, 70, 84, 94–95, 103, 136; "America Rocks the Vote," 95; *Crossfire*, 84, 94–96, 103, 135, 151; "Decision 2000," 70, 72

*The Colbert Report*, 2–3, 5, 7, 17, 31, 105, 107–9, 128, 153, 159–60; character of "Stephen Colbert," 2; criticism of news media, 52, 57, 120, 142; criticisms of Republicans in 2008 election cycle, 13, 113–17, 120, 153; criticism of Super PACs, 157; as news-desk style satire, 141; news media use of clips from, 11, 13, 157, 159; Peabody Award, 31, 159; politician appearances on, 7, 12; print journalism assessment of, 25, 143–44, 155

Colbert, Stephen, 127, 137, 142; 2006 White House Correspondents Dinner, 2, 147; on *The Daily Show*, 90; on *Meet the Press*, 135; move to *The Late Show*, 5, 157

Comedy Central, 4, 9, 47, 73, 83, 93, 96, 127, 136

Congress, 23, 41, 43, 62, 78, 97; government shutdown, 36, 145

content analysis, 13, 143, 159

Couric, Katie, 128–30

Cronkite, Walter, 83, 151

cultural omnivorousness, 138, 156

culture war, 45, 50

*The Daily Show*, 1–5, 12, 23, 31, 53, 59, 76, 79–81, 109, 123–24, 137, 141, 147, 156–57, 159–60; as alternative news source, 13, 83–84, 86, 142, 146, 151; character-based political humor, 61, 63, 88, 103; criticism of "infoganda," 52, 93; criticism of mainstream news media, 52, 94, 119, 151; criticism of "talking points," 68, 95, 135; influence on journalism, 17, 25, 56, 97–98, 113, 144, 155; influence on voters, 52, 71, 80–81, 92, 134, 137, 142, 146, 150–51; and news montage, 68, 119, 136, 146, 160; political discourse and, 92, 97, 106; politician appearances on, 5, 12, 73, 75, 98, 112, 127, 154; print journalism assessment of, 70–73, 79, 81, 84–85, 87, 90, 94, 101, 109, 143, 152, 155; substantive political humor, 12, 57, 64, 69, 73, 85–87, 90, 102–3, 106–7, 135, 146–47, 152,

155; use of clips by news media, 11, 13, 72, 81, 97, 152, 157, 159

Dean, Howard, 84, 87, 98–99; "Dean Scream," 89, 98

DeGeneres, Ellen, 111, 121

Democratic Party, 41, 51, 89, 91, 97, 115, 120–21, 122, 131, 134; candidates, 26, 28–29, 31, 56, 63, 85, 87, 99, 102, 114, 128, 147; infighting, 64, 84, 105, 116–17, 133, 138, 147–48; late-night slant towards, 17–18, 22, 36, 44, 56–59, 85, 107, 132, 145–47, 155; National Convention, 47, 93; and personal humor, 23, 86, 88, 144–45, 147, 152; and substantive humor, 90–91, 103, 108

Dole, Bob, 41–42, 44–45, 96, 153; parodied as elderly, 12, 31, 35, 44–45, 50, 52, 145–46; parodied as scary, 44, 154

Dole, Elizabeth, 42, 50, 153

Drudge, Matt, 117

*The Drudge Report*. See Drudge, Matt.

Dukakis, Michael, 20, 23; parodied as boring, 29–30, 152

Ebersol, Dick, 26, 31n1

Edwards, John, 84, 87, 89, 93, 95, 110

entertainment media, 2–3, 13, 24, 95; confluence of news media and, 11, 13, 47, 52, 72, 75, 81, 142, 150; as mass distraction, 16, 31, 143; political criticism in, 4, 47, 72; as pollution, 6, 72, 156; structural changes to, 53

Fallon, Jimmy, 4–5; on "Weekend Update," 55–58, 70, 79, 86

Ferraro, Geraldine, 22, 145

Ferrell, Will: portrayal of George Bush, 55, 60, 62, 66, 71, 78, 146; "strategery," 62, 78

"Fey Effect," 109, 139, 144

Fey, Tina: portrayal of Sarah Palin, 1–2, 5, 12, 80, 106, 109, 124–26, 129–31,

142–44; as substantively critical
comedian, 36, 100, 127; support of
Hillary Clinton, 122; on "Weekend
Update," 55–58, 70, 79, 80, 101
Florida: corruption in, 60, 67, 69, 92;
at the 2008 Democratic National
Convention, 116; Jeb Bush as
governor of, 69, 76; Supreme Court,
68–69, 79; voting results (2000
election), 56, 65, 67–69, 155
Forbes, Steve, 43, 46
Ford, Gerald, 1, 12, 87
Fox News, 94, 147; ideological
partisanship of, 118, 120, 136, 141;
as Republican mouthpiece, 109;
"Truth Squad," 94; use of Obama's
middle name, 120
Franken, Al, 20, 83

Gingrich, Newt, 38, 44
Gore, Al, 34, 56, 68, 71, 73–74, 80–81;
concession to George W. Bush, 159;
"Co-Presidents" sketch, 67; parodied
as boring, 39, 40, 60, 62–63, 68, 74,
77–78, 80, 100, 146, 154; parodied
as elite, 63, 66; substantive criticisms
of, 64, 68–69; and Yale University,
63, 100. *See also Bush v. Gore*
Gravel, Mike, 109–10
gun control, 10, 64

Hammond, Darrell, 71; portrayal of Al
Gore, 62; portrayal of Bill Clinton,
1, 43, 63
*Hardball*, 69; parody of, 69, 91
Harris, Katherine, 67–69, 82
Hart, Gary, 22–23, 27–29, 31, 80, 149,
151, 154
HBO, 7, 9, 11
Hicks, Bill, 10
Hussein, Saddam, 9, 89–91

internet, 12, 68, 84, 144
Iran-Contra scandal, 37–38, 145

Iraq, 1, 4, 11, 66, 84, 86, 89–91, 94, 98,
100–1, 103, 111–12, 116, 134–37

Jackson, Jesse, 19, 26, 110–11, 153
*Jimmy Kimmel Live!*. *See* Kimmel,
Jimmy
"Joe the Plumber," 115, 121, 126
journalists, 4, 25, 37, 51, 77–80,
83, 133–34, 139–40n2, 148–56;
awareness of late-night TV's
relevance, 35, 46–48, 52, 56, 70–76,
79–80, 105, 109, 134, 137–38, 141,
143, 145, 151, 154–56; concerns
about confluence of news and
entertainment, 11, 76, 142; criticism
of late night television, 13, 16–17,
24, 26, 30, 46, 50, 52, 102, 142, 146,
149–50, 153, 155–56; and political
access, 65, 136, 138; self-reflexivity
of, 142; uses of late night TV
political humor, 6, 17, 45, 49–51, 81,
84, 103, 105, 113, 126–27, 129–30,
138–39, 143, 147, 150, 152

Kennedy, John F., 6, 20, 46
Kennedy, Ted, 15–17, 23, 154; and
Chappaquiddick, 16–17, 25–26
Kerry, John, 84–85, 87, 89, 94–95,
99–100, 116; as "flip-flopper," 89,
100–1; military service, 84, 89, 92;
parodied as boring, 88, 98, 154;
parodied as elitist, 89–90, 101, 147;
similarities to George W. Bush, 98,
102, 155; "SwiftBoat" attack ads, 86,
91–92, 147
Kimmel, Jimmy, 2, 5
Koppel, Ted, 37, 96
Kucinich, Dennis, 87–88

L.A. riots, 35–37
late-night comedy television: influence
on journalism, 127, 134, 139,
144, 148, 151–52; influence on
election narratives, 70–72, 92, 127,

132, 150; influence on public, 17, 92–93, 127, 144, 151, 156; personal satire and, 5, 9, 16–17, 23–24, 41, 45–52, 56, 61, 73, 75, 77, 87, 99–102, 141, 145, 152, 154–55; politician appearances on, 5, 12, 46, 52, 61, 71, 73–74, 76–77, 101–2, 127–28, 132, 153–54; political slant of, 17, 36, 145; reflecting existing perceptions, 28, 152, 154; substantive satire and, 17, 23, 61, 93, 99, 134–35, 141, 152, 155, 159; transformation of, 1, 12–13, 56–57, 72, 76, 144, 149, 154, 159

*Late Night with David Letterman*, 4–5, 9–10, 13, 16, 27, 35, 47–51, 61, 72–73, 75–79, 98–100, 128, 145–46, 152–55, 159. *See also* Letterman, David

Lehrer, Jim, 3, 62

Leno, Jay, 4, 9, 14n5, 27, 35, 46–51, 70–73, 75–76, 79, 93–94, 97, 99–101, 135, 145, 153, 155; criticisms of "dumbing down" political humor, 14n5. *See also The Tonight Show*

Letterman, David, 61, 70, 94, 97, 100, 114, 128–29, 137, 146

Lieberman, Joe, 91, 98, 155

MacDonald, Norm, 36, 42–43, 50, 52, 145, 150

Madonna, 39–40

Maher, Bill, 9–10, 47

Matthews, Chris, 69, 119–20

McCain, John, 111, 114–15, 119–23, 126, 142, 154; appearances on late-night television, 12, 126, 128, 155; campaign bu on *The Daily Show*, 65, 75, 80; campaign suspension, 114, 137, 148; and *Late Night with David Letterman*, 5, 94, 128–29, 137, 154; "maverick" narrative, 124, 130; and mental health, 112; parodied

as elderly, 110, 135; pick of Sarah Palin as running mate, 105, 131–32, 138, 153

Medicare, 62, 62, 78

*Meet the Press*, 11, 135

Michaels, Lorne, 31n1, 125

Middle East, 139–40n2, 152

Miller, Dennis, 22–23, 83

Miller, Zell, 90–91

Mondale, Walter, 20, 22–23, 27, 45, 151–52

*Monty Python's Flying Circus*, 8–9, 11

MSNBC, 71–72, 79, 95, 136

Murphy, Eddie, 10, 26

narrative analysis, 143, 159

narrative: anti-Hillary Clinton, 43; election cycle, 17, 70, 77–78, 103, 145–46, 150, 152; of foreign threats, 115, 123; late-night comedy television as source of critical, 81, 103, 113, 144, 152, 156; racial, 106, 121, 148; simplistic, 119–20; "Washington insider," 113, 131; "working class," 90, 98, 118

NBC, 7, 20, 47, 71–72, 95, 110, 127, 157, 159

Nealon, Kevin, 36, 40, 42, 145

network television, 9–10, 109, 138, 156; cancellation of controversial shows, 7–9, 154; censorship on, 2, 4, 7–10; effects of profit motivation on, 7, 10; as mainstream media, 4, 10, 83, 142, 144

*NewsHour with Jim Lehrer. See* Lehrer, Jim

news media, 1, 5, 13, 79, 83, 86, 120, 133, 148, 155–56; criticism of gimmicks in, 20, 145; uncritical attitude of, 75, 84, 134, 138, 145

*New York Times* (NYT), 16–17, 24, 26, 29, 35, 48,

Nixon, Richard, 5–6, 8, 20, 46

nuclear weapons, 8, 21, 112

Obama, Barack: accused of "playing the race card," 121; as Arab, 122, 138; association with Jeremiah Wright, 111, 118, 123, 133; association with William Ayres, 121, 126; as biracial, 106, 110–11; and blackness, 111, 117, 120, 122; criticisms of elitism, 127–28, 134, 153; given a free pass by journalists, 120, 132–33, 138, 148, 155; *New Yorker* cover, 106, 119; and race, 106, 110–11, 117, 121, 127, 147–48; and religion, 106, 111, 123, 127, 147–48; and whiteness, 106, 111, 122

Obama, Michelle, 106, 127–28, 153

O'Brien, Conan, 4, 9, 35, 99, 135, 145

Paar, Jack, 7, 46

Palin, Sarah: accusing Obama of "palling around with terrorists," 121, 138; appearance on *Saturday Night Live*, 105, 129, 154; and the Bush Doctrine, 106, 113, 123–24, 130; "Caribou Barbie," 125; climate change and, 106, 123, 130; effect of Tina Fey's portrayal on the candidacy of, 12, 109, 126, 129–30, 139, 142, 144; inauthenticity of, 11, 105, 137–38; lack of foreign policy experience, 113, 116, 124, 130, 132; Vice Presidential unsuitability of, 2, 27, 131–32, 137

partisanship, 5, 94, 96, 103, 118, 135

PBS, 3, 8–9

Peabody Award, 4, 31, 159

Perot, Ross, 35, 38, 47–48, 52; choice of running mate, 34, 150; parodied as small, 33; parodied as strange, 33, 40, 145, 150, 154; parodied as wealthy, 33, 43; substantive humor about, 35

Pew Research Center for the People and the Press, 3, 48, 77, 81, 83–84, 92, 134, 137, 150–51

Poehler, Amy, 86, 124

political discourse, 17, 56, 80–81, 83, 96–97, 149

political humor, 1, 9, 16–17, 36, 42, 44, 77, 80, 143; concerns about, 24, 101, 143; importance of, 12, 159; influence of, 30, 48, 93, 143; personal, 5, 15, 33, 50; substantive, 1, 2, 15, 70, 83

*Politically Incorrect with Bill Maher.* *See* Maher, Bill

Powell, Colin, 15, 41

presidential candidates: appearing on late-night television, 5–6, 12, 24, 26, 46, 56, 71, 73–77, 80, 83, 98–99, 102, 105, 149, 153–54; authenticity of, 56, 73–74, 102, 137, 147–48, 153, 156; effect of portrayals on public opinion, 30, 62, 71, 81, 124, 133, 143, 149–50; parodies of, 2, 11, 17–21; personal humor about, 16, 21, 23, 38–40, 43, 49–50, 62–63, 71, 85–89, 100–1, 107, 109, 137, 147, 153–54; self-parodying, 25, 155; substantive humor about, 12, 24, 30, 35, 65–66, 68, 85–86, 107, 109, 112–13, 115, 134–35, 137, 152, 156; wives of, 42, 80, 87, 153

Pryor, Richard, 6–7

pundits, 2, 24, 55, 79, 83, 96, 99, 114, 121, 147

Quayle, Dan, 31, 34, 38, 40, 49, 77; criticism of *Murphy Brown*, 39, 145, 150; gaffes, 21, 27, 49, 150, 152; Indiana National Guard, 27; parodied as unintelligent, 35, 48, 52, 80, 145, 149, 154; Vice Presidential unsuitability, 27, 29, 48, 52, 152

Quinn, Colin, 55–58

racism, 127, 148

Rather, Dan, 72, 91

ratings, 3–5, 7–8, 14n5, 20, 23, 26, 94

Reagan, Ronald, 21, 45, 50, 144; economic recession and, 18, 38, 145;

and Johnny Carson, 24–27, 149, 151; jokes about acting career of, 19; parodied as elderly, 16, 18, 31, 35, 145, 150; parodied as senile, 17–20, 100, 114; substantive satire, 21, 38; and the Soviet Union, 18

*Real Time with Bill Maher. See* Maher, Bill

Republicans, 50, 114, 117, 129, 137, 153; as anti-science, 109; emotional vs. rational campaigning, 106, 115, 148; extremism, 105, 129, 152; moderate, 20, 112; National Convention, 41, 45, 50, 100; personal satire about, 18, 23–24, 37, 63, 85–86, 108, 152; substantive satire about, 17–18, 21, 24, 37, 47, 58–59, 85–86, 107–9, 116, 134–35, 144–45, 147–48; use of "Islamic Terrorism," 115; and young voters, 121, 134

Rice, Donna, 22, 28

Romney, Mitt, 5, 109, 114

Rove, Karl, 116–17, 124, 138

*Rowan and Martin's Laugh-In*, 5, 7, 75

Sahl, Mort, 30, 154

Sandler, Adam, 37, 40

*Saturday Night Live*, 10, 13, 25, 30, 35, 69, 122, 148; as opinion leader, 17, 78, 127, 133, 144; parodies of politicians, 1–2, 4, 9, 11, 22, 29, 35, 38–41, 50, 55, 62–63, 71, 78, 80, 87, 89, 106, 109, 117, 124–27, 141–42, 144, 149; personal satire and, 12, 16, 19, 21, 23–24, 30–31, 33–53, 47, 49–50, 58–61, 63, 67, 71, 85, 87, 102, 108–11, 114, 149–50, 154–55; politician appearances on, 5, 12, 19, 26, 71, 74, 80, 125–27, 129–30, 138, 153–54, 155; substantive satire and, 12, 15, 17–21, 24, 30–31, 35–38, 41, 44, 52, 56, 58–61, 63, 67, 79, 85, 91, 98–99, 101, 105, 108–11, 129–30, 145–49, 153, 156; ratings, 20, 23, 26

"Saturday Night News." *See* "Weekend Update"

September 11, 2001, 1, 3–6, 9, 31, 52–53, 57, 66, 70, 72, 81, 83–84, 86, 94, 102–3, 114–15, 129, 133–35, 138, 143, 146, 155–56

Sharpton, Al, 93, 110–11

Simpson, O. J., 42–43

*The Simpsons*, 4, 10

*The Smothers Brothers Comedy Hour*, 2–4, 7–8, 103

Social Security, 49, 60, 78

*Star Trek*, 39, 49

Stewart, Jon, 1, 4–5, 61–62, 64, 68–69, 88, 90–92, 97–99, 101, 106, 109, 112–14, 117–21, 123–24, 127, 132, 137, 139, 152–53, 155; criticism of mainstream news media, 2, 93–96, 102, 106–7, 120, 135–36, 138, 142; criticized as sanctimonious, 95; discomfort with "serious journalist" designation, 3, 72, 83, 103, 151; appearance on *Crossfire*, 94–96, 151. *See also The Daily Show*

talk radio, 9, 141, 144

television, structure of, 2, 4, 7, 11, 57, 81, 96, 144, 159

*The Tonight Show*, 4, 13, 46; journalist appearances on, 47; politician appearances on, 56, 76, 99. *See also* Carson, Johnny; Leno, Jay; Paar, Jack

Thompson, Fred, 133, 137

Trump, Donald, 2, 11, 136, 154–57

Tsongas, Paul, 38–39

United States Supreme Court, 20, 56, 67–70, 78, 147, 151

Vietnam War, 8, 63, 89, 100, 129

voters, 16, 21, 24, 27, 37, 39, 44–45, 48–50, 52, 63, 67, 70–71, 81, 87–88, 93, 98, 109, 112, 119, 121, 124, 128–32, 134, 139, 142–47, 149–51,

154; black, 65, 69; elderly, 110;
Republican, 65; women, 24, 50, 129,
131–32; young, 5, 75–76, 80, 92,
121, 134, 137, 143, 146, 151

War on Terror, 31, 52, 84, 91
*Washington Post* (WP), 16–17, 24–27,
29, 35, 48

Weapons of Mass Destruction, 84, 89,
91, 112
welfare, 21, 41
Whitewater, 42–43
Williams, Brian, 95–96, 110, 157
Wright, Jeremiah, 111, 118, 123, 133
Wurzelbacher, Samuel Joseph. *See* "Joe
the Plumber"

# About the Author

**Nickie Michaud Wild** (PhD, University at Albany, State University of New York) is visiting lecturer of sociology at Mount Holyoke College. Her publications include analyses of the rise of political humor in the post–9/11 era, the interaction of political humor with the journalistic public sphere, and popular culture. She is a faculty fellow at the Yale Center for Cultural Sociology. Her research interests include media, culture, the proliferation of conspiracy theories, fandom, politics, and moral panics. She has published articles in the *American Journal of Cultural Sociology*, the *Journal of Broadcasting and Electronic Media*, and the *European Journal of Cultural Studies*, as well as an edited reader on media and cultural perspectives on 9/11 and the War on Terror.

Printed in Great Britain

46653998R00108